1988

ORAL INTERPRETATION

Oral Interpretation

MARVIN R. GOTTLIEB

Professor of Speech and Theatre
Herbert H. Lehman College of The City University of New York

McGRAW-HILL BOOK COMPANY
New York □ St. Louis □ San Francisco □ Auckland □ Bogotá □ Hamburg
Johannesburg □ London □ Madrid □ Mexico □ Montreal □ New Delhi
Panama □ Paris □ São Paulo □ Singapore □ Sydney □ Tokyo □ Toronto

ORAL INTERPRETATION

1 2 3 4 5 6 7 8 9 0   KPKP   7 8 3 2 1 0 9

This book was set in Optima by Monotype Composition Company, Inc.
The editors were Richard R. Wright and Elisa Adams;
the designer was Nicholas Krenitsky;
the production supervisor was Leroy A. Young.
The cover photograph was taken by Laurence Tamaccio.
Kingsport Press, Inc., was printer and binder.

See Sources and Credits on pages 291–301.
Copyrights included on this page by reference.

Library of Congress Cataloging in Publication Data

Gottlieb, Marvin R
Oral interpretation.

Bibliography: p.
Includes index.
1. Oral interpretation.   I.   Title.
PN4145.G6   808.5'45   79-15646
ISBN 0-07-023838-3

For

GAIL, AARON, AND DAWN

Contents

CONTENTS

Preface

At the heart of this book is the conviction that the study of oral interpretation opens up possibilities for personal gratification and cultural rewards that may be elusive in other humanistic endeavors. A student of oral interpretation often discovers a talent for literary understanding and expression that may always have existed but never have been exercised before. As the beginning reader cuts through the weighty cloud of seriousness that hangs over much literary study, the fear of literature begins to disappear. The interpreter comes to know that, like any art form, literature is meaningless until it is engaged by the intellect and the senses, and that the life experiences and perceptions that are brought to this engagement are as important as the literature itself.

The great semanticist Korzybski tells us that language provides a map that allows us to navigate through the booming, buzzing confusion of the universe. In a sense we can view poems, stories, essays, and plays as wonderful maps that, when followed with care and sensitivity, will lead us into territories of feeling and experience that may otherwise remain unknown.

Teachers of oral interpretation can bring much creativity and individuality to their approach to this basic course. The material presented in this text can be reorganized in any way that makes it more compatible with each individual teaching style. This is particularly true of Part Three, which covers the various forms of literature. Each chapter in Part Three is a self-contained unit and can be taken out of sequence without destroying any developmental pattern. Part Two, however, includes three chapters that are arranged in a developmental pattern and should be used in sequence. One of the unique features of this text is that the basic principles of selection, analysis, preparation, and performance have been combined in a single section rather than interspersed throughout many chapters.

A suggested way to proceed is to assign Part One at the outset in order to provide a historical and theoretical foundation upon which to operate and then decide which genre to approach first and assign the appropriate chapter from Part Three to be used in conjunction with Part Two. In any event, the students will be continually referring to the principles in Part Two while covering each genre in detail in Part Three.

There are many approaches to the teaching of oral interpretation, and I have been fortunate, both as a student and as a professor, to have encountered many excellent teachers during the past 20 years. While differing in style, the most effective teaching approaches invariably contain these elements: the ability to develop a friendly and supportive creative climate, a critical approach that focuses first on what is good about a performance, the patience to allow the student to struggle all the way through a selection without being cut off, and, above all, the ability to project an enthusiasm for performance and a love of good literature.

ACKNOWLEDGMENTS

I am convinced that many books are proposed but few are finished without the help of others. This book is no exception. I am indebted, of course, to my many teachers in both literature and the performing arts. In particular, I am indebted to Alvina Kraus, who taught me how to shape experience into concrete action. I will be forever grateful to my friend and colleague Cj Stevens, who provided the help and prodding I needed at various stages, including the reading of several drafts of this manuscript, and to another friend and colleague, John F. Wilson, who provided much of the material on choral speaking as well as some sound advice about writing; and Barbara Emanuele, who worked on the permissions. Finally, I want to thank the reviewers: Gary Blake, New York City; Mrs. Ruth Menken; Dr. Patricia Stack, Nassau Community College; Dr. Maxine Trauernicht, University of Nebraska; and Professor David Willinger, Westchester Community College.

Marvin R. Gottlieb

ORAL INTERPRETATION

part One
Gaining a Perspective

PART ONE consists of two chapters. Chapter 1 covers the historical highlights of oral interpretation. It focuses on the growth of literature out of the oral tradition, and the relationship of literature to performance as it progressed from the time of the ancient Greeks to twentieth-century America.

While not providing a comprehensive history of oral interpretation, Chapter 1 points out the major shifts in style, with particular attention to some of the most important movements and concepts in the field: the Delsarte Method, the Natural School, the Mechanical School, and Elocution.

1

Chapter 2 puts forth a theoretical base upon which the student can build an understanding of the field of oral intepretation.

By the end of Part One, the beginning interpreter should have developed a concept and definition of oral intepretation which is uncontaminated by the usual comparisons with acting.

Chapter 1

The Role of Interpretation in History

KEY CONCEPTS

The growth of literature out of the oral
tradition

Interpretation and ritual

Major shifts in style

Interpretation in the modern world

GREECE

As the sun peers over the horizon it strikes across the face of a sleeping man stretched out upon a pallet. He twitches awake, yawns, folds the sheet upon which he has been sleeping around him as a garment, picks up a staff, and heads for the marketplace. It is Greece—Athens, in the fifth century before the birth of Christ, and books are rare. But, wonders of wonders, literature is abundant. As a matter of fact it is already considered to be an old and dependable form of expression, growing out of tribal ritual and religious ceremony. Our man, now fully awake, finds a high place on the base of a column, pulls out a scroll, and prepares to "publish" some poetry which he prepared the night before.

This was literature in ancient Greece, material to be spoken or heard—certainly not to be read in solitude. Material given voice by respected professionals: the minstrels. The minstrels not only functioned as welcome members of the royal court but also wandered from place to place taking part in contests.

Probably as a result of Homer's popularity, a new professional, the *rhapsode*, entered the traveling circuit. The *rhapsodes* carried the tales of gods and ancestors and were also history teachers and propagandists.[1] They banded together in guilds and were well established by the sixth century B.C. However, the fact that their recitations were limited to the works of Homer eventually left the field open to poets who wanted to recite their own works.

Throughout the classical period or Golden Age, oral interpretation played a large part in the cultural life of Greece. Its prominent role continued even after books became more readily available. In fact, the booksellers of the time would tempt passersby with readings from their wares.[2] This technique is very much alive today, with dramatizations of selected passages from books presented on television and on radio for the purpose of advertising potential best-sellers.

ROME

As the glory that was Greece passed from the scene, its cultural influence did not. Rome, as the next great power of the world, carried on many of the Greek cultural traditions. While Rome had its own oral tradition growing—

---

[1] Eugene Bahn and Margaret R. Bahn, *A History of Oral Interpretation*, Burgess, Minneapolis, 1970, p. 7.
[2] Ibid., p. 17.

as did that of all other peoples—from ancient rituals performed for the gods, still it was from the captive Greeks that Romans were to learn the fine arts of literature and oral interpretation. One captive, Livius Andronicus, translated Homer's *Odyssey* into Latin and thereby ensured Greek influence on world literature.[3]

In the hedonistic tradition of Rome, the oral interpretation of literature was most frequently practiced in the home for social entertainment. But, in time, public performances gained popularity, and in the years just before and after the birth of Christ they achieved enormous success. During this period, often referred to as the Augustan Age, occurring as it did during the reign of the emperor Augustus, oral interpretation was greatly enhanced by its association with the finest of Roman literature. Among the many who tried their hands at verse and recitation were Ovid, Horace, and Virgil.

While Virgil was writing the *Aeneid*, ". . . he read three books of it aloud to Augustus and Octavia. Octavia was so deeply affected by the verses about her son that she fainted as Virgil read them."[4]

As the Roman Empire began to crumble, the quality of literature and recitation deteriorated as well. But the Romans left us an important legacy. They revered the art of reading and speaking well and made it an essential part of their teaching. Quintilian, perhaps the most famous Roman teacher, gives special attention in his treatise on education to teaching boys to read well. He was also the first to state a basic concept that runs throughout this text: The reader must first experience the feeling encompassed in the literature before he or she can realistically convey it. Technique is used to convey that feeling, not to substitute for it.[5]

THE MIDDLE AGES

With the fall of Rome, civilization moved into the Middle Ages and literature was centered in one essential source—the Bible. Those who found salvation for themselves in the words of the Bible carried those words forth into the world for the salvation of mankind. Oral interpretation from the Bible was an important part of monastic life by the fourth century.[6]

The central figures of the period were all connected with the Church and subsequently became saints. Some, such as St. Jerome, were enthusiastic about oral interpretation. St. Jerome, like Quintilian, stressed the importance

---

[3] Ibid., p. 29.
[4] Ibid., p. 33.
[5] Quintilian, *Institutio Oratoria*, H. E. Butler (trans.), Harvard University Press, Cambridge, Mass., 1953, vol. 1, bk. 1, VIII, 2, p. 147.
[6] Bahn and Bahn, op. cit., p. 49.

of oral reading in the process of a young man's education. In addition, he felt that young girls could benefit considerably from rendering their lessons orally; they could improve their diction and their knowledge of literature.[7]

St. Augustine, another proponent of oral reading, admonished prospective readers of the Bible to be sure they understood the text, to select the proper style for communicating to a specific audience, to phrase well, and to employ proper vocal usage.[8]

As the influence of Christianity spread throughout the world, literacy increased with the need for oral excellence to carry the Word. At the same time, ancient oral traditions were still surviving and commanding a large following among the common people. In England, the old pagan tradition of the Druids and other pagan influences from the now departed Roman Empire still had a ready audience. In court it was the *scop* who entertained with legends of the old Germanic tribes. He also composed poems of a secular nature glorifying his master. His traveling counterpart, the *gleeman*, so called because he often accompanied himself on the harp or "glee wood," wandered about the land performing the work of others.

The earliest poems in the English language are attributed to the scops and gleemen. *Widsith, Deor'a Lament, Beowulf,* and *Cynewulf* all show evidence in their content and structure that they were constructed by these early professionals. Caedmon, the first early Christian poet whose name we know, employed the art of the scop and gleeman to extol the virtues of Christianity. During this period, from the middle of the seventh century to the beginning of the eighth century, several Christian leaders employed oral interpretation to help convert the heathen. Aldhelm, who was having difficulty holding on to his congregation when he began his sermon, positioned himself on a bridge which the retreating congregation had to cross and chanted popular verses to them. Having thus gained their attention, he recited verses from the Scriptures.[9]

Much political unrest and several invasions, including two by the Danes and one by the Normans, were to complicate England's cultural history for several hundred years. However, after the Norman conquest (1066), things began to settle down. The Normans were heavily influenced by the culture of southern Europe and carried on many of the traditions of ancient Rome, including that of the reciter-poet. They brought with them the minstrels, complete with schools and guilds. The minstrel was often a multitalented individual. In addition to turning his hand at reciting, chanting, and singing, it was not unusual for him to dance, juggle, and play a musical

---

[7] Ibid., p. 50.
[8] Ibid., p. 53.
[9] Ibid., p. 58.

instrument. In addition, depending upon his audience, he could shift his language quite easily from Norman-French to Latin to Anglo-Saxon.

With the coming of the crusades, the minstrel gradually added Oriental literature to his stock-in-trade. About the same time, a new form, the romance, was developed in France. Romance was considered a more delicate form than the ancient epic and heroic forms. These stories, some based on fact and others on fancy, gained much popularity during the twelfth, thirteenth, and fourteenth centuries.

Even though more and more people were learning to read, the primary medium for the "publication" of literature throughout the Middle Ages was the voice. In the manner of their Greek and Roman predecessors, the great thinkers and writers of the Middle Ages gave ample attention to the instruction of reading aloud. Throughout the period, oral interpretation remained an integral and important part of life in the monastery. The proselytizing Church actually adopted some of the more popular literary forms to carry the word of God to the people. So successful were these religious adaptations that they seriously competed with the minstrel's own tales. As the Middle Ages wore on, the minstrel's fortunes waned. He was replaced in court by members of the royal family. In the wealthy households, it was often the daughter who did the reciting. As the upper classes became more proficient at reading and providing their own entertainment, the minstrel slid continually down the social scale. At their lowest point, minstrels were considered to be ministers of the devil and on the same level as harlots.[10]

The Middle Ages have often been called the "Dark Ages," based on the notion that comparatively little significant cultural activity was then taking place. It is true that when one looks at the accomplishments of ancient Greece or those of the Renaissance, they appear far greater. However, without the accomplishments of the Middle Ages the Renaissance wouldn't have happened. We need to view the period of the Middle Ages as one of transition, a period of unprecedented social and religious upheaval. Those countries, such as England, which were to become in later centuries enormous cultural contributors, were beset with internal strife, invasion, and the dramatic assault of Christianity on their traditional culture and religious life.

In spite of all these conflicting forces, great works of art were produced during the Middle Ages and many of these were works of literature. It is a rare college student today who is unfamiliar with *The Canterbury Tales*, that ribald and wonderful tale of pilgrimage which forms a linguistic bridge

[10] Ibid., p. 76.

between the world of modern English and its Anglo-Saxon heritage. Written as it was in the fourteenth century, *The Canterbury Tales* provides us with a wealth of knowledge about the period. It confirms, in its content, the high regard still afforded the art of oral interpretation. It was the Church which came to adopt the methods of the oral interpreter to carry its message and, as the era came to a close, it was the content and method of the oral tradition which continued to carry what was most meaningful in literature to the heart and minds of people throughout the world.

THE RENAISSANCE

Sometime toward the end of the fourteenth century a new movement began in the field of literature. Classical authors began to be rediscovered—first the Roman and then the Greek. The focus began to shift from a view of mankind as essentially a sinning lot in need of reform to an acceptance of human frailty. Dante, Petrarch, and Boccaccio became the precursors of what was to become Humanism.

This return to classical sources began in Italy, for both written and oral literature. England did not begin to show the effects of the Renaissance until well into the sixteenth century. However, as the classical influence spread across Europe, so did the emphasis on oral interpretation, particularly in the schools. It was not unusual for students to begin to read and speak in Latin at the age of seven. By fourteen they were studying rhetoric, using Greek and Latin orations, reading from Homer, and taking part in frequent productions of Greek classical plays.[11]

As the Renaissance took hold in England, it was the influence of Quintilian, more than that of any other classical scholar, which established the prevailing attitude toward oral interpretation. It was deemed essential that the young man of the period who aspired to a position in either the Church or state should master the oral arts. To become an expert, he was read to by his masters, and, on his part, he read and memorized enormous amounts of material from the classics.

By the middle of the sixteenth century, only a little more than 5000 books had been printed in all of England. This kept the old teaching traditions, with their heavy emphasis on oral training, very much alive. Many students of the day didn't even own a book; they depended on their memories.

In addition to placing stress on good voice production and articulation

---

[11] Ibid., p. 88.

in the teaching of oral interpretation, Renaissance scholars became interested in the psychological aspects of gesture. Some theorists began to develop standardized systems of gestural communication. One of these theorists, John Bulwer, in his *Chirologia*, presented charts which depicted the proper hand gestures for expressing various emotions. These charts, although they appeared in 1644, maintained their influence into the nineteenth and early twentieth centuries.

However, the approach to oral interpretation in the Renaissance was far from a mechanical one. Just as Quintilian had advised centuries before, the reader was expected to experience the emotion inwardly before presenting a selection to an audience, and then to read with restraint and control in such a way that the members of the audience actually experienced more through their imaginations than was presented to them.

There were other developments during this period which were not wholly dependent upon the classical influence. For example, even though poetry continued as the dominant literary form, the art of both writing and reading prose became a significant factor, too. Also, in many countries, feelings of nationalism began to spawn a reaction to the pervasive influence of the classics. In England this reaction took the form of rising demands for instruction in the native tongue rather than in Latin and Greek. As part of this pattern, the first English Bible was published in 1535, and Henry VIII decreed in 1539 that a Bible should be available in every parish for anyone to read who might want to.

With the printing of the English Bible, the long-standing relationship between oral interpretation and the Church took on a new dimension. For the first time the common people had access to the Scriptures, and by all accounts they took advantage of the opportunity. The Bible was read aloud in the churches, in homes, and even in the taverns.

Perhaps inspired by the enormous amount of oral reading, new versions of the Bible began to appear: the Bishops' Bible during the reign of Queen Elizabeth, and later the King James Version. The latter was constructed through the combined techniques of oral interpretation and group discussion. Several scholars of the day each translated a portion of the Bible and then read the material aloud to the others. In this way the entire group was able to put forth criticism and maintain literary standards so that the various sections of the Bible didn't differ widely one from the other.

In sum, the Renaissance was a period of great advance for secular as well as religious literature. The rediscovery of the classics, the publishing of translations, the development of a national literature, the decrees of Henry VIII, and the inspiration of Queen Elizabeth—all conspired to create great changes in the relationship of humanity to the written word. At the center of these changes was oral interpretation. Aristocrat, or commoner—all felt the need to hear the word and speak the word and do it well.

The celebration of literature that was the mark of the seventeenth century spawned a reaction which set the tone of what was to become neoclassicism in the eighteenth century. To the taste of the eighteenth-century writer and theorist, the exuberance and romance of the seventeenth century was seen as an indulgence, an overstatement. After all, humanity had entered the age of reason, and reason must prevail, even in art. The history of oral interpretation in the eighteenth century is one of analysis and systematization. The rallying cry of the period was sounded by Alexander Pope, "The proper study of mankind is man."

Much of the literary activity centered in England. Unified and strong, the English prospered and developed an interest in self-improvement. Part of this self-improvement was learning to speak the language well. There was a great demand for teachers of the oral arts.

The eighteenth century also ushered in a new influence in oral interpretation—America—which will be discussed at length in a later part of this chapter.

Stirrings of what was to become eighteenth-century literature began as early as the Restoration (1660) with the poet John Dryden. Dryden represents the shift from ambiguity to open and direct statement, and from elaborate to plainer style. While the epic was recognized as the great classical form, Dryden and other neoclassic poets never wrote epics. What Dryden did write is more accurately called *heroic satire*. His greatest contribution to style was his simplicity, modernity, and lack of formality. This conversational style was a constant delight to his contemporaries.

Dryden set the tone for the age. He believed that there was a connection between morality and literary shoddiness. One of the major themes of the period was to be the association between morals and aesthetics.

Perhaps as a by-product of this secular concern for simplicity and directness, the Church came under serious criticism for the bad reading of scripture and the poor delivery of sermons. The most famous critics of the day, Thomas Betterton, Richard ("Dick") Steele, and Joseph Addison, placed the blame for this poor quality of delivery on the schools. They felt there was too much emphasis on the learning of Latin and not enough on oral interpretation. To correct this disparity, many textbooks were written and many theories were developed, sometimes bringing considerable fame to various teachers. The prevailing theory took its shape from the developing literary style, which was conversational in nature. The reader or speaker of the day was to sound as if the words were his or her own, coming naturally and spontaneously.

With so much activity surrounding the art of oral interpretation resulting in basic agreement as to its purposes and outcomes, the major arguments centered on secondary issues. Some teachers felt that a piece should be memorized, others did not. While everyone believed that the interpreter must convey understanding of the emotional content of the material, there was some argument about how much emotion should be portrayed. Among those who believed that emotion was an important part of delivery, there was argument about how this effect was best achieved. The major question of style during the eighteenth century was this: Should the interpreter depend on technique and remain at a distance from the material or should the interpreter fully experience the emotional content of the material and allow any actions to follow naturally from this experience? This question was at the heart of the differences between the Mechanical and Natural Schools.

Proponents of the Mechanical School devised marking systems which were supposed to determine vocal inflection and pauses. In addition rules were established for gesture. But even the foremost proponents of such rules, such as John Walker, admitted that all action could not be controlled.[12]

These rules, and others created in later centuries, are sometimes dismissed as historical curiosities, primarily because they generally led to excesses on the part of their more ardent followers. However, vestiges of such rules are still being taught to and used by many professional and amateur readers. Newscasters and announcers, for example, use marking systems as an aid for inflectional patterns and the placement of emphasis, in order to achieve a conversational quality with news copy and commercial messages.

ORAL INTERPRETATION IN AMERICA

England's influence on American education was very strong during the early years. As a colony, America was subject to British law and British cultural tradition. This influence persisted into the nineteenth century.

The criticism which was leveled at the oral interpreters in eighteenth-century England held true for their counterparts in the colonies as well. This comment from Joseph Addison sums up the case: "It proceeds perhaps, from our national virtue (modesty) that our orators are observed to make use of less gesture or action than those of other countries. Our preachers stand

---

[12] John Walker, *Elements of Elocution,* 3d. ed., J. Johnson, London, 1806, p. 282.

stock still in the pulpit, and will not so much as move a finger to set off the best sermons in the world."[13]

As in England, the demand for instruction in the oral arts was very strong in the colonies. After the American Revolution this demand took a more specific form. The new country needed lawyers, politicians, and educators to carry on the affairs of state. American colleges of the period, such as Kings College (now Columbia University) and the College of Philadelphia (now the University of Pennsylvania), broadened their curricula to include instruction which was designed to promote commerical and civic usefulness, as well as religious instruction. Some of this instruction involved the learning of voice production and gesture. This area of study was given the name *elocution,* after the Greek term *elocutio,* which means style. It is not entirely clear why the term elocution gained so much favor among teachers and writers during the late eighteenth and early nineteenth centuries, but it certainly caught on. Its usage continued well into the twentieth century. In fact, this author was present at an elocution lesson in 1949.

As the eighteenth century came to a close, oral interpretation was already established as an integral and important part of American higher education. The primary influence of England upon the teaching of oral interpretation in America began to decline, even though the important textbooks used in our colleges and universities were produced by English writers, actors, ministers, grammarians, and lexicographers. By this time America had begun to develop its own leaders in the field.

NINETEENTH-CENTURY AMERICA

The nineteenth century in America has been called the "Golden Age of Oratory." It began with the end of the War of 1812. The psychological ties with England had been pretty well cut, and the new country began to celebrate its existence with great energy. As the inhabitants began to explore and settle more and more of what was to be the America of the future, they also began to explore themselves and their actions. They developed an independent spirit that was at once both practical and romantic. There were enormous issues remaining to be settled: universal education, purchase of foreign lands, states rights, slavery, evolution. Some of these issues were to lead the nation to a bitter civil war before little more than half the century had passed. The intellectual climate was charged with controversy, providing fertile ground for great speakers.

The people were captivated by oratory in all its forms. Lectures,

---

[13] William Sanford, *English Theories of Public Address, 1530–1828,* H. L. Hedrick, Columbus, Ohio, 1931, p. 134

sermons, political speeches, and debates were attended regularly. Some great speakers became legends in their own time. It was reported by one writer of the period, Josiah Quincy, that during a court trial in 1821 Daniel Webster ". . . spoke for nearly four hours and held the great assembly breathless, and that he gave him [Quincy] the first idea of the electric force which might be wielded by a master of speech."[14]

Literary expression flourished, as well, in the form of a developing national literature. Poets, novelists, essayists, journalists, and historians all found an outlet for their efforts. Writing was considered a respectable way of earning a living, and printing became an important business. It was during this time that *Uncle Tom's Cabin* sold a million copies, still considered a notable achievement and particularly significant when one considers that there were only about 23 million people in the entire country at the time.

Colleges and universities, which, as we noted earlier, had included speech training in their programs from the start, began to endow special chairs for the purpose. John Quincy Adams was appointed to the Boylston Chair of Rhetoric and Oratory at Harvard in 1806. This was the first in a series of such endowments. A survey of forty-five college catalogs for the period 1835–1840 indicated that the average college requirement for speech work was 10 semester hours. A similar survey of ninety-seven colleges during the period 1860–1870 shows that even 20 years later an average of 8 hours of speech work was required, and much of this work was in oral interpretation.[15]

As in other periods and other countries, the interest in oral interpretation was not confined to colleges and universities. Elocution was taught in the public schools as well. The most famous beginning texts of the period, McGuffey's *Readers,* invariably included some instruction in elocution. One text, Epes Sargent's *Standard Speaker,* was reprinted sixty times within 20 years of its publication.

While many theorists on the speech arts commanded a large audience for the first 70 years of the nineteenth century, one man stands out as the central figure of the period. He was Dr. James Rush, one of the first American scientists to make a contribution to the field of speech. Mary Margaret Robb describes his influence and its decline in this way:

> Dr. James Rush, in his *Philosophy of the Human Voice,* published in 1827, introduced science into the teaching of elocution.

---

[14] Mary Margaret Robb, *Oral Interpretation of Literature in American Colleges and Universities,* H. L. Wilson, New York, 1941, pp. 73–74.
[15] Thomas E. Coulton, *"Trends in Speech Education in American Colleges 1835–1935,"* unpublished Ph.D. dissertation, New York University, 1935, pp. 42–43.

Although his book was not a textbook, it succeeded in analyzing the functions of the voice in such a minute fashion that it became the basis for most of the books written during this period. At first, physiology was the branch of science most emphasized and the training in elocution became not only a means of developing a useful and necessary skill, but in some cases was prescribed as therapy for bodily ailments. By 1870, however, the trend had changed and a psychological emphasis became evident which made the interpretation of literature primarily an intellectual process, much less mechanical than before and much more of a "liberal art."[16]

After the Civil War, America was left without much cultural leadership. The plantation master had been replaced by the captain of industry. As a new society was created by the machine, exploitation and progress came into being. This period, called by Mark Twain "The Gilded Age," was one of excess, display, and glitter. This tendency was expressed in the architecture and oratory favored by this new ruling class. "Victorian Gothic was like much of the oratory of the period, florid, vain and empty; characterized by over-decoration, over-ornamentation and ostentation."[17]

Oral interpretation was subjected to the same tendency through the influence of François Delsarte, a French music and acting teacher. He supposedly lost his voice because of faulty teaching methods used when he was a student. As a consequence, he developed his own system of bodily expression. He never wrote a book, but his system, as interpreted by his students, was brought to America and commanded a large following. The components of this system are extremely complicated, and it would be beyond our needs to describe them in detail. Briefly, Delsarte believed that gesture was the highest form of expression because it expressed the soul. He devised a series of exercises which his followers claimed produced poise, grace, beauty of face and figure, and health. Among these was an exercise called "statue-posing," which called for the performer to imitate several poses represented by Greek statues. It was believed that in this way all the basic emotions could be expressed. Other exercises supposedly produced various states of relaxation and helped in the development of the tone of the voice.

The Delsarte system became a fad with a following not only in the field of oral expression but also in physical education. Its extravagance was in tune with the desires of the period, and while it did not survive much

---

[16] Robb, op. cit., p. 122.
[17] Samuel Eliot Morison and Henry Steele Commager, *The Growth of the American Republic*, Oxford University Press, New York, 1937, p. 295.

beyond the 1890s, it was a significant part of the education in oral interpretation during the latter part of the century.

The new society wanted amusement, and a variety of lively and gaudy entertainment was readily available. Show business boomed in the cities, catering to the urban working population.

> Vaudeville shows, prize fights, circuses, dime museums, and cheap theatres like the spectacles of ancient Rome, kept countless millions happy in penury, not at public expense, as in Caesar's day, but at the expense of those who enjoyed them and to the advantage of those who owned them. Indeed, tickling the urban masses—creating popular tastes and standards of culture—now became one of the large and highly lucrative branches of Capitalistic enterprise.[18]

In addition to entertainment, the people also demanded "culture" and exposure to what they believed were the better things in life. Outside of the cities this demand created another extraordinary innovation—the *chautauqua*. People in the small towns from New York State to the far West developed a desire for adult education along with their entertainment. "Bishop Vincent, who had experience in camp meetings where people gathered under the trees for days or weeks to praise the Lord, realized that they were more than a religious gathering—a sort of community get-together where people enjoyed themselves as a by-product of religious experience."[19] With this in mind, he established the Sunday School Teachers Assembly in 1874 on the camp meeting grounds at Fair Point, Chautauqua Lake, New York. From this beginning grew the institution of the chautauqua.

The basic presentation of the chautauqua was the lecture, and the large crowds attracted most of the political and religious leaders of the period to the lecture platform. "Russell H. Conwell delivered his famous lecture 'Acres of Diamonds' five thousand times before chautauqua audiences and earned four million dollars."[20]

In addition to the lecture, one or two readings were included on every program. These were delivered primarily by professional oral interpreters; however, several poets, including Emerson Brooks, Edmund Vance Cooke, Lew Sarett, and Carl Sandburg, performed their own poetry.

The influence of the chautauqua on America is difficult to measure except to say that it was great. One of the oral interpreters who experienced the movement firsthand, Gay McLaren, describes it this way:

---

[18] Charles A. Beard and Mary Beard, *The Rise of American Civilization,* Macmillan, New York, 1927, p. 397.
[19] Mary Margaret Robb, op. cit., p. 128.
[20] Ibid., p. 130.

While the original purpose was the study of the Bible, the fame of the institution grew and its patronage increased when the course of study was expanded to include secular subjects. Lectures, music and readings were added to furnish "pure, wholesome entertainment" for the Bible students. Boating, bathing, and outdoor games were provided to encourage healthful exercise. Thus the Assembly developed a uniquely American blending of religion, education, and recreation. . . .

Chautauquas now began to spring up all over the country in groves of trees and by lakesides. The original idea of a combined studying and entertainment with the health-making influences of trees and water seemed the keynote of Chautauqua's appeal, because when the idea was tried in cities it was almost always a failure.[21]

Several professional schools of oral interpretation were established to fulfill the need created by the chautauqua and the regular lecture circuit, the *lyceum*. These schools were separate and distinct from the colleges and universities and offered specialized adult training in oral interpretation and public speaking. Many of these schools were later merged with universities. An example is the School of Speech at Northwestern University, originally founded by Robert McLain Cumnock in 1878.

As the nineteenth century drew to a close, a new and powerful influence came upon the scene—psychology. Psychology has created such an impact on our lives that it is hard to imagine a world without it. But in the speech arts of the nineteenth century the great concern was physiology. Students of oral interpretation learned about the speech mechanism: they systematically developed "proper" breathing; learned elaborate notation systems for pauses, inflection, and emphasis; and followed the "rules" for correct posture, movement, and gesture. The nation grew, tore itself apart, and then flung itself wildly into the industrial age. The history of the nineteenth century is a rich history, and the art of oral interpretation was a part of that history.

TWENTIETH-CENTURY AMERICA

Even before the end of the nineteenth century, some of the major forces which were to shape the character of the twentieth century had begun to take hold. Psychology, as has already been mentioned, caused people to begin to examine themselves and their actions with a different set of tools. It was probably the almost universal concern with introspection that brought

---

[21] Gay McLaren, *Morally We Roll Along*, Little, Brown, Boston, 1938, pp. 74–77.

the mechanical approaches to oral interpretation into disfavor. Literature itself had become an intensely introspective exercise. The literary heroes and heroines of the period engaged in unrelenting examination of themselves, their motives, and those of their fellow characters. It was to be expected, then, that a more "natural" approach to oral interpretation would begin to take over.

There had always been advocates of such an approach. In fact, the conflict between the Mechanical and Natural Schools had been raging since the eighteenth century. However, nineteenth-century preoccupation with science and the machine had caused the natural approach to take a back seat for most of the century.

The shift to the natural approach was gradual, but, by the end of the nineteenth century, textbooks were beginning to reflect the attempts at reconciliation between the two approaches. However, the vitality of the Mechanical School cannot be discounted, and only since 1950 has it been safe to say that this approach has passed completely from the scene.

The chautauqua lasted well into the first quarter of the twentieth century, as did the professional nature of the schools it spawned. But oral interpretation was once again becoming an integral part of the college curriculum and moving away from strictly professional applications.

Not only were students studying the art of oral interpretation, but also interest was aroused in its history. Scholars such as Alfred Lord in his *The Singer of Tales* made significant contributions to classical study by deciphering the patterns in oral poetry. Lord also makes a convincing case for the existence of these ancient poetic traditions even today. The Yugoslavian Guslars are creating oral poetry in the same way that Homer did over 2000 years ago. Studies are being conducted now which indicate that the same Homeric forms exist among the Somali tribes in Africa. But, far from being a historical curiosity or an anachronism, oral interpretation has played a large part in the twentieth century.

In a sense, the "Golden Age of Radio" was a golden age for oral interpretation as well. Dramatic shows and reading hours abounded. Even though television brought a halt to the massive doses of oral interpretation that the American public encountered, dramatic readings continue to be a part of television variety fare. The increasing use of animated fiction provides another significant outlet for the oral interpreter.

New forms have been developed, sometimes called Readers' Theatre or Chamber Theatre. Almost any Broadway season since 1951, when *Don Juan in Hell* was read to an audience by a distinguished group of actors and actresses, includes productions which employ oral interpretation techniques.

In the colleges and universities, more students than ever before are taking courses in oral interpretation. A recent informal survey indicates that most teachers of oral interpretation expect the enrollments in their courses to continue growing throughout the next several years.

There is no way to predict what the future holds for the art of interpretation. But it is hoped that this chapter will leave you with the understanding that oral interpretation is a territory of its own. It derives from a tradition that goes far back. One can only guess how many hundreds or thousands of years before recorded history the first human stood before others and recounted a tale or a myth. Oral interpretation has its roots in the very same soil as the rudiments of language. It has a rich and varied history. During many periods it was considered to be of greater importance than music or theatre. It now enjoys a vibrant and expanding presence in the modern world, and, if history is any judge, it will always be with us.

Chapter 2
The Concept of Performance in Literature

KEY CONCEPTS

Oral interpretation as a creative art

The relationship of the interpreter to the literature

The relationship of the interpreter to the audience

Novels, essays, poems—in fact, all written material, including plays and textbooks—are created from some combination of memory, imagination, and organizational structure. When literature is read aloud, the resulting performance will be unique. The act of oral interpretation is a creative art, and, above all, a performing art. As such, it can be judged by the criteria of any performing art as set forth in any aesthetic doctrine. For the Aristotelians, it is mimetic; for the most modern aestheticians, it occupies "artspace."

We must begin with a question: Who is this person, the interpreter? Is he or she the author? A person created by the author? What is the function of the interpreter? One theorist in the field, Paul M. Pearson, answers this way:

> The interpreter must work under the limitations of time and place. His audience is before him. They are dependent upon him. It is not of his choosing. For the moment at least he is the medium through which they are to understand and enjoy what he presents. The interpreter's business is to get hold and develop enthusiasm in his audience. He cannot turn away to another audience. His moral obligation is to realize from the material before him the possibilities of a combination of the poem, the hearer, and the interpreter.[1]

The interpreter, then, is the medium through whom the audience experiences the literature. Like the medium at a séance, the interpreter contacts the spirit that lives within the literature, assumes its voice and body, and allows it to flow through him or her and communicate with the audience. The interpreter may or may not represent the author and can be human, nonhuman, or superhuman as the literature demands, but, for the duration of the performance, the interpreter must appear to be real. The creation of reality is the primary concern of the interpretive artist.

We live in a scientific age, and the influence of technology on modern art forms is unmistakable. The "scientific method" is highly revered and is applied to all areas of inquiry. In the study of literature, this application of scientific method, or *empiricism,* has brought us insights which have greatly enriched our understanding of literature from all periods and cultures.

As interpreters we are greatly aided by empiricism in defining the reality we seek. We owe a great debt to the "new critics" who have espoused and employed this method throughout much of this century and have taught us to pay rigorous attention to the text. But as interpretive artists

---

[1] Paul M. Pearson, "Artistic Interpretation," *Studies in the Art of Interpretation* edited by Gertrude E. Johnson (New York: Appleton-Century Co., 1940), p. 40.

we are only partially critics. We cannot maintain the distance from our subject that a good critic must. We cannot just admire the gown; we must wear it. We cannot just explain its shape and size; we must tailor it to fit our dimensions.

The concept of performance disturbs literary critics because of the element of unpredictability. Wellek and Warren in their text, *Theory of Literature,* make this clear in their discussion of the sound elements in poetry: they attempt to separate literature from any notion of performance.

> In analysing these sound effects, we have to bear in mind two principles, important but frequently ignored. We must initially distinguish between performance and pattern of sound. The reading aloud of a literary work of art is a performance, a realization of a pattern which adds something individual and personal and, on the other hand, may distort or even entirely ignore the pattern.[2]

Such statements not only hinder advancements in the study of literature but are counterproductive to the study of oral interpretation.

There is no distinction between performance and pattern of sound. There is only good (true) performance or bad (false) performance on either end of a continuum. Granted that a poor performance of a poem will lead to distortion, a good performance will most likely lead to comprehension, feeling, knowledge, and experience. The experiential aspects of literary engagement cannot be ignored. Whether one hears a poem performed in an auditorium by a reader, in some cases by the actual poet, or in the privacy of the voice inside one's head ("auralizing"), one hears the poem performed. The words, rhythms, and sound patterns mingle with "what one is," and out of this engagement comes comprehension and the resulting manifestations on a feeling level.

It is not unlikely that most of us, during our lifetime, confront more literature than any other art form. Perhaps as a result of this familiarity, we tend to think of poems, novels, plays, and the like, as commonplace, not having the same importance or stature as painting or sculpture. Or perhaps it is the ready access to literature, its relatively low cost to possess, that leads some of us to feel that it is somehow less important than other art forms. We can leave it to others to argue which art form is greater than the others, but literature is art. Like all art, literature has its raw materials. Some of these raw materials, such as experience and organization, are shared with other art forms; language is wholly its own. Language is the pigment

---

[2] Rene Wellek and Austin Warren, *Theory of Literature,* Harcourt, Brace & World, New York, 1956, p. 158.

and clay of the literary artist. Through an understanding of the function of language, we move to the essence of what literature is.

Richard Ohmann, generally associated with stylistics, presents a workable theory that "the locus of language is in the minds of its speakers" and, therefore, the various literary forms and structures are meaningless until they are interpreted in someone's mind; "literary criticism is the study of mental structures." He concludes:

> A literary work is a discourse whose sentences lack the illocutionary force that would normally attach to them. Its illocutionary force is *mimetic*. By "mimetic" I mean purportedly imitative. Specifically, a literary work purportedly imitates (or reports) a series of speech acts, which in fact have no other existence. By doing so, it leads the reader to imagine a speaker, a situation, a set of ancillary events, and so on.[3]

Ohmann divides the speech act into three aspects: *locutionary*, the physical act of saying or writing something, of producing the sound or marks; *illocutionary*, the act of using language to state, warn, question; and *perlocutionary*, the effect of what one says on the hearer.

If Ohmann is correct that a reader—in this case a silent solitary reader free of the contamination of any external performance—imagines a speaker (or speakers), a situation, and a set of "ancillary events," then a performance of a very real kind is taking place. This supports the contention that there is no engagement with literature without performance. The interpreter's function, then, is to bring this implicit performance to life for the audience.

As an artist, the interpreter possesses skills and insights which the average reader does not. Through the application of these skills and insights, the interpreter stimulates the imagination and creates an illusion of reality. For the duration of the performance, the audience believes that the words being heard are the words of the person before them. By manipulating the audience's imagination the interpreter leads them toward the meaning, knowledge, feeling, and experience contained within the text. In so doing, he or she satisfies the requirements of art, and, at the same time, the responsibility to the author.

It is useful for beginning students to think of themselves as musicians. Their instruments are their voices and bodies. The literature on the page before them is their "score." Like musicians, interpreters bring something of themselves to this score. They filter it through their consciousness and coax forth its essence, its feeling, its life, its meaning. For the duration of

---

[3] Richard Ohmann, "Speech Acts and the Definition of Literature," *Philosophy and Rhetoric*, vol. 4, 1971, pp. 1–19.

their performance the "song" belongs to them; they have made it their own. And they are special, because while everyone can sing, the interpreter can do it better. And the song, perhaps known, perhaps heard many times before, is once again heard as if for the first time.

QUESTIONS FOR STUDY AND DISCUSSION

1

How does the interpretive artist differ from a literary critic?

2

What similarities can you discover between the interpretive artist and the medium at a seance?

3

In what way has science contributed to the study of literature?

4

What does Ohmann mean by ". . . the locus of language is in the mind of its speakers"?

5

How does literature compare or contrast with painting? With sculpture? With music?

SUGGESTED ACTIVITIES

1

Choose a poem and list the "events" reported within it.

2

Become familiar with your own storytelling style. Tell an auto-biographical incident to the class.

Part Two
The Steps to Performance

P ART TWO consists of Chapters 3 to 6. Chapter 3 covers the problems of choosing and analyzing a selection for performance. Chapter 4 develops the interpreter's technique through rehearsal. Chapter 5 shows how to correctly train and use the communication mechanism for interpretation. Chapter 6 uses a narrative approach and takes the student through the process of preparing and performing a selection before an audience.

Part Two also introduces the concept of **Gottlieb's**

25

Principles, which are signposts and rules of thumb easily retained and turned into action by the beginning interpreter.

Chapter 3
Approaching Performance

KEY CONCEPTS

Choosing material

Analyzing for performance

CHOOSING A SELECTION

With the whole wide range of literature open to them, beginning readers can find choosing a selection to be a perplexing task. However, a few general rules will bring the problem down to manageable proportions.

First, and most important, the interpreter is always dealing with a time limit and should choose a selection accordingly. While time limits will vary according to the type of literature being studied, generally the beginning reader chooses a 5- to 10-minute selection of prose or a 2- to 4-minute selection of poetry. Each has its merits as a starting point, but poetry may be the better choice. The beginning student has difficulty sustaining longer selections because of a natural tendency to stage fright. Therefore, for many students it is easier to work with shorter selections, even though the content may be more difficult. A selection from a play should be avoided altogether, particularly the first time around.

Second, the material chosen should have literary merit and stir some feeling in the reader. The initial experiences with performing literature will be more successful if the selection has been encountered before—perhaps in an English class—and has already affected the reader in some way.

The question of literary merit may be difficult for the beginning interpreter to answer. Just because a poem or story is printed in an anthology does not ensure that it is a "good" piece of literature. However, the interpreter has a responsibility to the audience. By presenting a selection the interpreter gives it credibility, and this is a responsibility which should not be taken lightly. Be prepared to justify your choice based on its value as literature. Obviously, you are in a better position if your selection has been judged worthy by others in the literary world. Selections from the works of well-known authors or from anthologies where judgments other than your own were made about the selection are your best choices. If you feel strongly that a selection has merit, by all means read it. Just be sure that you have considered the question of literary value before making a final choice.

Third, the material chosen should have been written during the past 50 years. The beginning interpreter should not add language problems to the already existing difficulties. Language changes significantly during the course of 50 years, so that choices of words, phrasing, and even meanings alter. This problem, of course, is one that should not be avoided for long. It is a great challenge to the intermediate interpreter to bring to life a Shakespearean sonnet, a passage from Milton's "Paradise Lost", or Wordsworth's "Prelude." It is also one of the great sources of satisfaction in this kind of performing.

Fourth, the interpreter should choose a selection which has narrative content. Whether a poem or short story is selected, the beginning reader is better off with content that describes a specific incident or an action of some kind. The following poem is a good example:

EVERYONE SANG
SIEGFRIED SASSOON

Everyone suddenly burst out singing;
And I was filled with such delight
As prisoned birds must find in freedom
Winging wildly across green fields; on; on;
   and out of sight.
Everyone's voice was suddenly lifted,
And beauty came like the setting sun.
My heart was shaken with tears, and horror
Drifted away. . . . O, but everyone
Was a bird; and the song was wordless; the singing
   will never be done.

The narrator (speaker) is describing what appears to be an incident witnessed at some time in the past: a moment ago, a week ago, 10 years ago. This description includes the speaker's feelings about that incident. In the process of testing this poem as a possible selection, the interpreter should ask the following questions:

1
Have I had a similar experience?

2
Have I had a similar feeling?

3
Can I picture the situation in which these words could logically be spoken?

The following poem is an example of a different kind of incident:

BUFFALO BILL
e. e. cummings

Buffalo Bill's
defunct

Who used to
ride a water-smooth-silver
                                    stallion
and break onetwothreefourfive pigeons just like that
                                                            Jesus

he was a handsome man
                              and what i want to know is
how do you like your blueyed boy
Mister Death

With this poem, you, the reader, must bring more of yourself to the visualization of the narrator. Why is the narrator saying these words? Can you picture a situation in which you might say these words? Do you know someone else who might? Once again the narrator is describing an action and a feeling.

In the following excerpt from a short story, the same principles apply. There is a narrator describing an event from memory.

From SENOR PAYROLL
WILLIAM E. BARRETT

Larry and I were Junior Engineers in the gas plant, which means that we were clerks. Anything that could be classified as paper work came to the flat double desk across which we faced each other. The Main Office downtown sent us a bewildering array of orders and rules that were to be put into effect.

Junior Engineers were beneath the notice of everyone except the Mexican laborers at the plant. To them we were the visible form of a distant, unknowable paymaster. We were Señor Payroll.

Those Mexicans were great workmen; the aristocrats among them were the stokers, big men who worked Herculean eight-hour shifts in the fierce heat of the retorts. They scooped coal with huge shovels and hurled it with uncanny aim at tiny doors. The coal streamed out from the shovels like black water from a high-pressure nozzle, and never missed the narrow opening. The stokers worked stripped to the waist, and there was pride and dignity in them. Few men could do such work, and they were the few.

The Company paid its men only twice a month, on the fifth and on the twentieth. To a Mexican, this was absurd. What man with money will make it last fifteen days? If he hoarded money beyond the spending of three days, he was a miser—and when, Señor, did the blood of Spain flow in the veins of misers? Hence, it was the custom for our stokers to appear every third or fourth day to draw the money due to them.

There was a certain elasticity in the Company rules, and Larry and I sent the necessary forms to the Main Office and received an "advance" against a man's pay check. Then, one day, Downtown favored us with a memorandum:

"There have been too many abuses of the advance-against-wages privilege. Hereafter, no advance against wages will be made to any employee except in a case of genuine emergency."

We had no sooner posted the notice when in came stoker Juan Garcia. He asked for an advance. I pointed to the notice. He spelled it through slowly, then said, "What does this mean, this 'genuine emergency'?"

I explained to him patiently that the Company was kind and sympathetic, but that it was a great nuisance to have to pay wages every few days. If someone was ill or if money was urgently needed for some other good reason, then the Company would make an exception to the rule.

Juan Garcia turned his hat over and over slowly in his big hands. "I do not get my money?"

"Next payday, Juan. On the twentieth."

He went out silently and I felt a little ashamed of myself. I looked across the desk at Larry. He avoided my eyes.

In assessing this selection as a possible choice for performance, the interpreter examines the narrator and again questions: Could I logically be saying these words? In what hypothetical situation might I be saying these words?

In summary, when selecting a piece of literature for performance the beginning interpreter should consider these guidelines:

1

Select something short: either a poem less than 4 minutes in length or a short story less than 10 minutes in length. The selection should be complete and uncut.

2

Choose material about which you have some feeling.

3

Consider the literary merit of your selection.

4

Choose a selection in which the language is relatively contemporary. Don't further complicate matters with unfamiliar words
and syntax.

5

Choose a selection with obvious narrative content, something
which tells a story.

THE ANALYSIS

Chances are, the interpreter already has a good acquaintance with the
selection. Many times this is the primary reason for making a selection.
Readers naturally feel more comfortable performing something which they
feel they know well. However, the approach to performance requires a
different kind of analysis from the approach used in most literature classes.
Assume for the moment that you are looking at your selection for the very
first time. What strikes you as the most obvious characteristic it has? Even
before you have any idea what a selection says, you know its genre—that
is, whether it is a selection of prose, poetry, or drama.

Each genre provides its own problems for analysis. These will be
covered in more detail in later chapters. However, the basic performance
approach to any selection is the same and will apply to all three genres in
much the same way.

Let's assume that you have chosen a poem. Again, you must begin
your approach with questions. What is happening in the poem? Does it tell
a story? Describe an action? Paint a picture? Give a character sketch?

When you believe you can answer these questions, put the poem
aside and, in your own words, write down what you believe it's about—not
what you think it means! You can think of this exercise as *extended
paraphrasing*—extended because you should feel free to add as much to
your version as comes to mind, without confining yourself to simply finding
synonyms for the words in the poem. While doing this exercise, remember
that you are the narrator; use the first-person point of view. The following
is a short example of a poem and its extended paraphrase.

ANIMALS
From SONG OF MYSELF
WALT WHITMAN

I think I could turn and live with animals, they are so placid
    and self-contained;

I stand and look at them long and long.
They do not sweat and whine about their condition;
They do not lie awake in the dark and weep for their sins;
They do not make me sick discussing their duty to God;
Not one is dissatisfied—not one is demented with the mania of
    owning things;
Not one kneels to another, nor to his kind that lived thousands
    of years ago;
Not one is respectable or industrious over the whole earth.

      I really think that I could turn my back on the human race and go and live with the animals. They all seem to have a great sense of self. They're confident and self-reliant. I stand and look at them for long periods of time, and I wish I could be like them. They don't sweat and whine about their condition like a lot of people I know. Or can't get to sleep because they think they're guilty about something. And the ones that really make me sick are the superreligious types, always talking about what they have to do for God. Well, animals aren't like that. They don't seem to be dissatisfied with what they have, and they certainly aren't materialistic. They might have leaders, but they don't bow and scrape all the time. When they die, they're gone and the living animals don't feel the need to remember. They don't worry about being respectable or industrious in the "middle-class" way. All in all, it seems like a better life.

    If you had chosen a short story rather than a poem, you would ask the same questions. However, it would be impractical to rewrite the entire short story in your own words. The short story provides you with most of the narrative elements you need. The extended paraphrase would be used only for those passages that are particularly difficult.

    Having produced your extended paraphrase, compare it with the original. Be sure you are satisfied that you have discussed all the actions and feelings contained in the original, being particularly careful that your account is free of logical inconsistencies.

    Next, note all the *transitions* in your selection. Each time within the "story" of your selection there is a change of place, time, action, mood, or character, a transition has occurred. Again, check your paraphrase against the original to be sure that it covers everything, including the transitions in their proper sequence. Now, put your version aside for the moment and turn to the original text. (However, since you will be using your version for rehearsal, keep it handy.) At this point, with your noted transitions, your text should resemble the following:

AN OLD MAN'S WINTER NIGHT
ROBERT FROST

All out of doors looked darkly in at him.
Through the thin frost, almost in separate stars,
That gathers on the pane in empty rooms.
What kept his eyes from giving back the gaze
Was the lamp tilted near them in his hand.
What kept him from remembering the need
That brought him to that creaking room was age.
He stood with barrels round him—at a loss.

(transition)

And having scared the cellar under him
In clomping here, he scared it once again
In clomping off;—and scared the outer night,
Which has its sounds, familiar, like the roar
Of trees and crack of branches, common things,
But nothing so like beating on a box.

(transition)

A light he was to no one but himself
Where now he sat, concerned with he knew what,
A quiet light, and then not even that.

(transition)

He consigned to the moon, such as she was,
So late arising, to the broken moon
As better than the sun in any case
For such a charge, his snow upon the roof,
His icicles along the wall to keep;
And slept.

(transition)

The log that shifted with a jolt
Once in the stove, disturbed him and he shifted,
And eased his heavy breathing, but still slept.

(transition)

One aged man—one man—can't keep a house,
A farm, a countryside, or if he can,
It's thus he does it of a winter night.

Your next analytical task is to discover the narrator. Once again, begin with a question. Who is speaking these words? To answer, "the poet," is an oversimplification. Sometimes the speaker is the poet, but more often than not the speaker is a person created by the poet through whom the poet presents a message. Try to imagine the person who logically would be speaking the words of this poem. Is the person male or female? How old? In what state of mind? Happy or depressed? Tall or short? Mortal or God? **Gottlieb's First Principle** states that the key to a quality performance is detail, and nowhere is this more important than in your picturization of the narrator. You might thumb through magazines or other picture sources, run through your memory, or watch people pass on the street for a while, but before you go any further, be sure you know who your narrator is. With this accomplished, you are ready to move on to the rehearsal stage.

QUESTIONS FOR STUDY AND DISCUSSION

1

Why is it important for the interpreter to have some feeling for the material?

2

Explain why it's helpful to choose a selection with narrative content.

3

What is meant by "genre"?

4

What is an "extended paraphrase"?

5

How does the interpreter "discover the narrator"?

SUGGESTED ACTIVITIES

1

Select a poem and bring a picture of the narrator, cut from a magazine or other source, to class.

2

Several students should do extended paraphrases of the same poem and compare.

3

Select a short story and write a synopsis of the events. Read your synopsis to the class.

Selections for Analysis and Performance

THE SNIPER
LIAM O'FLAHERTY

The long June twilight faded into night. Dublin lay enveloped in darkness but for the dim light of the moon that shone through fleecy clouds, casting a pale light as of approaching dawn over the streets and the dark waters of the Liffey. Around the beleaguered Four Courts the heavy guns roared. Here and there through the city, machine-guns and rifles broke the silence of the night, spasmodically, like dogs barking on lone farms. Republicans and Free Staters were waging civil war.

On a roof-top near O'Connell Bridge, a Republican sniper lay watching. Beside him lay his rifle and over his shoulders were slung a pair of field glasses. His face was the face of a student, thin and ascetic, but his eyes had the cold gleam of the fanatic. They were deep and thoughtful, the eyes of a man who is used to looking at death.

He was eating a sandwich hungrily. He had eaten nothing since morning. He had been too excited to eat. He finished the sandwich, and, taking a flask of whiskey from his pocket, he took a short draught. Then he returned the flask to his pocket. He paused for a moment, considering whether he should risk a smoke. It was dangerous. The flash might be seen in the darkness and there were enemies watching. He decided to take the risk.

Placing a cigarette between his lips, he struck a match. There was a flash and a bullet whizzed over his head. He dropped immediately. He had seen the flash. It came from the opposite side of the street.

He rolled over the roof to a chimney stack in the rear, and slowly drew himself up behind it, until his eyes were level with the top of the parapet. There was nothing to be seen—just the dim outline of the opposite housetop against the blue sky. His enemy was under cover.

Just then an armored car came across the bridge and advanced slowly up the street. It stopped on the opposite side of the the street, fifty yards ahead. The sniper could hear the dull panting of the motor. His heart beat faster. It was an enemy car. He wanted to fire, but he knew it was useless. His bullets would never pierce the steel that covered the gray monster.

Then round the corner of a side street came an old woman, her head covered by a tattered shawl. She began to talk to the man in the turret of the car. She was pointing to the roof where the sniper lay. An informer.

The turret opened. A man's head and shoulders appeared, looking toward the sniper. The sniper raised his rifle and fired. The head fell heavily on the turret wall. The woman darted toward the side street. The sniper fired again. The woman whirled round and fell with a shriek into the gutter.

Suddenly from the opposite roof a shot rang out and the sniper dropped his rifle with a curse. The rifle clattered to the roof. The sniper thought the noise would wake the dead. He stopped to pick the rifle up. He couldn't lift it. His forearm was dead.

"Christ," he muttered, "I'm hit."

Dropping flat onto the roof, he crawled back to the parapet. With his left hand he felt the injured right forearm. There was no pain—just a deadened sensation, as if the arm had been cut off.

Quickly he drew his knife from his pocket, opened it on the breast-work of the parapet, and ripped open the sleeve. There was a small hole where the bullet had entered. On the other side there was no hole. The bullet had lodged in the bone. It must have fractured it. He bent the arm below the wound. The arm bent back easily. He ground his teeth to overcome the pain.

Then taking out the field dressing, he ripped open the packet with his knife. He broke the neck of the iodine bottle and let the bitter fluid drip into the wound. A paroxysm of pain swept through him. He placed the cotton wadding over the wound and wrapped the dressing over it. He tied the ends with his teeth.

Then he lay against the parapet, and, closing his eyes, he made an effort of will to overcome the pain.

In the street beneath all was still. The armored car had retired speedily over the bridge, with the machine-gunner's head hanging lifelessly over the turret. The woman's corpse lay still in the gutter.

The sniper lay still for a long time nursing his wounded arm and planning escape. Morning must not find him wounded on the roof. The enemy on the opposite roof covered his escape.

He must kill that enemy and he could not use his rifle. He had only a revolver to do it. Then he thought of a plan.

Taking off his cap, he placed it over the muzzle of his rifle. Then he pushed the rifle slowly over the parapet, until the cap was visible from the opposite side of the street. Almost immediately there was a report, and a bullet pierced the center of the cap. The sniper slanted the rifle forward. The cap slipped down into the street. Then catching the rifle in the middle, the sniper dropped his left hand over the roof and let it hang, lifelessly. After a few moments he let the rifle drop to the street. Then he sank to the roof, dragging his hand with him.

Crawling quickly to the left, he peered up at the corner of the roof. His ruse had succeeded. The other sniper, seeing the cap and rifle fall, thought he had killed his man. He was now standing before a row of chimney pots, looking across, with his head clearly silhouetted against the western sky.

The Republican sniper smiled and lifted his revolver above the edge of the parapet. The distance was about fifty yards—a hard shot in the dim light, and his right arm was paining him like a thousand devils. He took a steady aim. His hand trembled with eagerness. Pressing his lips together, he took a deep breath through his nostrils and fired. He was almost deafened with the report and his arm shook with the recoil.

Then when the smoke cleared he peered across and uttered a cry of joy. His enemy had been hit. He was reeling over the parapet in his death agony. He struggled to keep his feet, but he was slowly falling forward, as if in a dream. The rifle fell from his grasp, hit the parapet, fell over, bounded off the pole of a barber's shop beneath and then clattered on the pavement.

Then the dying man on the roof crumpled up and fell forward. The body turned over and over in space and hit the ground with a dull thud. Then it lay still.

The sniper looked at his enemy falling and he shuddered. The lust of battle died in him. He became bitten by remorse. The sweat stood out in beads on his forehead. Weakened by his wound and the long summer day of fasting and watching on the roof, he revolted from the sight of the shattered mass of his dead enemy. His teeth chattered, he began to gibber to himself, cursing the war, cursing himself, cursing everybody.

He looked at the smoking revolver in his hand, and with an oath he hurled it to the roof at his feet. The revolver went off with the concussion and the bullet whizzed past the sniper's head. He was frightened back to his senses by the shock. His nerves steadied. The cloud of fear scattered from his mind and he laughed.

Taking the whiskey flask from his pocket, he emptied it at

a draught. He felt reckless under the influence of the spirit. He decided to leave the roof now and look for his company commander, to report. Everywhere around was quiet. There was not much danger in going through the streets. He picked up his revolver and put it in his pocket. Then he crawled down through the sky-light to the house underneath.

When the sniper reached the laneway on the street level, he felt a sudden curiosity as to the identity of the enemy sniper whom he had killed. He decided that he was a good shot, whoever he was. He wondered did he know him. Perhaps he had been in his own company before the split in the army. He dicided to risk going over to have a look at him. He peered round the corner into O'Connell Street. In the upper part of the street there was heavy firing, but around here all was quiet.

The sniper darted across the street. A machine-gun tore up the ground around him with a hail of bullets, but he escaped. He threw himself face downward beside the corpse. The machine-gun stopped.

The the sniper turned over the dead body and looked into his brother's face.

Interpreter's Notebook

"The Sniper" is an exciting adventure which depends heavily on the interpreter's ability to handle the omniscient narration. The moments of pain and frustration, and the startling twist at the end, require that the interpreter experience each moment fully, carefully illustrating each realization by the central character.

Don't rush it. Build slowly throughout and then pick up pace at the end. Strive for a "documentary" tone.

COMPOSED UPON WESTMINSTER BRIDGE
WILLIAM WORDSWORTH

Earth has not anything to show more fair:
Dull would he be of soul who could pass by
A sight so touching in its majesty:
This City now doth, like a garment, wear
The beauty of the morning; silent, bare,
Ships, towers, domes, theatres, and temples lie
Open unto the fields, and to the sky;

All bright and glittering in the smokeless air.
Never did sun more beautifully steep
In his first splendour, valley, rock, or hill;
Ne'er saw I, never felt, a calm so deep!
The river glideth at his own sweet will:
Dear God! the very houses seem asleep;
And all that mighty heart is lying still!

Interpreter's Notebook

"Composed upon Westminster Bridge" might not be immediately recognized
as a sonnet. Count the lines and plot the rhythm and rhyme scheme.
Wordsworth has enhanced the conversational quality of the poem by
periodically breaking the traditional iambic pentameter pattern. Note the
bold stroke of using a mixture of metric feet in line 6 and then tacking the
unaccented syllable "lie" onto the end of the line. "Lie open" actually
forms the first iamb of line 7. The effect is to sweep the poem along and
provide a build at its geometric center.

Give in to it. Trust Wordsworth's judgment here. He is showing you
how to read it. Make sure you know why you are saying these words. Your
inner life must be up to the level of the two exclamation points in the last
two lines.

INCIDENT
COUNTEE CULLEN

Once riding in old Baltimore,
    Heart-filled, head-filled with glee,
I saw a Baltimorean
    Keep looking straight at me.

Now I was eight and very small,
    And he was no whit bigger,
And so I smiled, but he poked out
    His tongue and called me, "Nigger."

I saw the whole of Baltimore
    From May until December:
Of all the things that happened there
    That's all that I remember.

ROTATION
JULIAN BOND

Like plump green floor plans
the pool tables squat
Among fawning mahogany Buddhas with felt heads.
Like clubwomen blessed with adultery
The balls dart to kiss
and tumble erring members into silent oblivion.
Right-angled over the verdant barbered turf
Sharks point long fingers at the multi-colored worlds
and play at percussion
Sounding cheap plastic clicks
in an 8-ball universe built for ivory.

Interpreter's Notebook

These two short poems capture a quick perception of the black experience in America. "Incident" confronts the problem directly, openly. "Rotation" uses a more abstract approach and employs metaphor and analogy. Play with emphasis until you can highlight ". . . 8-ball universe built for ivory." in the most effective way.

Both poems require a solid improvisational background. Make the stories longer and keep your subtext going.

THE ROAD NOT TAKEN
ROBERT FROST

Two roads diverged in a yellow wood,
And sorry I could not travel both
And be one traveler, long I stood
And looked down one as far as I could
To where it bent in the undergrowth;

Then took the other, as just as fair,
And having perhaps the better claim,
Because it was grassy and wanted wear;
Though as for that, the passing there
Had worn them really about the same,

And both that morning equally lay
In leaves no step had trodden black.
Oh, I kept the first for another day!
Yet knowing how way leads on to way,
I doubted if I should ever come back.

I shall be telling this with a sigh
Somewhere ages and ages hence:
Two roads diverged in a wood, and I—
I took the one less traveled by,
And that has made all the difference.

THE PLEASURE
DAVID IGNATOW

With broken tooth he clawed it,
with crooked finger held it,
and with naked eyes watched it
as he chewed, hair disheveled,
tie loose, shirt open, socks down—
a bum, greedy, therefore knowing.
How he chewed and how he swallowed
and wiped his lips with the back of his palm,
then spat blood of the raw-veined
brick-red lump meat; and went
looking for more down the side streets
of the market where the trash cans stank,
and came up with chunks greening
at the center and edges, but he chewed
and swallowed and dug for more,
a bum greedy, a bum alive,
a hungry one.

A LONDON THOROUGHFARE TWO A.M.
AMY LOWELL

They have watered the street,
It shines in the glare of lamps,
Cold, white lamps,
And lies

Like a slow-moving river,
Barred with silver and black.
Cabs go down it,
One,
And then another.
Between them I hear the shuffling of feet,
Tramps doze on the window-ledges,
Night walkers pass along the sidewalks.
The city is squalid and sinister,
With the silver-barred street in the midst,
Slow-moving,
A river leading nowhere.

Opposite my window,
The moon cuts,
Clear and round,
Through the plum-colored night.
She cannot light the city;
It is too bright.
It has white lamps,
And glitters coldly.
I stand in the window and watch the moon.
She is thin and lusterless,
But I love her.
I know the moon,
And this is an alien city.

Interpreter's Notebook

"A London Thoroughfare Two A. M." provides a good example of the "historical present." Don't try to set it up as if you are making observations now. Sometimes we use the present tense to describe past events in order to give them a sense of immediacy. Recall the details of the scene slowly. The layout of the poem on the page suggests the tempo. Also the repetition of "slow-moving" and words like "shuffling," "doze," "pass," and "leading nowhere" suggest a slow pace.

Note how the alliteration sets the tone:

The city is squalid and sinister,
With the silver-barred street in the midst,
Slow-moving, . . .

The *s* sound is used nine times in the preceding fourteen words. Try some subtle emphasis, but don't overdo it.

THE BATH TUB
EZRA POUND

As a bathtub lined with white porcelain,
When the hot water gives out or goes tepid,
So is the slow cooling of our chivalrous passion,
O my much praised but-not-altogether-satisfactory lady.

THE UNKNOWN CITIZEN
(To JS/07/M/378 This Marble Monument
Is Erected by the State)
W. H. AUDEN

He was found by the Bureau of Stastics to be
One against whom there was no official complaint,
And all the reports on his conduct agree
That, in the modern sense of an old-fashioned word, he was a
    saint,

For in everything he did he served the Greater Community.
Except for the War, till the day he retired
He worked in a factory and never got fired,
But satisfied his employers, Fudge Motors Inc.
Yet he wasn't a scab or odd in his views,
For his Union reports that he paid his dues,
(Our report on his Union shows it was sound)
And our Social Psychology workers found
That he was popular with his mates and liked a drink.
The Press are convinced that he bought a paper every
    day
And that his reactions to advertisments were normal
    in every way.
Policies taken out in his name prove that he was fully insured,
And his Health-card shows he was once in hospital but left it
    cured.
Both Producers Research and High-Grade Living declare

He was fully sensible to the advantages of the Installment Plan
And had everything necessary to the Modern Man,
A phonograph, a radio, a car and a frigidaire.
Our researchers into Public Opinion are content
That he held the proper opinions for the time of year;
When there was peace, he was for peace; when there was
    war, he went.
He was married and added five children to the population,
Which our Eugenist says was the right number for a parent of
    his generation,
And our teachers report that he never interfered with their
    education.
Was he free? Was he happy? The question is absurd:
Had anything been wrong, we should certainly have heard.

Interpreter's Notebook

To properly approach the poem "The Unknown Citizen," begin your improvisation with the questions at the end. The poem is an attempt to answer these questions. The tone is defensive. The narrator needs some characterization; who are you?

Chapter 4. Preparing the Performance: The Rehearsal Stage

KEY CONCEPTS

Auralizing

Meaning clusters

Improvisation

Picking up the line

47

THE IMAGINARY AUDIENCE

The main thing to keep in mind during the rehearsal stage is that you are moving toward a performance before an audience. Create an imaginary audience and have it present throughout your rehearsal period. If you are like most people, your imaginary audience will be far more critical of your work than a real one. Keeping an audience in mind during rehearsal gives a performer objectivity, and you must quickly learn to be objectively critical about your own performance.

If you own recording equipment, it can be useful in giving you a more objective point of view. However, if it cannot be set up unobtrusively, it will be more of a hindrance than a help. Under no circumstances should you confine yourself to one small area in front of a microphone, or hold a microphone in your hand.

AURALIZING

Pick up your selection and read it out loud. From this point on all work on the selection should be done orally. **Gottlieb's Second Principle** states: *If you are not reading out loud, you are not rehearsing.* Continue reading the selection two or three times, or until the sound of your own voice no longer surprises you.

You will have noted by now whether you can pronounce all the words in the selection with relative ease. You will also be aware of words whose meaning may not be clear to you. In either case, consult your dictionary immediately. Nothing will destroy an otherwise good performance more quickly than a mispronounced or misunderstood word.

If your selection is a poem, you may notice that the lines end before the sentence, and it sounds awkward to stop at the end of each line.

IN WASTE PLACES
JAMES STEPHENS

As a naked man I go
Through the desert, sore afraid;
Holding high my head, although
I'm as frightened as a maid.

The lion crouches there! I saw
In barren rocks his amber eye!
He parts the cactus with his paw!
He stares at me as I go by!

He would pad upon my trace
If he thought I was afraid!
If he knew my hardy face
Veils the terrors of a maid.

He rises in the nighttime, and
He stretches forth! He snuffs the air!
He roars! He leaps along the sand!
He creeps! He watches everywhere!

His burning eyes, his eyes of bale
Through the darkness I can see!
He lashes fiercely with his tail!
He makes again to spring at me!

I am the lion, and his lair!
I am the fear that frightens me!
I am the desert of despair!
And the night of agony!

Night or day, whate'er befall,
I must walk that desert land,
Until I dare my fear and call
The lion out to lick my hand.

Stopping consistently at the end of each line, particularly when there is a rhyme scheme, produces an undesirable sing-song effect. As a reader, try to ignore the rhyme scheme, or, at least, do not stress it.

A similar problem occurs with prose. You may find that it is awkward or unnatural to pause only at the punctuation marks.

From HOW GRANDPA CAME INTO THE MONEY
ELSE ZANTNER

He was a sweet soul, my grandfather, but when the brains were passed out he must have been absent. I still marvel how Grandmother could raise a family on his earnings.

We all lived in one little house and we were a scrawny lot. Nobody ever had to coax any of us children to eat. In fact, after having had lunch at my mother's, I would go upstairs to Grandmother and have another one. And then I would visit Aunt Bertha, who lived a few doors away, and eat some more.

What a ripe apple tasted like I found out only when I was well over fifteen and apprenticed to a shopkeeper in the city. Apples did not ripen in our village—they never had a chance. They were so sour they would have pulled the holes in our stockings together. But no apples ever tasted as good again as those little green ones!

One time in my entire childhood I felt good and full: Aunt Bertha had forgotten to lock the larder and I detected, disappeared with, and devoured twenty-two doughnuts. The rest of the family never forgot nor forgave me. Years later when I would arrive at family gatherings someone would always shout, "Watch the doughnuts!"

Perhaps you can imagine what it meant when, one fine day, fortune smiled on Grandfather. He got himself in a trainwreck!

Now, if something like that happened to you (and you survived) you had it made. The railroad would pay! So all of the lucky passengers knew exactly what to do: they commenced to groan piteously and writhe upon the ground while waiting for the doctors and stretcher bearers to arrive.

All but Grandfather!

He had a better appetite than the rest of us combined. Never in his life had he missed a meal and he was not going to start now. No sir! Not for a puny trainwreck. So he cut himself a stout walking stick and set out for home—a three-hour walk.

In the meantime, the news of the wreck had already reached the village and the telegram had said, "No fatalities."

I cannot describe the many looks that passed across my grandmother's face when she saw her husband come striding in the door, covered with dust, a bit tired from his long walk, but sound of limb and smiling broadly for he was just in time for dinner. First came relief at seeing her man unharmed. Then the relief mingled with and finally was replaced by fury.

Grandfather had passed up his one and only golden opportunity!

So she turned into a kind of tornado. Before he knew what was happening, he found himself minus his pants and in bed. His plaintive protests did him no good. Grandma slapped a wet towel on his head while Mother went to search for the only medicine we had in the house—castor oil!

Your next task is to mark the *meaning clusters*. Using a pencil, make a slash mark (/) at the end of each meaning cluster. There is no "right" way to select meaning clusters. While in most cases there will be a high level of consensus, each individual is free to phrase in a way that is comfortable and compatible with his or her own natural phrasing pattern, as long as the phrasing doesn't alter the meaning in a way that is inconsistent with the text.

> As a naked man/ I go
> Through the desert, sore afraid;/
> Holding high my head,/ although/
> I'm as frightened as a maid./

He was a sweet soul, my grandfather,/ but/ when the brains were passed out/ he must have been absent./ I still marvel how Grandmother could raise a family on his earnings./

While it may not be necessary to mark the meaning clusters for an entire selection of prose, be sure to mark the more difficult passages.

As you can see, sometimes clusters will conform to the punctuation and line stops, and sometimes not. Having marked the clusters, put your selection aside momentarily and read through (aloud!) the paraphrase you prepared during the analysis.

Do you still feel that your version is accurate? If not, make whatever changes you feel are necessary, and read it aloud again. At this point, most beginning readers become aware of a discrepancy in "sound" between the original and the paraphrase. The original tends to sound stilted, while the paraphrase, primarily because of word choice, sounds more natural—more like speech. Your problem at this moment is to make the original text sound more like the paraphrase. This brings us to **Gottlieb's Third Principle:** *The final product should sound as if you were saying the words for the first time—*spontaneously, naturally.

IMPROVISATION

The creation of this "spontaneous" effect is the primary goal at this stage of rehearsal. It is accomplished through a step-by-step process. First, do a simple improvisation. Imagine yourself as the narrator you have already visualized in your analysis. Now, as the narrator, with one eye on your paraphrase, invent a situation within which you could logically be saying the words of your selection. Ask yourself (1) who am I? and (2) why am I saying these things to this group of people? Here again a few general rules apply.

It is usually more productive for a reader to accept the notion that the creation of nearly all literature is a retrospective exercise. The writer does not, as a rule, take pen and paper and fashion a poem, story, novel, or play at the moment of experience. The writer first lives through the experience or group of experiences which form the impression, and later, in retrospect, casts them into written form. The reader's job is not to recreate the moment of experience, but to illustrate the process of literary creation as that moment is called forth from memory.

Many beginning readers make the mistake of considering the creation of literary art a solitary enterprise. It is true that an author usually works in solitude, but there is an implicit audience present. The literature has a voice, and this voice is addressing someone. The reader is not portraying the author, he is portraying this voice; and the implicit audience becomes the actual audience during performance. The audience should be perceived not as passive recipients of your performance, but rather as participants in a complex series of events which culminate in the necessity for you to say the words of the text. **Gottlieb's Fourth Principle** states: *The audience is always part of the performance.*

For the purpose of the improvisation, think of the actual words of your selection as part of a continuum. What events or words have just preceded the words of the selection? What follows? What question might someone in your audience have asked to which the first line of your selection is the logical answer? Work through the poem or short story, adding parts of your paraphrase when necessary to make it real. Try to remember each word, each image. Let the event happen first in your mind, find a reason to communicate it, then speak. Throughout, you should hear a voice saying, "Take your time, think it through, remember." It is the voice of **Gottlieb's Fifth Principle:** *Thought precedes verbalization.* Do not allow the words to jump from the text into your mouth without stopping a moment in your brain.

What follows is one student's improvisation and extended paraphrase for Malcolm Cowley's "The Long Voyage." First, here is the actual poem.

THE LONG VOYAGE
MALCOLM COWLEY

Not that the pines were darker there,
nor mid-May dogwood brighter there,
nor swifts more swift in summer air;
    it was my own country,

having its thunderclap of spring,
its long midsummer ripening,
its corn hoar-stiff at harvesting,
　　almost like any country,

yet being mine; its face, its speech,
its hills bent low within my reach,
its river birch and upland beech
　　were mine, of my own country.

Now the dark waters at the bow
fold back, like earth against the plow;
foam brightens like the dogwood now
　　at home, in my own country.

Well, I'm on this ship, and I've been away from home for a long time. Today, the sun is shining and the air has a balmy warmth to it. I've just spent about an hour looking over the rail at the water and wishing I were home. Since I'm usually very outgoing and talkative, you, the others on the ship with me, ask me what's wrong. I tell you I'm homesick, and you want to know what's so special about where I come from. I try to explain that it's not the features of my country which make it so important to me. That it's *Not that the pines were darker there, nor mid-May dogwood brighter there, nor swifts more swift in summer air;* it's not that these things are different but *it was my own country,* and that's the difference. There's just nothing particularly great about its features. I think about its *having its thunderclap of spring, its long midsummer ripening,* and I remember *its corn hoar-still at harvesting,* and I think it's probably *almost like any country. Yet,* and this is the main point, *being mine; its face, its speech, its hills bent low within my reach, its river birch and upland beech were mine, of my own country.* And now, see, things are reminding me of home. *Now the dark waters at the bow* of this ship *fold back,* and to me it looks *like earth against the plow;* the *foam brightens* in the sun and looks *like the dogwood now at home, in my own country*—and these images are making me homesick.

The process is to continue rehearsing in this manner, moving always closer to the words of the text. It is useful to think of those parts of your improvisation and extended paraphrase which are not actual lines from the poem or phrases from the prose as thought or *subtext*—something which you say to yourself, but not to your audience.

PICKING UP THE LINE

At this point in the rehearsal process, the interpreter has usually committed large sections of the selection to memory without even trying. Except in specialized instances, where it is necessary for the interpreter to perform some complicated action or to be away from the text for a long period of time, a conscious attempt at memorization is not advisable. When we set out to memorize something, we often memorize patterns of inflection and emphasis along with the words of the text. In performance, these set patterns of inflection and emphasis can rob a reading of its spontaneity.

We are trying to give our audience the impression that the words we are saying are our own, or the words of the character we have created to be our narrator. Further, we are creating the illusion that these words—the words of the literature—are being said for the very first time, that they are being generated out of the circumstances and necessities of the moment and the narrator's need to say these things to this audience.

Of course, in most cases the audience is not really fooled. Audiences bring a set of assumptions with them to a performance, and they experience more or less what they expect to experience. In a sense, the interpreter enters into a conspiracy with the audience members, who willingly suspend their disbelief in what is taking place. In short, if the interpreter does not call attention to the fact that the words being spoken are not his or her own, the audience will readily respond to them as if they were. If the interpreter's performance sounds like reading or looks like reading, the purpose will be defeated. The previous material will help you avoid sounding as if you're reading, but if you are to avoid looking as if you're reading, you must learn to pick up the line.

Look at the first line of your poem, or the first phrase or sentence of your prose. Depend on your short-term memory and lift your eyes from the page. Now, say the line, phrase, or sentence aloud. Return your eyes to the page and pick up the second line, phrase, or sentence, and do the same thing. Repeat this procedure throughout the entire selection. ***Gottlieb's Sixth Principle*** states: *Speak to your audience, not to your book.*

This technique must be practiced until it no longer feels awkward. This usually occurs when you no longer worry about losing your place in the text. Keeping your place should not be a problem if the selection is well rehearsed. Simply place your thumb along the margin as a guide to where you left off. As you become more familiar with your selection, you will be able to "pick up" larger chunks of the manuscript.

Until you master this technique, you will not be able to progress as an interpretive artist. Once mastered, it will soon become second nature and give a luster of professionalism to your performance. For those of you who subject yourselves to tryouts of various kinds, the pick-up technique will allow you to give superb "cold" readings.

QUESTIONS FOR STUDY AND DISCUSSION

1
Why are you not rehearsing if you are not reading aloud?

2
What is a sing-song effect? Why is it undesirable?

3
Why don't meaning clusters always conform to punctuation marks?

4
Why is the audience always part of the performance?

5
What is meant by the phrase "willing suspension of disbelief"?

SUGGESTED ACTIVITIES

1
Select a poem or piece of prose and practice picking up the line.

2
Develop an improvisation involving the events of a poem and two or more people.

3
Select a poem and mark the meaning clusters.

4
Repeat the above using prose.

Selections for Analysis and Performance

AN ATTEMPT AT REFORM
AUGUST STRINDBERG

She had noticed with indignation that girls were solely brought up to be housekeepers for their future husbands. Therefore she had learned a trade which would enable her to keep herself in all circumstances of life. She made artificial flowers.

He had noticed with regret that girls simply waited for a husband who should keep them; he resolved to marry a free and independent woman who could earn her own living; such a woman would be his equal and a companion for life, not a housekeeper.

Fate ordained that they should meet. He was an artist and she made, as I already mentioned, flowers; they were both living in Paris at the time when they conceived these ideas.

There was style in their marriage. The took three rooms at Passy. In the centre was the studio, to the right of it his room, to the left hers. This did away with the common bedroom and double bed, that abomination which has no counterpart in nature and is responsible for a great deal of dissipation and immorality. It moreover did away with the inconvenience of having to dress and undress in the same room. It was far better that each of them should have a separate room and that the studio should be a neutral, common meeting-place.

They required no servant; they were going to do the cooking themselves and employ an old charwoman in the mornings and evenings. It was all very well thought out and excellent in theory.

"But supposing you had children?" asked the sceptics.

"Nonsense, there won't be any!"

It worked splendidly. He went to the market in the morning and did the catering. Then he made the coffee. She made the beds and put the rooms in order. And then they sat down and worked.

When they were tired of working they gossiped, gave one another good advice, laughed and were very jolly.

At twelve o'clock he lit the kitchen fire and she prepared the vegetables. He cooked the beef, while she ran across the street to the grocer's: then she laid the table and he dished up the dinner.

Of course, they loved one another as husbands and wives do. They said good night to each other and went into their own rooms, but there was no lock to keep him out when he knocked at her door; but the accomodation was small and the morning found them in their own quarters. Then he knocked at the wall.

"Good morning, little girlie, how are you today?"

"Very well, darling, and you?"

Their meeting at breakfast was always like a new experience which never grew stale.

They often went out together in the evening and frequently met their countrymen. She had no objection to the smell of tobacco, and was never in the way. Everybody said it was an ideal marriage; no one had ever known a happier couple.

But the young wife's parents, who lived a long way off, were always writing and asking all sorts of indelicate questions; they were longing to have a grandchild. Louisa ought to remember that the institution of marriage existed for the benefit of the children, not the parents. Louisa held that this view was an old-fashioned one. Mama asked whether she did not think that the result of the new ideas would be the complete extirpation of mankind? Louisa had never looked at it in that light, and moreover the question did not interest her. Both she and her husband were happy; at last the spectacle of a happy married couple was presented to the world, and the world was envious.

Life was very pleasant. Neither of them was master and they shared expenses. Now he earned more, now she did, but in the end their contributions to the common fund amounted to the same figure.

Then she had a birthday! She was awakened in the morning by the entrance of the charwoman with a bunch of flowers and a letter painted all over with flowers, and containing the following words:

"To the lady flower-bud from her dauber, who wishes her many happy returns of the day and begs her to honor him with her company at an excellent little breakfast—at once."

She knocked at his door—come in!

And they breakfasted, sitting on the bed—his bed; and the charwoman was kept the whole day to do all the work. It was a lovely birthday!

Their happiness never palled. It lasted two years. All the prophets had prophesied falsely.

It was a model marriage!

But when two years had passed, the young wife fell ill. She put it down to some poison contained in the wall-paper; he suggested germs of some sort. Yes, certainly, germs. But something was wrong. Something was not as it should be. She must have caught cold. Then she grew stout. Was she suffering from tumour? Yes, they were afraid that she was.

She consulted a doctor—and came home crying. It was indeed a growth, but one which would one day see daylight, grow into a flower and bear fruit.

The husband did anything but cry. He found style in it, and then the wretch went to his club and boasted about it to his friends. But the wife still wept. What would her position be now? She would soon not be able to earn money with her work and then she would have to live on him. And they would have to have a servant! Ugh! those servants!

All their care, their caution, their wariness had been wrecked on the rock of the inevitable.

But the mother-in-law wrote enthusiastic letters and repeated over and over again that marriage was instituted by God for the protection of the children; the parents' pleasure counted for very little.

Hugo implored her to forget the fact that she would not be able to earn anything in future. Didn't she do her full share of the work by mothering the baby? Wasn't that as good as money? Money was, rightly understood, nothing but work. Therefore she paid her share in full.

It took her a long time to get over the fact that he had to keep her. But when the baby came, she forgot all about it. She remained his wife and companion as before in addition to being the mother of his child, and he found that this was worth more than anything else.

Interpreter's Notebook

"An Attempt at Reform" is a very carefully constructed story. Pay close attention to the images and the choice of words. In the beginning the couple "conceives" ideas, and she makes "artificial flowers." At the end they "conceive" in the real sense of the word, and the "lady flower-bud" develops a "growth . . . which would one day see daylight, grow into a flower and bear fruit."

Lead the audience with subtle shades of emphasis to make sure they note the progression from the artificial to the real. Consider your attitude as the omniscient narrator. Are you amused? Ironic? Sarcastic?

THE LOST SOUL
BEN HECHT

It would be dawn soon.

The man in the cell was unable to sleep. He had dressed himself. He stood looking out of a small barred window at the waning night and the winter stars going away.

Two heavy-set men with tired puffy unshaven faces were also in this cell. They stared at the cell walls with a remarkable ox-like persistency.

Then, as if overcome by a secret curiosity, they turned their eyes on the man at the barred window and looked shyly over his shoulder at the first colours of dawn.

Yet a fourth man appeared.

The two heavy-set men greeted him with unexpected dignity in their voices.

"Hello, Doc," said one.

"What time is it?" said the other.

The cell door was unlocked. The doctor came in. He took a small silver pencil out of his vest pocket and began rolling it back and forth between his thumb and fingers. Then he cocked his eye at the unshaded electric light burning high up in the cell. He was very nervous.

"Hello," he said.

The one at the window turned. He was smiling.

"How do you feel?" the doctor asked, continuing with the silver pencil.

The one at the window shook his head with a rather queer good-humoured politeness.

"I didn't sleep well," he answered. "I suppose it doesn't help any to worry. But . . . well . . . I was just talking to these two men here who have been good enough to keep me company. You see, I'm in a very awkward predicament . . . I don't know who I am."

The doctor blinked. Then he turned and stared at the two heavy-set men. They looked remarkably inscrutable—even for oxen. The doctor put the silver pencil away and removed a black leather case from his coat pocket. He opened it and took out a stethoscope.

"Just a formality," he muttered. "Open your shirt, please."
He put the instrument on the man's chest and listened.

"Very remarkable," he spoke after a long pause of listening.
"Normal. Absolutely normal heart action."

The two heavy-set men nodded mechanically but correctly.
There is a certain etiquette of nodding and staring which the
laity proudly observe in their relation with the professions.

"I don't know who I am," the man at the window resumed
in a slightly high-pitched tone, rebuttoning his shirt. "I feel all
right, doctor. But I haven't the faintest idea"—the queer, good-
natured smile played apologetically behind his words—"I haven't
the slightest idea what my name is. I presume the officials are
working hard and doing all they can . . . to determine. But it's
getting a little on my nerves. It's lucky I have a sense of humour.
Otherwise. Well. Imagine finding yourself in jail. And just not
knowing who the deuce you are or where you come from. I
suppose I was picked up roaming around. Nevertheless it doesn't
seem right to me to put a man in jail. They might have been
decent enough to think of a hospital. Or a hotel. I unquestionably
have a family who are worrying. You know, I've been trying to
figure out what sort of man I am. It's very interesting. For
instance, I'm obviously educated and unused to jails."

The doctor turned to the two heavy-set men. They shrugged
their shoulders. The doctor looked at his wrist-watch hurriedly.

"What time is it?" one of the heavy-set men asked in a shy
voice.

The one at the window sighed and went on talking as the
doctor, with a secretive gesture, held his wrist-watch for the two
heavy-set men to look at. They looked and nodded.

"I've searched through my pockets," he was saying from
the window, "and not a shred of identification. No pocketbook
or handerchief or any marks. Of course—my hands. Not those
of a working man, I should say. And—a—"

He stopped and began rubbing the back of his head.

"Don't you remember coming here?" the doctor asked,
looking intently at the man.

"No, I can't say I do," he answered. "I feel quite aware of
everything in the present. But the past. Well! the past—"

He closed his eyes and frowned. A slightly bewildered and
contemptuous chuckle started his words again.

"Of course, efficiency is more than one has a right to
expect from the police. Or they would have had me photo-
graphed. As I was telling these two men. And my picture put in
the newspapers so that my family would see it and sort of claim
me. Obviously"—he stared at the doctor with some anger—
"obviously I'm somebody of importance."

"The doctor drew a deep breath.

"Don't you remember," he began.

"Nothing," the man at the window interrupted irritably. "Pardon me. I don't mean to get angry. But it's damned awkward. You know, I might be somebody very important—with all sorts of people dependent and worried. There's some medical term for this condition, isn't there, doctor? I forget at the moment. The sensation is decidedly queer. And amusing."

He was staring at the beginning of morning light beyond the barred window.

"I don't know why I should feel amused," he chuckled. "In reality what it amounts to, I suppose, is that I have lost my soul. Or, that is, misplaced it for the time being. A most serious matter, it seems to me. But, damn it, I must be a humorist or something. Because the situation makes me want to laugh. I'm sure most men would be wailing and tearing their hair if they suddenly lost their soul. But really, I—"

His face spread in a grin and he began laughing softly.

"By God, what a beautiful morning," he murmured, his eyes again on the world outside. "Doctor,"—he crossed to where the doctor stood regarding him, the silver pencil again working between his thumb and fingers. "Doctor, if I could only get hold of my name," he whispered, "who am I . . . who . . ."

The doctor cleared his throat.

"Your name is," he began, "is—"

He stopped. There were footsteps in the corridor. People were coming.

A group of six men came walking toward the cell. The two heavy-set men stood up and shook their legs. The doctor grew excited. He stepped into the group and began talking hurriedly and in a lowered voice.

"Don't read it," he repeated, "it'll just give us a lot of trouble, sheriff. He's amnesic. It'd just be borrowing trouble to wake him up. Let him go this way."

"Well, he'll find out pretty soon," said the sheriff.

"I doubt it," the doctor whispered. "Anyway, by the time he does you'll have him strapped and—"

"All right"—the sheriff thrust a sheet of typewritten paper in his pocket—"let's go."

"Come on." The doctor returned to the cell.

The man at the window nodded good-naturedly. The doctor took his arm and led him into the group.

They fell into place around him—two on each side, two in front, the two heavy-set men behind and the doctor still holding his arm and watching his face.

"You see," the man in the centre began talking at once,

eagerly, quickly, as if a dizziness swayed the edges of his words, "I haven't the least idea who I am, gentlemen. But if you'll be patient with me, I'm sure my family or some other clue . . . I dislike being such a bother. Is that a clergyman? Where, by the way, are you taking me? Please . . . I insist! I must know! Where are you taking me? Good God!"

Silently, without answer to this amazing question, the marchers escorting James Hartley to the gallows continued on their way.

And in the tall, gloomy death chamber a hundred or more spectators sat waiting for the hanging of the creature known as the Axe Fiend who a few months ago had murdered his wife and two children in their sleep.

The group of marchers stepped through an opened door on to the gallows platform.

A confusion ensued. Figures moved about on the platform. Then, out of the bustle on the high platform, an amazed face looked down on the spectators. The mouth of this face was opened as if it were about to scream. Its eyes moved wildly as if they had become uncentred. Gasps came from it.

A shiny yellow rope was being tightened around its neck.

A man was adjusting a voluminous white wrapper about the figure under the rope.

Another man was stepping forward with a white hood in his hands. Suddenly the face screamed.

Three words filled the smoke-laden air—three words uttered in a sob so pitiful, so agonized, so startled that the sheriff paused with the white hood.

"This ain't me!" screamed the face. "This ain't ME!"

The spectators held their breaths, and stared.

A white bundle was swaying and twisting on the end of a long thin yellow rope.

RICHARD CORY
EDWIN ARLINGTON ROBINSON

Whenever Richard Cory went down town,
We people on the pavement looked at him:
He was a gentleman from sole to crown,
Clean favored, and imperially slim.

And he was always quietly arrayed,
And he was always human when he talked;

But still he fluttered pulses when he said,
"Good-morning," and he glittered when he walked.

And he was rich—yes, richer than a king—
And admirably schooled in every grace:
In fine, we thought that he was everything
To make us wish that we were in his place.

So on we worked, and waited for the light,
And went without the meat, and cursed the bread;
And Richard Cory, one calm summer night,
Went home and put a bullet through his head.

RICHARD CORY
With Apologies to E. A. Robinson
PAUL SIMON

They say that Richard Cory owns
One half of this old town,
With elliptical connections
To spread his wealth around.
Born into Society,
A banker's only child,
He had everything a man could want:
Power, grace and style.

Refrain
But I, I work in his factory
And I curse the life I'm livin'
And I curse my poverty
And I wish that I could be
Oh I wish that I could be
Oh I wish that I could be
Richard Cory.

The papers print his picture
Almost everywhere he goes:
Richard Cory at the opera,
Richard Cory at a show
And the rumor of his party
And the orgies on his yacht—

Oh he surely must be happy
With everything he's got.   *(Refrain.)*

He really gave to charity,
He had the common touch,
And they were grateful for his patronage
And they thanked him very much,
So my mind was filled with wonder
When the evening headlines read:
    "Richard Cory went home last night
    And put a bullet through his head."   *(Refrain.)*

Interpreter's Notebook

In performing "Richard Cory" the key is to begin with your surprise and disbelief already in place. In both versions you already know Richard Cory is dead. The poem and the song lyric based on it are reactions to news.

Handle the song lyrics the same way you would any poem. You will need to work for some justification which will allow you to repeat the refrain three times realistically.

FROG AUTUMN
SYLVIA PLATH

Summer grows old, cold-blooded mother.
The insects are scant, skinny.
In these palustral homes we only
Croak and wither.

Mornings dissipate in somnolence.
The sun brightens tardily
Among the pithless reeds. Flies fail us.
The fen sickens.

Frost drops even the spider. Clearly
The genius of plenitude
Houses himself elsewhere. Our folk thin
Lamentably.

EXILED
EDNA ST. VINCENT MILLAY

Searching my heart for its true sorrow,
  This is the thing I find to be:
That I am weary of words and people,
  Sick of the city, wanting the sea;
Wanting the sticky, salty sweetness
  Of the strong wind and shattered spray;
Wanting the loud sound and the soft sound
  Of the big surf that breaks all day.

Always before about my dooryard,
  Marking the reach of the winter sea,
Rooted in sand and dragging driftwood,
  Straggled the purple wild sweet pea;

Always I climbed the wave at morning,
  Shook the sand from my shoes at night,
That now am caught beneath great buildings,
  Stricken with noise, confused with light.

If I could hear the green piles groaning
  Under the windy wooden piers,
See again the bobbing barrels,
  And the black sticks that fence the weirs,

If I could see the weedy mussels
  Crusting the wrecked and rotting hulls,
Hear once again the hungry crying
  Overhead, of the wheeling gulls,

Feel once again the shanty straining
  Under the turning of the tide,
Fear once again the rising freshet,
  Dread the bell in the fog outside,

I should be happy—that was happy
  All day long on the coast of Maine.
I have a need to hold and handle
  Shells and anchors and ships again!

I should be happy, that am happy
Never at all since I came here.
I am too long away from water.
I have a need of water near.

THE LEADEN-EYED
VACHEL LINDSAY

Let not young souls be smothered out before
They do quaint deeds and fully flaunt their pride.
It is the world's one crime its babes grow dull,
Its poor are oxlike, limp, and leaden-eyed.
Not that they starve, but starve so dreamlessly,
Not that they sow, but that they seldom reap,
Not that they serve, but have no gods to serve;
Not that they die, but that they die like sheep.

Interpreter's Notebook

"The Leaden-Eyed" requires some characterization for the narrator. Ask yourself, "What situation could I be in that would require me to say these words?" The tone is both formal and passionate. You cannot approach the poem timidly.

SPRING AND FALL: TO A YOUNG CHILD
GERARD MANLEY HOPKINS

Margaret, are you grieving
Over Goldengrove unleaving?
Leaves, like the things of man, you
With your fresh thoughts care for, can you?
Ah! as the heart grows older
It will come to such sights colder
By and by, nor spare a sigh
Though worlds of wanwood leafmeal lie;
And yet you will weep and know why.
Now no matter, child, the name:
Sorrow's springs are the same.
Nor mouth had, no nor mind, expressed

What heart heard of, ghost guessed:
It is the blight man was born for,
It is Margaret you mourn for.

Interpreter's Notebook

Hopkins is often referred to as the originator of *sprung rhythm,* a poetic form based on stress rather than on the metric foot. As in "Spring and Fall: To a Young Child," each line has four stressed syllables, but many of the lines follow no particular metric pattern. Tucked in the middle, however, are four lines of pure iambic pentameter (lines 5 through 8). Be careful not to get caught up in a sing-song pattern as you move through these lines. Yet, it is clear that the poet sees these lines as a unit.

You cannot trust the ends of lines to define your sense units. Many times the thought is carried over into the next line, as with "It will come to such sights colder/by and by, . . ."

NOBODY LOSES ALL THE TIME
e. e. cummings

nobody loses all the time

i had an uncle named
Sol who was a born failure and
nearly everybody said he should have gone
into vaudeville perhaps because my Uncle Sol could
sing McCann He Was a Driver on Xmas Eve like Hell Itself
   which
may or may not account for the fact that my Uncle

Sol indulged in that possibly most inexcusable
of all to use a highfalootin phrase
luxuries that is or to
wit farming and be
it needlessly
added

my Uncle Sol's farm
failed because the chickens
ate the vegetables so

my Uncle Sol had a
chicken farm till the
skunks ate the chickens when

my Uncle Sol
had a skunk farm but
the skunks caught cold and
died and so
my Uncle Sol imitated the
skunks in a subtle manner

or by drowning himself in the watertank
but somebody who's given my Uncle Sol a Victor
Victrola and records while he lived presented to
him upon the auspicious occasion of his decease a
scrumptious not to mention splendiferous funeral with
tall boys in black gloves and flowers and everything and

i remember we all cried like the Missouri
when my Uncle Sol's coffin lurched because
somebody pressed a button
(and down went
my Uncle
Sol

and started a worm farm)

MY LAST DUCHESS
Ferrara
ROBERT BROWNING

That's my last Duchess painted on the wall,
Looking as if she were alive, I call
That piece a wonder, now: Fra Pandolf's hands
Worked busily a day, and there she stands.
Will't please you sit and look at her? I said
"Fra Pandolf" by design, for never read
Strangers like you that pictured countenance,
The depth and passion of its earnest glance,
But to myself they turned (since none puts by
The curtain I have drawn for you, but I)

And seemed as they would ask me, if they durst,
How such a glance came there; so, not the first
Are you to turn and ask thus. Sir, 'twas not
Her husband's presence only, called that spot
Of joy into the Duchess' cheek: perhaps
Fra Pandolf chanced to say, "Her mantle laps
Over my lady's wrist too much," or "Paint
Must never hope to reproduce the faint
Half-flush that dies along her throat": such stuff
Was courtesy, she thought, and cause enough
For calling up that spot of joy. She had
A heart—how shall I say?—too soon made glad,
Too easily impressed; she liked whate'er
She looked on, and her looks went everywhere.
Sir, 'twas all one! My favour at her breast,
The dropping of the daylight in the West,
The bough of cherries some officious fool
Broke in the orchard for her, the white mule
She rode with round the terrace—all and each
Would draw from her alike the approving speech,
Or blush, at least. She thanked men,—good! but thanked
Somehow—I know not how—as if she ranked
My gift of a nine-hundred-years-old name
With anybody's gift. Who'd stoop to blame
This sort of trifling? Even had you skill
In speech—(which I have not)—to make your will
Quite clear to such an one, and say, "Just this
Or that in you disgusts me; here you miss,
Or there exceed the mark"—and if she let
Herself be lessoned so, nor plainly set
Her wits to yours, forsooth, and made excuse,
—E'en then would be some stooping; and I choose
Never to stoop. Oh sir, she smiled, no doubt,
Whene'er I passed her; but who passed without
Much the same smile? This grew; I gave commands;
Then all smiles stopped together. There she stands
As if alive. Will't please you rise? We'll meet
The company below, then. I repeat,
The Count your master's known munificence
Is ample warrant that no just pretence
Of mine for dowry will be disallowed;
Though his fair daughter's self, as I avowed

At starting, is my object. Nay, we'll go
Together down, sir. Notice Neptune, though,
Taming a sea-horse, thought a rarity,
Which Claus of Innsbruck cast in bronze for me!

Interpreter's Notebook

In "My Last Duchess", Browning has chosen to put forth his message in the form of a dramatic monologue. Someone else is assumed to be present even though this other person doesn't speak. Think of your audience as this other person, and address them as if they had asked the questions or expressed the curiosity to which the words of this poem are the answer.

The first-person narrator in this poem requires characterization. Remember, you are a duke. You are stiff, formal, snobbish, and perhaps a little crazy. Take your time to work through each assertion. Spontaneity is an absolute requirement. The thoughts must appear to come from your mind, not the page.

Chapter 5
Tuning the Instrument: Your Voice and Your Body

KEY CONCEPTS

Breathing

Volume and projection

Pitch

Articulation, pronunciation, and dialect

Physical awareness

Physical action

Empathy

As pointed out in Chapter 1, there have been periods in the history of oral interpretation which stressed the techniques of presentation over other values of the interpretive performance. It should be apparent by now that this is not the approach of this text. The best interpretive performances grow out of a union of the interpreter and the text, creating the illusion that the words of the text are the words of the narrator created by the interpreter to say them. This union can be achieved only by internalizing the experience contained within the text, and presenting that experience with as much reality as possible.

However, interpretation is a performing art, and, as such, some attention must be paid to the techniques of projecting that internalized experience to the audience. In short, the experience of the text must be communicated. After employing mind and emotion, the interpreter must turn his or her attention to voice and body, those parts of the instrument which will ultimately convey the experience in the performance setting.

It is highly recommended that any serious student of interpretation take courses in voice and articulation as well as courses which focus on bodily awareness, such as dance, mime, or fencing. This chapter highlights some of the important technical considerations of the interpretive performance, but is not intended to be comprehensive.

THE INTERPRETER'S VOICE

What a wonderful thing the voice is. It speaks, it cries, it laughs, it yells. It expresses love and hate, fear and anxiety. It sets us apart from others; there are no two exactly alike. It makes us human. The interpreter depends on the voice and all its capabilities to communicate the text. The better the interpreter uses the voice, the better the performance will be. We may never achieve the virtuosity of operatic singers, but, in a very real sense, we are singers. We are singers of words; the author has given us the guidelines, but we must provide our own music.

BREATHING

One might think that something as natural as breathing would not have to be studied in order to become an effective interpreter of literature. However, the performance situation includes factors that are not encountered in everyday speech. For instance, the interpreter is usually much farther from the audience during a performance than in a conversational situation. The increased distance requires, among other things, more volume, which, in turn, requires more breath. In addition, some selections require that long streams of words be said without a breath in between. In order to convey the text properly the interpreter must know how to capture and gain control over breathing.

In order to accomplish this control, we must begin with a basic understanding of how the breathing mechanism works. In normal breathing, the chest alternately expands and contracts, bringing air into the lungs and pushing it out. Breathing is a muscular activity. Muscles in the chest wall lift the ribs and expand the chest cavity. The diaphragm, a curved and partially dome-shaped layer of muscle and tissue, forms the floor of the chest cavity. When the diaphragm is contracted, it flattens out, increasing the vertical dimension of the chest cavity. It is the expansion of the available space in the chest cavity that draws air into the lungs. The reverse occurs in order to expel the used air from the lungs. The diaphragm relaxes and the chest cavity contracts. It is the contraction of the available space in the chest cavity which forces the air out of the lungs; then the process begins again.

When the interpreter adapts breathing for the purpose of more effective presentation, the normal pattern is changed. Performance usually requires that air be drawn into the lungs at a more rapid rate than normal. Also, the interpreter needs to get more air into the lungs: the usual amount necessary to sustain life and an additional amount necessary to produce speech.

Each breath is held longer and released gradually as the interpreter produces the words and other sounds necessary for effective performance. Retaining the breath and releasing it gradually in a controlled way is the chief problem in performance. The interpreter must work to improve the strength and coordination of the breathing muscles so that a ready supply of air for speaking is always at hand. Give yourself a test. Take a lungful of air and begin to count seconds. See how far you can get without overstraining or otherwise losing your composure. If you have your breath under control and are acquiring enough air for the purpose, you should be able to count to fifty. If you have difficulty with this exercise, take an objective view of how you are breathing. As always, we begin with questions. Are you standing or sitting as straight as possible? If you have poor posture, your chest cavity will not be able to expand to its full capacity. Have you really acquired as much air as possible? Many untrained breathers do not fill the entire chest cavity because they depend entirely on chest expansion. After you have acquired a chestful of air, transfer your attention to your abdominal muscles and force them out away from your body. This should cause additional air to flow into the chest cavity. If you have trouble focusing on your abdominal muscles, take your hand and press it against your midsection. Try to push your hand away using only your stomach muscles.

Are you allowing your chest to collapse too quickly? When you expel air for speech, as with the counting exercise, you reverse the process you used for intake. Collapse your abdominal muscles first, and maintain as large a chest expansion as possible for as long as you can. In fact, there should always be some chest expansion. The trained performer never allows the chest cavity to collapse completely. This maintains a ready reserve of air and, because the cavity is larger, produces more tonal resonance.

When you breathe, do you tend to raise and lower your shoulders? Good breath control involves only the chest and abdominal regions. If you raise and lower your shoulders, you are employing extraneous muscular activity which gains you no additional air, tends to tire you out sooner, and looks funny to the audience. Continual practice with the counting exercise and other exercises suggested at the end of this chapter will ultimately give you the kind of control you need over one of the interpreter's most important resources—air.

VOLUME AND PROJECTION

The terms *volume* and *projection* tend to be used interchangeably. They both relate to the problem of getting your words and other pertinent sounds to your audience. However, it is more useful to the interpreter to think of projection as the primary goal, and volume as one important way of achieving projection. Later in the chapter, we will be discussing projection as it relates to body movement.

Volume means loudness, the amount of sound the interpreter produces to project the words and other utterances toward the audience. The interpreter adjusts his or her degree of loudness to adapt to the physical surroundings where the performance takes place and to provide emphasis or other dramatic effects.

Enough sound must of course be produced for the interpreter to be heard easily. Exactly how much sound is needed will vary according to the size and acoustical qualities of the performance space. A small intimate reading room may require less volume than a large classroom or auditorium. If the performance is taking place outside in the open air, more volume is required than indoors. While acoustics vary widely from place to place, the interpreter should be able to hear a slight echo coming back a split second after speaking, which indicates that the sound is reaching the back wall and rebounding. Practice bouncing your voice off of the back wall using sharp sounds. Stand in front of the room and repeat *da . . . da . . . da . . . da* at various volume levels until you hear the echo. Whenever possible, "tune up" in the performance space before you have to go on for real.

PITCH

Pitch refers to the "highs" and "lows" the interpreter uses to produce variety, expression, and character elements during the course of a performance. As with singers, the pitch an interpreter uses can be compared with the notes on a piano. Control of pitch is very important. The careful use of high and low notes during a reading can help point out connotations of meaning within a particular selection.

One common fault among beginning interpreters is their lack of pitch variety, which produces a quality called *monotone,* the dependence upon too narrow a range of notes. This narrow range of notes works against the interpreter's objective of producing a natural, spontaneous quality of speech and helps call attention to the fact that the interpreter is *reading,* rather than *telling* the audience something.

Another common fault is that many beginning interpreters do not use their *optimum pitch* as a starting point. To determine whether or not you are using your optimum pitch, that level which falls in the middle between your highest and lowest producible notes, try this exercise. Read and record a short selection of prose. Then, with a piano, sing up and down the scale to determine your highest and lowest producible notes. Your optimum pitch centers around the note which falls exactly in the middle. That is, there are as many usable notes above the optimum as there are below it. Using that middle note as your guide, reread the passage and record it. Now, play back the two versions to determine if the first one is generally higher or lower than the second.

If there is a noticeable difference, you must practice to get your voice in line with what is more natural for you. By not using your most effective range, you restrict your ability for expression and run the risk of producing sounds during the performance that will both strain your voice and sound unpleasant to your audience.

As with so many aspects of performance, a large part of the cure is the recognition of the problem. Another thing to keep in mind is that the tension created by the performance situation often causes the interpreter to raise the voice. Monitor yourself very carefully, and keep your throat as relaxed and open as possible.

The interpreter with good pitch control can use changes in pitch to indicate character. For example, if you are reading a two-character scene from a play, or a selection that includes both narration and dialogue, using a slight change in pitch when you "change" from one character to another will help the audience to keep the characters separate and add to the effectiveness of the performance.

ARTICULATION

Articulation means the precise rendering of speech sounds as they are meant to be uttered. Interpretation, or, more accurately, reading aloud, has often been used for the purpose of improving articulation. Speech improvement, while an important by-product of oral interpretation, is not the focus of this text. However, good articulation is a major part of the interpretive performance. The interpreter who articulates well will have less problem with projection and will be more easily understood.

Articulation is a muscular activity involving the tongue, lips, teeth, and the hard and soft palates. The interpreter must prepare the muscles of the tongue and the lips for action, in the same way an athlete warms up before running a race or jumping a hurdle.

Try some of the following limbering-up exercises and other tongue twisters of the same type with which you may already be familiar. Repeat each exercise several times with constantly increasing speed.

Rubber baby buggy bumpers.
Black bug's blood.
Shave a cedar shingle thin.
How much wood could a woodchuck chuck if a woodchuck
could chuck wood.

PRONUNCIATION AND DIALECT

As was stated in the preceding chapter, nothing will destroy an otherwise good performance more quickly than a mispronounced or misunderstood word. If you are unsure of a pronunciation, consult your dictionary, or ask your instructor to pronounce the word for you. The pronunciation of the English language varies to some degree from region to region within the United States and from country to country outside of the United States where English is spoken. It is useful for the interpreter to have a command of the so-called "standard" pronunciation of English, which can be learned in a voice and articulation class. However, regionalisms and other dialect differences do not necessarily interfere with the performance. If both the interpreter and the audience share the same dialect, differences from standard pronunciation will not be noticed.

There are many times when dialect can be used by the interpreter to advantage. It can sketch in character or add realistic flavor to the presentation. Some authors build dialect into the syntax and rhythm of their work. The interpreter who employs dialect should be careful not to become "stereotypic" and run the risk of offending some members of the audience.

In summary, as part of the normal process leading to performance, the interpreter must consider the technical aspects of voice production. Students of interpretation must include voice and articulation work as a regular part of their program. The technical aspects of performance, while not primary, are nonetheless essential to consider if the end result is going to be successful.

THE INTERPRETER'S BODY

As with the voice, the key to effective muscular activity is control. The interpreter is always communicating something. In many instances, more is communicated during the "silences" of a performance than when the words of the text are being spoken. Even before the text is put in motion, the interpreter establishes a presence, an attitude, and a set toward action. From the moment the interpreter comes into view, the audience begins to make inferences about how the performance is going to go. A strong but relaxed stance and a confident attitude at the outset can make a significant difference in how the total performance is perceived.

Effective use of the body in interpretation is extremely important. At least half of what is being communicated is generated by physical activity. Facial expressions, gestures, shifts of weight, tension, and relaxation all "speak" to the audience, and those physical messages must be as clear, distinct, and purposeful as the spoken messages. Physical action is any muscular activity which can be observed during a performance.

The interpreter develops body technique with two objects in mind: the control to exclude unnecessary or distracting physical activity and the control to use planned physical activity for a specific end. Both kinds of control are acquired through the development of strength, coordination, agility, and physical awareness.

Proper control of the body is not accomplished without serious work. Physical training should be a regular part of the interpreter's routine. At one time or another, we have all experienced what it feels like to be in shape or, conversely, what it feels like to be out of shape. The serious student of interpretation must be in shape. Or, to put it another way, the interpreter, like the dancer, the actor, and the mime, is part athlete. Jogging, tumbling, dancing, calisthenics, and other types of noncompetitive physical conditioning activities build strength and agility and focus the interpreter's attention on specific muscles in the body. *It is **Gottlieb's Seventh Principle** that the prospect of an excellent performance is enhanced when the interpreter has a general sense of physical well-being.*

The effective use of physical activity during the oral interpretation performance enhances understanding, creates empathy, and develops the illusion of reality. During the elocutionary period, a great deal of emphasis was placed on using the "proper" movement or gesture to match the specific word, phrase, or concept being spoken from the text. The application of elocutionary movements would appear stilted or even comic to most of us today. However, the necessity to use physical action to support understanding is as important as it always has been. Physical action clarifies meaning and provides emphasis. A shrug of the shoulders, a toss of the head, a roll of the eyes can do more than words to reveal the narrator's mood and attitude toward the material.

POSTURE

While posture will vary from performance to performance depending on the requirements of characterization, the interpreter must be familiar with what good basic posture is. Posture means the alignment of the various parts of the body. Good posture places the head, shoulders, spine, pelvis, legs, and feet in a balanced relationship. Beginning interpreters should fight the tendency to put weight on one leg at the expense of the other, or to lean forward with their elbows on the lectern. A strong, well-balanced appearance at the outset of a performance will produce a very positive effect on the audience. This, along with some thought to clothing and other grooming aspects, indicates that the performer is in control—has cared enough about the performance to make a special effort.

GESTURE

Gestures are overt physical actions, usually involving the hands and arms, which occur spontaneously along with speech. Beginning interpreters tend to suppress gesture, and, in so doing, remove from their performances an extremely important component. Gesture is as naturally a part of communication as the spoken word. Perhaps more than any other physical action, gesture enhances the understanding, creates the empathy, and develops the illusion of reality that marks the superior oral interpretation performance. Once the interpreter has adequately prepared the "internal" psychological components of the performance, gesture should grow naturally out of the response to the material.

In some cases the interpreter might need to focus more specifically on gesture. The interpreter who uses too much gesture, for example, dilutes the overall effect of the physical action. Self-monitoring will help cut down on the activity so that it is not distracting and it regains its power of emphasis.

In another circumstance, the interpreter may want to "plan in" a few gestures at appropriate points for specific dramatic or clarifying effects. A planned gesture is always in danger of losing its spontaneity. Get a good mental image of what you want to do, and then let the gesture grow as naturally as possible out of the circumstances of the moment. Don't stand in front of the mirror for half an hour practicing one gesture; the results are almost always disappointing.

In the case of characterization, however, some focus should be placed on the gestures which may be appropriate to convey that character. Where possible, this should grow naturally out of the psychological preparation. But sometimes the adopting of a characteristic gesture will give the interpreter the key to all the other character elements. A further discussion of developing character through technique is found in Chapter 7.

EMPATHY

For clarity, the concept of empathy is being handled separately here. In actuality empathy is not a technique: it is the desired end result of good physical action working in unity with good internal preparation. If the interpreter has been responsive to the text and has conveyed that response effectively through physical action, the audience will experience a corresponding physical reaction. Of the many examples available, the yawn is still the best. What makes it almost irresistible to yawn when you see someone else doing it? The yawn communicates powerfully and specifically a state of mind that is immediately recognizable. Given the opportunity, we will always attempt to experience what other individuals are experiencing; therefore we will yawn along with them. If the physical action of the performance is specific, appropriate and powerful, the audience will attempt, at a covert level, to replicate that action, so as to connect with the experience more intimately. As important as empathy is to the audience's enjoyment, it is equally important to the interpreter. It is through empathy that the interpreter "feels" the audience. Empathy is power. There is no experience quite like sensing the crowd in the palm of your hand, moving them, coaxing them to ever higher levels of experience and emotional response. This exchange of empathy between performer and audience is basic to the art of interpretation. Response builds upon response like the endless mirror, until nothing exists but this time, this place, these feelings. The text, the audience, and the interpreter are one entity. Your voice, your body, and your mind have created this moment. You are the artist. This is where the work pays off. It's worth it. Do it.

In summary, the effective use of physical action combined with the voice projects the experience contained within the selection to the audience.

The best application of technique does not call attention to itself. Instead, it helps the interpreter create not merely the illusion of spontaneity but a spontaneity that is communicated. No matter how beautiful the score and the conception, the tune must be played on an instrument. If the instrument is faulty, all that is good will go unheard.

QUESTIONS FOR STUDY AND DISCUSSION

1

How does breathing for performance differ from normal breathing?

2

What part is played by the abdominal muscles in breathing for performance?

3

What is meant by "tuning up" before a performance?

4

What is your optimum pitch?

5

How can jogging help you improve your oral interpretation?

6

How does physical action help create empathy?

SUGGESTED ACTIVITIES

1

Take a large breath and say *ah*. Try to sustain the sound at the same pitch and intensity for a long time. Repeat with *oo*, and then with *ee*.

2

Light a candle. Read a short paragraph keeping your face within one foot of the candle, trying not to expel enough air to blow it out or make the flame waver too much.

3

Become more physically aware. Try to pantomime several of your normal daily activities (combing hair, brushing teeth, etc.), noting which muscles you use.

4

Try to explain several items without gesture: a spiral stair, a paper clip, a rubber band, an explosion. Then explain with gesture.

5

Pretend your audience is the opposing team in a tug-of-war match. Pull on your imaginary rope in a way that makes them feel as if they are pulling back.

Selections for Analysis and Performance

PLAYER PIANO
JOHN UPDIKE

My stick fingers click with a snicker
And, chuckling, they knuckle the keys;
Light-footed, my steel feelers flicker
And pluck from these keys melodies.

My paper can caper; abandon
Is broadcast by dint of my din,
And no man or band has a hand in
The tones I turn on from within.

At times I'm a jumble of rumbles,
At others I'm light like the moon,
But never my numb plunker fumbles,
Misstrums me, or tries a new tune.

Interpreter's Notebook

"Player Piano" is a great poem for practicing articulation skills. Try moving
it along at a fairly rapid pace, being careful to pronounce each syllable.

LA BELLE DAME SANS MERCI
JOHN KEATS

O what can ail thee, knight-at-arms,
    Alone and palely loitering?
The sedge has wither'd from the lake,
    And no birds sing.

O what can ail thee, knight-at-arms,
  So haggard and so woe-begone
The squirrel's granary is full,
  And the harvest's done.

I see a lilly on thy brow,
  With anguish moist and fever dew,
And on thy cheeks a fading rose
  Fast withereth too.

I met a lady in the meads,
  Full beautiful—a faery's child,
Her hair was long, her foot was light,
  And her eyes were wild.

I made a garland for her head,
  And bracelets too, and fragrant zone;
She look'd at me as she did love,
  And made sweet moan.

I set her on my pacing steed,
  And nothing else saw all day long,
For sidelong would she bend, and sing
  A faery's song.

She found me roots of relish sweet,
  And honey wild, manna dew,
And sure in language strange she said—
  'I love thee true.'

She took me to her elfin grot,
  And there she wept, and sigh'd full sore,
And there I shut her wild wild eyes
  With kisses four.

And there she lulled me asleep,
  And there I dream'd—Ah! woe betide!
The latest dream I ever dream'd
  On the cold hill side.

I saw pale kings and princes too,
  Pale warriors, death-pale were they all;

They cried—'La Belle Dame sans Merci
   Hath thee in thrall!'

I saw their starved lips in the gloam,
   With horrid warning gaped wide,
And I awoke and found me here,
   On the cold hill's side.

And this is why I sojourn here,
   Alone and palely loitering,
Though the sedge has wither'd from the lake,
   And no birds sing.

THE SHELL
JAMES STEPHENS

I.
And then I pressed the shell
Close to my ear,
And listened well.

And straightway, like a bell,
Came low and clear
The slow, sad murmur of far distant seas,

Whipped by an icy breeze
Upon a shore
Windswept and desolate.

It was a sunless strand that never bore
The footprint of a man,
Nor felt the weight

Since time began
Of any human quality or stir,
Save what the dreary winds and waves incur.

II.
And in the hush of waters was the sound
Of pebbles, rolling round;
Forever rolling, wth a hollow sound:

And bubbling seaweeds, as the waters go,
Swish to and fro
Their long cold tentacles of slimy grey;

There was no day;
Nor ever came a night
Setting the stars alight

To wonder at the moon:
Was twilight only, and the frightened croon,
Smitten to whimpers, of the dreary wind

And waves that journeyed blind . . .
And then I loosed my ear.—Oh, it was sweet
To hear a cart go jolting down the street!

THE FIREBIRD
Cj STEVENS

The delicate dancers arabesque,
Lightly they lean on the lyric strings.
The sweet and smiling faces bask
beneath the soft and shining sounds.
The harps and the horns glid the stage.

This is love in a fairy-fancy,
music muted, and passion stilled
to painless pleasure.
               The Wizard comes!
Terror tosses the orchestra.
Ivan is torn from tender dreaming,
worried and snatched by the wicked goblins.

And where is she? the Shimmering Bird?
Ah, she will come, she has surely heard,
rescue is certain.
              After the curtain,
Princesses will reach for programs,
will search for gloves and grope for shoes,
then rise and go, remembering awhile,
in the afterglow of music's magic,
tomorrow's possible, but improbable, loves.

THE WINDHOVER: TO CHRIST OUR LORD
GERARD MANLEY HOPKINS

I caught this morning's minion, king-
  dom of daylight's dauphin, dapple-dawn-drawn Falcon, in
  his riding
  Of the rolling level underneath him steady air, and striding
High there, how he rung upon the rein of a whimping wing
In his ecstasy! then off, off forth on swing,
  As skate's heel sweeps smooth on a bow-bend: the hurl and
  gliding
  Rebuffed the big wind. My heart in hiding
Stirred for a bird,—the achieve of, the mastery of the thing!

Brute beauty and valour and act, oh, air, pride, plume, here
  Buckle! AND the fire that breaks from thee then, a billion
Times told lovelier, more dangerous, O my chevalier!

  No wonder of it: sheer plod makes plough down sillion
Shine, and blue-bleak embers, ah my dear,
  Fall, gall themselves, and gash gold-vermilion.

Interpreter's Notebook

"The Windhover" combines the effects of sound and physical tension. You must be excited by the imagery and the music of the alliteration. Look up all unfamiliar words.

THE SCOOP
JAMES T. FARRELL

A large *Chicago Questioner* delivery truck parted the traffic as it roared northward toward the Clark Street bridge. It shook the street, emitted carbon monoxide gas from its exhaust pipe, punctuated the atmosphere with the shrillness of an open cutout. And thundered onward.

It was the first truck to be used for deliveries. Dennis McDermott, a circulation slugger, stood on the tail gate and hung onto a stout rope. Husky and handsome, he expressed his pride in a characteristic leering frown. He enjoyed the honor of having been assigned to his new truck while the other sluggers remained at work on horse-drawn vehicles.

Bumping, the truck rattled over the Clark Street bridge. Dennis was tearing through the scenes of his boyhood. He had grown up on the Near North Side, been educated on its streets, and he had served as an altar boy at the Holy Name Cathedral. Nuns had even looked at him with masked wonderment, incapable of understanding why such a intelligent-looking boy, who seemed so holy and devout in his acolyte's cassock, should always be fighting the way he was. That had been before he had been ejected from school for the third and final time in his seventh grade. His father had been an Irish immigrant and an unskilled worker. A precinct Captain in Bart Gallivan's organization had gotten him a job as a street cleaner, and that had elevated Dennis' father to one of the most minor positions in the neighborhood political aristocracy. Dennis had always had before him the example of the local hoodlums, and in his small-boy manner he had emulated them, leading his gang in expeditions to roll drunks, and in fights against neighborhood gangs of Jews and Wops. Reckless and possessed of volatile courage, he had grown to be a tough guy, hired as a slugger and strikebreaker, employed in the taxicab wars, and then by *The Questioner* in the newspaper circulation war. Twice, he had been arrested in hold-ups. Duke O'Connell, from Dennis' own neighborhood, had become State's Attorney, and he had sprung Dennis both times. He stood on the tail gate of the truck, delivering papers to the old corners, even to corners where he had sold newspapers himself. And just as earlier sluggers had gypped him by subtracting papers from his order and charging him for them, so he was now gypping newsboys who were acquiring an education similar to his own in the same kind of system.

He clutched his supporting ropes more tightly as the truck curved about a corner. It drew up to a newstand and Dennis flung down a bundle containing forty-five copies of the paper.

"How many?" asked the newsboy, a tired-looking kid of twelve or thirteen with a hole in the knee of his left stocking.

"What you ordered. Fifty!" Dennis said in his habitually bullying voice.

"Last night there was only forty-five. I counted 'em," the kid said with a nervous and uncertain air of defiance.

"I said there was fifty!"

"Well, I counted 'em!" the kid said, a whine creeping into his voice.

Dennis squeezed the boy's left ear between two strong fingers, and asked him how many there had been.

"I counted 'em!" the kid said, his voice cracking.

Dennis gave him a back-handed slap in the mouth and

said that there had been fifty copies. He collected for the papers and jumped on the truck as the sniffling newsboy opened the bundle.

"How's it going, Wop?" Dennis asked Rocko Martini, at the next stop.

"All right, Irish," Rocko replied, winking.

While Rocko opened his bundle of papers, Dennis quickly said that he and a pal were pulling an easy house job on Saturday night and they needed somebody for a lookout. He'd been watching Rocko, and he knew he was all right. If Rocko wanted, they'd let him in with a fourth of the take. Rocko agreed, and Dennis made a date to meet him after work to give him the lowdown.

After two uneventful stops, the truck drew up to a stand where two newsboys were jawing each other. Dennis leaped down and stood over them, sneering, his hands on his hips. He noticed that a freckle-faced kid had a bundle of *The Chicago Clarion*.

"What's the idea, huh?"

"This guy's trying to bust into my business," *The Questioner* kid said.

Dennis looked at the freckle-faced boy, and the latter drew back a few paces.

"This is my corner, ain't it, Denny?"

"Well, I can sell my papers where I wanna. It's a free country, ain't it?"

"So that's the story!" Dennis said, grabbing the freckle-faced kid's papers, and shoving him. The kid reached for his papers, Dennis twisted his arm, booted his tail, and warned him not to be seen selling papers on this corner again. He tore the papers and told *The Questioner* kid to let him know if the punk came back.

Dennis delivered papers to Shorty Ellis, the punk he didn't like. Ellis was always giving *The Questioner* inside place on his stand. He told his driver to go around the block, and jumped off the tail gate. He sauntered back to Ellis. He pointed to the copies of *The Questioner* which were placed on the inside.

"Didn't I tell you where to place our papers?"

"Well, Muggs was around and told me to place his in the same spot."

"He did?"

"Yes."

"What did I tell you?"

"I don't see why you guys can't leave a kid alone to sell his papers."

"You don't, huh!" Dennis said, catching a look in Ellis'
eyes that he didn't like.

"Change 'em!"

"And then Muggs'll come around and crack my puss."

"Change 'em!"

Ellis did not obey the command. Dennis slapped his face.
Touching the red flush on his cheeks, Ellis drew back, pulled out
a pocketknife and, waving it before him defensively, told Dennis
to let him alone. Dennis advanced on the boy. Ellis, still
brandishing his knife, scratched Dennis' wrists. Dennis lost his
temper and flashed a razor. When the boy again struck out
defensively, Dennis slashed his throat, almost from ear to ear.
The boy fell, his head nearly dismembered, his blood gushing
over the sidewalk. Dennis looked around. No one had seen the
fracas. He knew the kid would die quickly. He hastened away
and leaped onto his truck. It raced back to *The Questioner* office.
He saw the night editor, Kelly Malloy, who had worked himself
up from a copy boy and was now only in his thirties. Malloy
always talked hard, but he had a soft, womanish face. He had
been given the job in a change that was calculated to jack up
circulation, and Dennis was the best circulation man on the
force. When Dennis assured him for the fourth time that no one
had seen him slash the boy, he breathed a sigh of relief. Then
he slapped his hands together and said that the story was worth
an extra. He became a dynamo of energy.

Very soon Dennis was back on the truck with an extra
which bore the headline:

NEWSBOY MURDERED;
SLAYER UNAPPREHENDED
North-Side Boy Slashed with Razor in Suspected
Neighborhood Gang Fight.

At that time *The Questioner* was conducting, as a circulation
stunt, one of its wars on crime. On the editorial page there was
a flamboyant editorial demanding that the police enforce the
laws and reduce crime.

Interpreter's Notebook

There is an enormous amount of physical activity in "The Scoop." Resist
the temptation to act out the action. However, use enough movement and
gesture to create pictures in the audience's mind. Take a look at the section
Indicating Character in Chapter 8.

HURT HAWKS
ROBINSON JEFFERS

I.

The broken pillar of the wing jags from the clotted shoulder,
The wing trails like a banner in defeat,
No more to use the sky forever but live with famine
And pain a few days: cat nor coyote
Will shorten the week of waiting for death, there is game
    without talons.
He stands under the oak-bush and waits
The lame feet of salvation; at night he remembers freedom
And flies in a dream, the dawns ruin it.
He is strong and pain is worse to the strong, incapacity is
    worse.
The curs of the day come and torment him
At distance, no one but death the redeemer will humble that
    head,
The intrepid readiness, the terrible eyes.
The wild God of the world is sometimes merciful to those
That ask mercy, not often to the arrogant.
You do not know him, you communal people, or you have
    forgotten him;
Intemperate and savage, the hawk remembers him;
Beautiful and wild, the hawks, and men that are dying,
    remember him.

II.

I'd sooner, except the penalties, kill a man than a hawk; but
    the great redtail
Had nothing left but unable misery
From the bone too shattered for mending, the wing that trailed
    under his talons when he moved.
We had fed him six weeks, I gave him freedom.
He wandered over the foreland hill and returned in the
    evening, asking for death,
Not like a beggar, still eyed with the old
Implacable arrogance. I gave him the lead gift in the twilight.
                      What fell was relaxed,
Owl-downy, soft feminine feathers; but what
Soared: the fierce rush; the night-herons by the flooded river
    cried fear at its rising
Before it was quite unsheathed from reality.

PROSPICE
ROBERT BROWNING

Fear death?—to feel the fog in my throat,
   The mist in my face,
When the snows begin, and the blasts denote
   I am nearing the place,
The power of the night, the press of the storm,
   The post of the foe;
Where he stands, the Arch Fear in a visible form,
   Yet the strong man must go:
For the journey is done and the summit attained,
   And the barriers fall,
Though a battle's to fight ere the guerdon be gained,
   The reward of it all.
I was ever a fighter, so—one fight more,
   The best and the last!
I would hate that death bandaged my eyes, and forbore,
   And bade me creep past.
No! let me taste the whole of it, fare like my peers,
   The heroes of old,
Bear the brunt, in a minute pay glad life's arrears
   Of pain, darkness, and cold.
For sudden the worst turns the best to the brave,
   The black minute's at end,
And the elements' rage, the fiend-voices that rave,
   Shall dwindle, shall blend,
Shall change, shall become first a peace out of pain,
   Then a light, then thy breast,
O thou soul of my soul! I shall clasp thee again,
   And with God be the rest!

LEDA AND THE SWAN
WILLIAM BUTLER YEATS

A SUDDEN blow: the great wings beating still
Above the staggering girl, her thighs caressed
By the dark webs, her nape caught in his bill,
He holds her helpless breast upon his breast.

How can those terrified vague fingers push
The feathered glory from her loosening thighs?
And how can body, laid in that white rush,
But feel the strange heart beating where it lies?

A shudder in the loins engenders there
The broken wall, the burning roof and tower
And Agamemmon dead.
                              Being so caught up,
So mastered by the brute blood of the air,
Did she put on his knowledge with his power
Before the indifferent beak could let her drop?

Interpreter's Notebook

"Leda and the Swan" is one of the great poems in the English language, and
a test of the interpreter's skill. The key is to develop the proper level of
physical excitement and tension before the first line. The improvisation
technique will help you here. It doesn't have to be paced quickly; just keep
the tension going strong until it begins to fade in the last stanza.

THE HEAVENLY CHRISTMAS TREE
FÉDOR DOSTOEVSKI

I am a novelist, and I suppose I have made up this story. I write
"I suppose," though I know for a fact that I have made it up, but
yet I keep fancying that it must have happened on Christmas Eve
in some great town in a time of terrible frost.

I have a vision of a boy, a little boy, six years old or even
younger. This boy woke up that morning in a cold damp cellar.
He was dressed in a sort of little dressing-gown and was shivering
with cold. There was a cloud of white steam from his breath,
and sitting on a box in the corner, he blew the steam out of his
mouth and amused himself in his dullness watching it float away.
But he was terribly hungry. Several times that morning he went
up to the plank bed where his sick mother was lying on a
mattress as thin as a pancake, with some sort of bundle under
her head for a pillow. How had she come here? She must have
come with her boy from some other town and suddenly fallen
ill. The landlady who let the "corners" had been taken two days
before to the police station, the lodgers were out and about as
the holiday was so near, and the only one left had been lying
for the last twenty-four hours dead drunk, not having waited for

Christmas. In another corner of the room a wretched old woman of eighty, who had once been a children's nurse but was now left to die friendless, was moaning and groaning with rheumatism, scolding and grumbling at the boy so that he was afraid to go near her corner. He had got a drink of water in the outer room, but could not find a crust anywhere, and had been on the point of waking his mother a dozen times. He felt frightened at last in the darkness: it had long been dusk, but no light was kindled. Touching his mother's face, he was surprised that she did not move at all, and that she was as cold as the wall. "It is very cold here," he thought. He stood a little, unconsciously letting his hands rest on the dead woman's shoulders, then he breathed on his fingers to warm them, and then quietly fumbled for his cap on the bed, he went out of the cellar. He would have gone earlier, but was afraid of the big dog which had been howling all day at the neighbour's door at the top of the stairs. But the dog was not there now, and he went out into the street.

Mercy on us, what a town! He had never seen anything like it before. In the town from which he had come, it was always such black darkness at night. There was one lamp for the whole street, the little, low-pitched, wooden houses were closed up with shutters, there was no one to be seen in the street after dusk, all the people shut themselves up in their houses, and there was nothing but the howling of packs of dogs, hundreds and thousands of them barking and howling all night. But there it was so warm and he was given food, while here—oh, dear, if he only had something to eat! And what a noise and rattle here, what light and what people, horses and carriages, and what a frost! The frozen steam hung in clouds over the horses, over their warmly breathing mouths; their hoofs clanged against the stones through the powdery snow, and everyone pushed so, and—oh, dear, how he longed for some morsel to eat, and how wretched he suddenly felt. A policeman walked by and turned away to avoid seeing the boy.

There was another street—oh, what a wide one, here he would be run over for certain; how everyone was shouting, racing and driving along, and the light, the light! And what was this? A huge glass window, and through the window a tree reaching up to the ceiling; it was a fir tree, and on it were ever so many lights, gold papers and apples and little dolls and horses; and there were children clean and dressed in their best running about the room, laughing and playing and eating and drinking something. And then a little girl began dancing with one of the boys, what a pretty little girl! And he could hear the music through the window. The boy looked and wondered and laughed, though his toes were aching with the cold and his fingers were red and stiff so that it hurt him to move them. And all at once the boy remembered how his toes and fingers hurt him, and began crying, and ran on; and again through another window-pane he saw another Christmas tree, and on a table cakes of all sorts—almond cakes, red cakes and yellow cakes, and three grand young ladies were sitting there, and they gave the cakes to any one who went up to them, and the door kept opening, lots of gentlemen and ladies went in from the street. The boy crept up, suddenly opened the door and went in. Oh, how they shouted at him and waved him back! One lady went up to him hurriedly and slipped a kopeck into his hand, and with her own hands opened the door into the street for him! How frightened he was. And the kopeck rolled away and clinked upon the steps; he could not bend his red fingers to hold it right. The boy ran away and went on, where he did not know. He was ready to cry again but he was afraid, and ran on and on and blew his fingers. And he was miserable because he felt suddenly so lonely and terrified, and all at once, mercy on us! What was this again? People were standing in a crowd admiring. Behind a glass window there were three little dolls, dressed in red and green dresses, and exactly, exactly as though they were alive. One was a little old man sitting and playing a big violin, the two others were standing close by and playing little violins, and nodding in time, and looking at one another, and their lips moved, they were speaking, actually speaking, only one couldn't hear through the glass. And at first the boy thought they were alive, and when he grasped that they were dolls he laughed. He had never seen such dolls before, and had no idea there were such dolls! And he wanted to cry, but he felt amused, amused by the dolls. All at once he fancied that some one caught at his smock behind: a wicked big boy was standing beside him and suddenly hit him on the head, snatched off his cap and tripped him up. The boy fell down on the ground, at once there was a shout, he was numb with fright, he jumped up and ran away. He ran, and not knowing where he was going, ran in at the gate of some one's courtyard, and sat down behind a stack of wood: "They won't find me here, besides it's dark!"

He sat huddled up and was breathless from fright, and all at once, quite suddenly, he felt so happy: his hands and feet suddenly left off aching and grew so warm, as warm as though he were on a stove; then he shivered all over, then he gave a start, why, he must have been asleep. How nice to have a sleep here! "I'll sit here a little and go and look at the dolls again," said the boy, and smiled thinking of them. "Just as though they were alive! . . ." And suddenly he heard his mother singing over him. "Mammy, I am asleep; how nice it is to sleep here!"

"Come to my Christmas tree, little one," a soft voice suddenly whispered over his head.

He thought that this was still his mother, but no, it was not she. Who it was calling him, he could not see, but someone bent over and embraced him in the darkness; and he stretched out his hands to him, and . . . and all at once—oh, what a bright light! Oh, what a Christmas tree! And yet it was not a fir tree, he had never seen a tree like that! Where was he now? Everything was bright and shining, and all round him were dolls; but no, they were not dolls, they were little boys and girls, only so bright and shining. They all came flying round him, they all kissed him, took him and carried him along with them, and he was flying himself, and he saw that his mother was looking at him and laughing joyfully. "Mammy, Mammy; oh, how nice it is here, Mammy!" And again he kissed the children and wanted to tell them at once of those dolls in the shop window.

"Who are you, boys? Who are you, girls?" he asked, laughing and admiring them.

"This is Christ's Christmas tree," they answered. "Christ always has a Christmas tree on this day, for the little children who have no tree of their own . . ." And he found out that all these little boys and girls were children just like himself; that some had been frozen in the baskets in which they had as babies been laid on the doorsteps of well-to-do Petersburg people, others had been boarded out with Finnish women by the Foundling and had been suffocated, others had died at their starved mother's breasts (in the Samara famine), others had died in third-class railway carriages from the foul air; and yet they were all here, they were all like angels about Christ, and He was in the midst of them and held out His hands to them and blessed them and their sinful mothers. . . . And the mothers of these children stood on one side weeping; each one knew her boy or girl, and the children flew up to them and kissed them and wiped away their tears with their little hands, and begged them not to weep because they were so happy.

And down below in the morning the porter found the little dead body of the frozen child on the woodstack; they sought out his mother too. . . . She had died before him. They met before the Lord God in heaven.

Why have I made up such a story, so out of keeping with an ordinary diary, and a writer's above all? And I promised two stories dealing with real events! But that is just it, I keep fancying that all this may have happened really—that is, what took place in the cellar and on the woodstack; but as for Christ's Christmas tree, I cannot tell you whether that could have happened or not.

Chapter 6
The Oral Interpretation Performance

KEY CONCEPTS

Preparing the script

Stage fright

Sensing audience feedback

Beginning

Self-monitoring

George and Jean are sophomores. Before this term they didn't even know each other, but now they share a common experience. They are both taking oral interpretation. George had done some debating in high school, and Jean had been in the class play, so both felt that they could handle this business of getting up in front of an audience.

The class had been through the historical material, so they felt that they had a pretty good idea of what oral interpretation was. But now the time had come for performing, and neither one was as sure as before. Having received the reading schedule from the instructor, they went to the cafeteria for a cup of coffee and some discussion of the forthcoming event.

"Well, in a way I envy you," began George, as he stirred his coffee. "At least you'll get it over with early. I have to squirm all week." Jean was not so enthusiastic. "Are you kidding? I'll trade places with you if you think it's so great to perform the first day."

"No thanks. Anyway, you're the actress."

Jean thought of the play she had been in. How good she looked in that ruffled costume. She thought of the excitement in the dressing room, and putting on all that make-up. She remembered being frightened on stage, but then the audience had seemed so far away. They were all in the dark. Even when she came close to the front of the stage she could see only faint glimmers of light reflecting off the faces of the people in the front row. How different this would be: standing before everyone in broad daylight, without costume, without make-up, without scenery or props, without other actors.

"This is not acting, George, and anyway, I only did one play. I thought this would be more like acting; I'm surprised."

"You know, the way the instructor describes it, it sounds a lot like what I went through on the debating team. All the talk about the interpreter's relationship with the audience, about eye contact, sensing feedback—it's the same thing they tell you when you're giving a speech." He began to develop his thought. "The lectern, the fact that you have the printed material with you for reference: the similarities are incredible. I thought it would be more like acting, too." He thought for a moment. "Have you decided what you're going to read?"

"I haven't looked completely through the book yet, but I hope there's a poem in it that I already know. I don't want to start from scratch the first time up."

"I hate poetry anyway," George said slightly defensively. "I can never understand it." He thought of those long afternoons in high school English when Miss Verbliss—the students called her Miss Word-List—droned on about Shakespeare and about iambic pentameter, when he would much rather have been outside kicking a soccer ball around the field. "I just want to get through this. I'll probably do a lot better with the short stories."

Jean replied, somewhat mockingly, "Where's your sensitivity? Don't you know that some of the most beautiful images ever put into language are to be found in poetry?" She gathered her books, pushed her chair away from the table, and said, "Well, I've got to have this thing ready in two days, so I'd better do it. I'll see you later."

Jean returned to her room, picked up her oral interpretation textbook, and settled comfortably into an easy chair. She quickly leafed through the chapter containing the material on selecting a piece of literature. She then leafed through her notebook and compared her class notes with the suggestions in the text. There were no great discrepancies. Both the text and her instructor confirmed that she should select something that fell within the realm of her experience. She began turning through the sections of the text which contained selections for study and performance.

Jean was pleased that there were several poems in the book with which she was familiar. She narrowed her selections down to two or three and began trying them out loud. She began to imagine herself in front of the class, and, as she read, she imagined the audience's response. At first she wasn't too thrilled about any of the selections, but she kept coming back to one in particular.

It was a poem by John Updike. It told a story of a young man who had been a great basketball player in high school, but, because he never learned a trade, ended up pumping gas for a living. She read it again.

EX-BASKETBALL PLAYER
JOHN UPDIKE

Pearl Avenue runs past the high school lot,
Bends with the trolly tracks, and stops, cut off
Before it has a chance to go two blocks,
At Colonel McComsky Plaza. Berth's Garage
Is on the corner facing west, and there,
Most days, you'll find Flick Webb, who helps Berth out.

Flick stands tall among the idiot pumps—
Five on a side, the old bubble-head style,
Their rubber elbows hanging loose and low,
One's nostrils are two S's, and his eyes
An E and O. And one is squat, without
A head at all—more of a football type.

Once, Flick played for the high school team, the Wizards.
He was good: in fact, the best. In '46,

He bucketed three hundred ninety points,
A county record still. The ball loved Flick.
I saw him rack up thirty-eight or forty
In one home game. His hands were like wild birds.

He never learned a trade; he just sells gas,
Checks oil, and changes flats. Once in a while,
As a gag, he dribbles an inner tube,
But most of us remember anyway.
His hands are fine and nervous on the lug wrench.
It makes no difference to the lug wrench, though.

Off work, he hangs around Mae's Luncheonette.
Grease-grey and kind of coiled, he plays pinball,
Sips lemon cokes, and smokes those thin cigars;
Flick seldom speaks to Mae, just sits and nods
Beyond her face towards bright applauding tiers
Of Necco Wafer, Nibs, and Juju Beads.

Yes, she would read this one. She had dated a basketball player for a while in high school. She thought about him: the way he looked, the way he talked. She hadn't seen him for a couple of years. She wondered what had happened to him. Yes, she would read this one. She grew excited. She remembered sitting in the stands watching him play. She had once thought that she would always love him. She thought about his hands. Yes, "like wild birds," that's just what they were.

She turned her attention once more to the poem. "I can say these words," she thought. "It could be me saying these words."

She found herself involuntarily pacing the room and repressed an almost irresistible urge to get something to eat. She knew she didn't want to be hampered with the heavy textbook, and she couldn't get to the xerox machine in the library until the next day, so she sat down at her typewriter and began to copy the poem. She double-spaced between the lines and triple-spaced between the stanzas. After finishing typing, she took a pencil and began to search for moments of transition. She decided that there were three and that they coincided with the last three stanzas. She marked them.

Next, she began to play with different phrasing possibilities and penciled in slash marks to enclose the sense units. She thought, "This is pretty conversational; the line stops seem arbitrary." She began to scan the poem.

Pearl Avenue runs past the high school lot,
Bends with the trolly tracks, and stops, cut off . . .

She was amazed, "It's iambic pentameter. I don't think I'll follow the pattern of emphasis, but there is a plan in operation here."

Suddenly she remembered her old high school yearbook. "Don's picture is in there," she thought. She rummaged around in the closet and came up with it. Flipping rapidly through the book, she finally came to a page with the basketball team grouped around the smiling coach, and there in the left-hand corner was Don. She looked at it for a moment. Thoughts and remembrances mingled together in a confusing array. She set the book aside and returned to the poem.

She thought about the three questions the instructor had emphasized: "Who am I?" "Where am I?" "Why am I saying these things?" She thought, "I've already answered 'who': the narrator is me. There doesn't seem to be anything in the poem that inhibits that." She looked at the opening lines of the poem again.

> Pearl Avenue runs past the high school lot,
> Bends with the trolly tracks, and stops, cut off
> Before it has a chance to go two blocks,
> At Colonel McComsky Plaza.

"I'm giving directions," she said out loud. "I'm out on the street—maybe shopping—and someone has asked me directions, someone is trying to find Flick Webb." She thought for a moment. "Some newspaper reporter wants to do a story on what's happened to some great high school athletes and has come to town to interview Flick Webb."

Jean continued to build detail into her story. She remembered Gottlieb's First Principle: "The key to quality performance is detail." She thought about what kind of day it was, what she was wearing. Using the poem as a guide she began her extended paraphrase. As she thought, halted, and searched for words, she listened to herself—trying to tune into her phrasing patterns.

After a half hour or so she was pretty tired, but she noticed that she had memorized large portions of the poem without even trying. She decided to call it a night. As she set the poem aside and sat in the easy chair, the phone rang.

"Hi, Jean." It was George.

"Hi," Jean yawned.

"You sleeping?"

"No, just tired. I've been working on my poem."

"What did you pick?"

"'Ex-Basketball Player' by John Updike."

"Basketball," George thought for a moment. "I didn't know you were such a sports fan."

"It's not a poem about sports, really. It's kind of sad. There's a warning in it. Read it—you'll see what I mean. You'd better not pick it, though!"

"Why do you care? You're performing the first day. If I read it, I'd be doing it three days later."

Jean thought for a moment, "Yes, you're right. I don't know why, but somehow it just seems like my poem. Do you know what I mean?"

"Well, not exactly, but you sure are involved in it. I'll bet you're going to be fantastic."

"In my room I'm fantastic, but every time I think of performing in front of the class I get a terrible hollow feeling in the pit of my stomach."

"Stage fright."

"What?"

"You've got stage fright."

"Terrific. What am I supposed to do about that?"

"Don't ask me. Gottlieb isn't talking about it until tomorrow. He probably has a principle for it."

"At least one."

"Listen, not to change the subject, but are we going to that open house this weekend?"

They settled their weekend plans and said goodby, and Jean settled down for the night. She was amazed that she couldn't get the poem off of her mind. She decided to try it once more before going to bed. She picked it up from the table where it was lying face down. She turned it over. Why did it look so strange all of a sudden? She couldn't get herself to say the words out loud. The room was too quiet. Fear swept over her. Would this happen in front of the class? Would she make a complete fool of herself? "I'm making much too big a thing of this," she thought, "I'm just tired and out of the mood. I guess you can't just pick something up and perform it without going through all the preparation. I hope I haven't lost the knack; it was really beginning to sound good—at least to me."

The following day, as predicted, Gottlieb dealt with the problem of stage fright. ". . . it is a phenomenon which no one escapes. Singers, actors, speakers, anyone who has to get up in front of an audience for some reason. It is one of the paradoxes of human nature that in our fantasies most of us want an audience, yet we fear it. In the privacy of our thoughts we lead armies and sway mobs, but we break out in a cold sweat at the thought of reading a poem in front of the class."

Jean thought to herself, "I'm not sure this is helping."

"Stage fright is both mental and physical," he continued. "It is the same feeling you get if you hear someone coming up behind you in the dark, and the response your body makes is also the same—you are preparing yourself to either fight or run. Potent doses of hormones are secreted from the endocrine glands, adrenalin is shot into the blood stream, and the liver adds glycogen to the mixture. When these secretions reach your heart, it starts to thump. When they reach the respiratory center of the brain, you start to gasp. Your muscles may tense because of all the extra blood being sent to them, your mouth may become dry, and you may have a tendency to perspire. There is both good news and bad news about stage fright. Which do you want first?"

Almost as a chorus the class responded, "The good news."

"The good news is that there is a principle for stage fright" (chorus of titters and groans). "*Gottlieb's Seventh Principle states: Stage fright controlled and put to use is the interpreter's best source of creative energy.* The bad news is that stage fright can never be totally overcome.

"Obviously there is no simple answer to the question of how to control stage fright. As you continue to rehearse and perform you become more confident. As your confidence grows, you will find that you are able to concentrate this energy source in a positive way. Almost all of you will have gained a significant measure of control by the end of this course. Many of you will actually begin to feel relatively comfortable in front of an audience. A few of you will experience the feeling of exhilaration and power that comes from being in complete control of yourself, your material, and your audience. There is no substitute for practice, practice, practice. But here are a few suggestions that will help you initially.

"*Select literature of interest to you*, and about which you have some feeling. Many readers who experience acute stage fright are actually suffering partially from 'selection fright.' In other words, they have made an inappropriate selection.

"*Be well prepared.* Nothing will heighten your anxiety more than not being well rehearsed.

"*Warm up.* Some minutes before you have to read, sit upright, and begin forcing yourself to breathe deeply and regularly. Relax your hands by shaking them out and pressing your fingertips together. Relax your face and jaw muscles by letting your jaw drop and yawning.

"*Take a strong stance.* When you go before your audience, set both feet firmly on the floor, stand up to your full height, and draw in a deep breath. Make sure the first sound you make is strong. A tentative or squeaky beginning is hard to overcome.

"*Use physical action.* Remember your body is prepared to do something physical, and you must provide constructive outlets for the tension. Hand gestures, head movement, facial expression, and body movement are essential outlets, not only to help you relax, but also to make you more fully communicative."

The lesson continued with examples of various kinds of stage-fright manifestations: the wobbly foot, the lectern clutcher, the change jingler, and the frozen face. It ended with a discussion of the need for self-monitoring. "Monitor thyself!" Gottlieb had thundered at them, "Know where your feet are and what your face is doing. Your audience is a mirror. Look deep into them and you will see what you need to know."

At the end of the lesson, Gottlieb read off the names of the people who were to perform the next day. Jean heard her name read, and, even though she was well aware that she was going to perform the next day, she still felt a sinking feeling when she heard her name. "Well," she thought, "by this time tomorrow this will no longer be my biggest problem in life."

That evening, Jean rushed through her other assignments and finally turned her attention to her poem. She read it through to herself a couple of times and then remembered **Gottlieb's Eighth Principle:** *If you are not reading out loud, you are not rehearsing.* He had said, "As an interpreter you have enough to contend with without being surprised by the sound of your own voice." She read aloud, but stopped after a few lines. "Why do I feel so self-conscious?" She decided to start from the very beginning. She opened her high school annual and stared for a long time at the picture of Don. Her eyes drifted to other pictures on the page, and her mind began to develop images, scenes, remembrances. She turned to the poem and began her improvisation. "I'm in a small town. I'm shopping, and someone has asked me directions. Someone is trying to find Flick Webb. . . . "

The following day there was an air of expectancy in the classroom. The readers were joking about how awful they were going to be. Jean resolved that she would perform first if the student whose name preceded hers on the list didn't mind. "I'll just get more nervous if I have to wait," she reasoned. It was settled: she would go first. The other student seemed grateful. Jean informed the instructor as he came into the room.

The roll was called, and then—it seemed so sudden—she was before the audience. She began setting the poem in a logical stream of circumstances. She told who and where she was, and she assigned the audience the role of the reporters who had asked where to find Flick Webb. She moved into the poem. She heard herself saying the words, but they seemed to be strangely distant—almost as if someone else were saying them. She felt a bit uneasy. The audience was looking at her, but they too seemed uneasy. Jean found herself constantly fighting the urge to keep her eyes on the page.

However, as she began the third stanza, she felt the gap between herself and her voice close. She began to slow down. As she spoke about how talented Flick was, she recalled pictures of her high school gymnasium, and she saw Don's face. "The ball loved Flick," she read, and a small tingling sensation began at the base of her spine and traveled slowly up her back. She began to look more intently at her audience. "They seemed to have settled down; their faces seemed more relaxed," she thought. She read, "His hands are fine and nervous on the lug wrench." Her right hand suddenly sprang up from the lectern and startled her. She squelched the gesture. She finished. The class applauded. She started for her seat. She heard the instructor say, "Stay there." She returned to the lectern.

"All right," Gottlieb was addressing the class, "this is a very good beginning. What did you like about it?" Comments were made on the clarity of Jean's delivery, her genuine involvement, the appropriateness of the story she had created to fit the poem in, and her smooth transition from the story to the poem. Gottlieb continued questioning, "What portion of the poem did you like the best?" George raised his hand, "Well, I liked it all, really, but the second half was better. It seemed as if she relaxed a bit, and it was easier for me to follow what was going on."

"How do you feel about that, Jean?"

"Well, I felt better about the second half—actually, I started to feel that it was going better about the time I got to the third stanza."

"Why?"

"The audience seemed suddenly more attentive, and I began to relax and experience the feelings of the poem more."

"Jean, have you ever been to the ocean?"

"Yes."

"Did you dive into the waves?"

"Yes."

"How did you do it?"

"Well, I let the waves come to me, and then I dove through them just as they crested."

"You see, you were learning something very important about performing without even knowing it."

"How's that?"

"It is the basic principle upon which is built **Gottlieb's Ninth Principle:** *Good beginnings are made by riding the crest of your audience's attention.* An audience's attention comes at you in waves. As with all communicative acts, there is a process. When you get up to perform, your audience has a great deal to adjust to. This is especially true if you are the first or only performer, since your audience isn't at all prepared, initially, for what is about to happen. They need to complete conversations with a neighbor, adjust to you visually, and make room in their busy minds for the receipt of new information. Beginning performers make the mistake of diving too quickly—before the wave has arrived. Now, I know that there is nothing more terrifying to an unseasoned performer than the prospect of simply standing silent before an audience; however, that is what you must do until you sense the wave coming in. And you will sense it. It may seem like a sudden silence, or even a subtle pressure on your skin, but you will sense it. One big reason why you began to feel better by the third stanza is that the unwaited-for wave finally arrived.''

''Jean,'' he continued, ''this is a very good first effort, and I don't want to run it into the ground with too much criticism. However, bear with me while I make one more point. I want you to tell me, in your own words, the events of the poem.''

''You don't want me to read?''

''No, use the poem as a guide, but tell me what happens.''

''Well, as I see it, this person is standing . . .''

''No.''

''No?''

''It is *your* story; *you* are telling it. Who is this person?''

''Me. Oh, I see. I'm standing on the corner after finishing some shopping, and a car drives up with two men in it. They're looking for directions. They're trying to find Flick Webb. You see, he was this really great basketball player, and they are reporters writing a feature on what happeaned to some of yesterday's promising athletes. Anyway, I begin giving them directions, and I really get caught up talking about Flick because he and I used to go out, you know? Well, so, I start to remember all these things . . .''

''Okay, hold it there.'' Gottlieb turned to the class. ''What's different about what she's doing now?''

George spoke up, ''She's really talking to you.''

''How do you know?''

''Well, she was looking directly at you, for one thing, and she seemed more natural.''

''Why?''

''She seemed more animated.'' George thought for a moment. ''She was gesturing.''

''George, you have just made two points which are most important to the intepreter. First, you are right—it is more natural for most of us to gesture when we speak. At one point during the reading, Jean began to gesture and then held back.''

''Yes,'' said Jean, ''I remember doing that.''

''Of course, as with everything else we do in front of the audience, the gestures we use must be purposeful. However, at this stage, I would prefer seeing too much gesture rather than none at all. The sooner you free your body from artificial constraints, the sooner you will satisfy the requirements of Gottlieb's Third Principle, which states . . .''

Several students rapidly flipped through their notes, and then a chorus of voices, not quite together, responded, "The final product should sound as if you were saying the words for the first time."

"Right!"

"Do we get an A?" asked one.

"You get a C−," retorted Gottlieb.

"Why?" feigning hurt, "we got it right, didn't we?"

"Yes, but you read it abominably."

There were a few groans and some laughter. Gottlieb continued, "Yes, making it sound like the first time, natural, spontaneous, that's what it's all about. Whatever will help you achieve that effect, that 'reality,' must be brought to bear on the interpretive performance. Gesture, bodily communication of all kinds, in fact any device which brings you closer to your audience, will enhance the effect of your performance. The second point which George made relates to one such device.

"He said, 'She was looking directly at you.' I had asked Jean if she could paraphrase the poem, so she spoke directly to me in response. As an interpreter, you need to extend this concept to the entire audience: Treat your audience as if they have asked a question which demands a response. When possible, deliver some small portion of your performance directly to each member of the audience. When we think of eye contact, the emphasis must be on the *contact*. It is **Gottlieb's Tenth Principle** *which states that total contact is achieved when each member of the audience feels that some part of the performance has been delivered exclusively to him or her.*"

He returned his attention to Jean. "You made a big step by fighting the tendency to hide in the book. You need to carry it one step further. Let's try it again from the top."

That evening, as Jean thought over the events of the day, she was quite pleased with herself. Her reading wasn't perfect, but then, neither was anyone else's. The second time through had been a little choppy, not as she had planned it, but she had experienced more, felt freer. The class had liked it better than the first reading, and Gottlieb had said that she took direction very well. She was better able to see what was meant by spontaneity as she watched the other performances and the instructor working through them. She thought, "Yes, I will be able to do this." She felt that she had just joined a very special club. She was thinking of a world tour, bringing the message of poetry to all humanity when she drifted off to sleep.

QUESTIONS FOR STUDY AND DISCUSSION

1

Why did looking in her high school annual help Jean prepare her reading?

2

In what ways is oral interpretation like giving speeches?

3

Why did Jean make up the story about the newspaper reporter looking for Flick Webb?

4

Why can't we control stage fright?

5

Why are gesture and eye contact important to the intepretive performance?

SUGGESTED ACTIVITIES

1

Each student takes a turn in front of the class and says "now" when he or she experiences total attention.

2

Select several poems and create logical situations within which the events of these poems could actually take place.

3

All the students work with the same poem, and each student creates his or her own set of given circumstances.

Selections for Analysis and Performance

THE HOUR OF LETDOWN

E. B. WHITE

When the man came in, carrying the machine, most of us looked up from our drinks, because we had never seen anything like it before. The man set the thing down on top of the bar near the beerpulls. It took up an ungodly amount of room and you could see the bartender didn't like it any too well, having this big, ugly-looking gadget parked right there.

"Two rye-and-water," the man said.

The bartender went on puddling an Old-Fashioned that he was working on, but he was obviously turning over the request in his mind.

"You want a double?" he asked, after a bit.

"No," said the man. "Two rye-and-water, please." He stared straight at the bartender, not exactly unfriendly but on the other hand not affirmatively friendly.

Many years of catering to the kind of people that come into saloons had provided the bartender with an adjustable mind. Nevertheless, he did not adjust readily to this fellow, and he did not like the machine—that was sure. He picked up a live cigarette that was idling on the edge of the cash register, took a drag out of it, and returned it thoughtfully. Then he poured two shots of rye whiskey, drew two glasses of water, and shoved the drinks in front of the man. People were watching. When something a little out of the ordinary takes place at a bar, the sense of it spreads quickly all along the line and pulls the customers together.

The man gave no sign of being the center of attraction. He laid a five-dollar bill down on the bar. Then he drank one of the ryes and chased it with water. He picked up the other rye, opened a small vent in the machine (it was like an oil cup) and poured the whiskey in, and then poured the water in.

The bartender watched grimly. "Not funny," he said in an even voice. "And furthermore, your companion takes up too much room. Whyn't you put it over on that bench by the door, make more room here."

"There's plenty of room for everyone here," replied the man.

"I ain't amused," said the bartender. "Put the goddam thing over near the door like I say. Nobody will touch it."

The man smiled. "You should have seen it this afternoon," he said. "It was magnificent. Today was the third day of the tournament. Imagine it—three days of continuous brainwork. And against the top players of the country, too. Early in the game it gained an advantage; then for two hours it exploited the advantage brilliantly, ending with the opponent's king backed in a corner. The sudden capture of a knight, the neutralization of a bishop, and it was all over. You know how much money it won, all told, in three days of playing chess?"

"How much?" asked the bartender.

"Five thousand dollars," said the man. "Now it wants to let down, wants to get a little drunk."

The bartender ran his towel vaguely over some wet spots. "Take it somewheres else and get it drunk there!" he said firmly. "I got enough troubles."

The man shook his head and smiled. "No, we like it here." He pointed at the empty glasses. "Do this again, will you, please?"

The bartender slowly shook his head. He seemed dazed but dogged. "You stow the thing away," he ordered. "I'm not ladling out whiskey for jokestersmiths."

"'Jokesmiths,'" said the machine. "The word is 'jokesmiths.' "

A few feet down the bar, a customer who was on his third highball seemed ready to participate in this conversation to which we had all been listening so attentively. He was a middle-aged man. His necktie was pulled down away from his collar, and he had eased the collar by unbuttoning it. He had pretty nearly finished his third drink, and the alcohol tended to make him throw his support in with the underprivileged and the thirsty.

"If the machine wants another drink, give it another drink," he said to the bartender. "Let's not have haggling."

The fellow with the machine turned to his new-found friend and gravely raised his hand to his temple, giving him a salute of gratitude and fellowship. He addressed his next remark to him, as though deliberately snubbing the bartender.

"You know how it is when you're fagged out mentally, how you want a drink?"

"Certainly do," replied the friend. "Most natural thing in the world."

There was a stir all along the bar, some seeming to side with the bartender, others with the machine group. A tall, gloomy man standing next to me spoke up.

"Another whiskey sour, Bill," he said. "And go easy on the lemon juice."

"Picric acid," said the machine, sullenly. "They don't use lemon juice in these places."

"That does it!" said the bartender, smacking his hand on the bar. "Will you put that thing away or else beat it out of here. I ain't in the mood, I tell you. I got this saloon to run and I don't want lip from a mechanical brain or whatever the hell you've got there."

The man ignored this ultimatum. He addressed his friend, whose glass was now empty.

"It's not just that it's all tuckered out after three days of chess," he said amiably. "You know another reason it wants a drink?"

"No," said the friend. "Why?"

"It cheated," said the man.

At this remark, the machine chuckled. One of its arms dipped slightly, and a light glowed in a dial.

The friend frowned. He looked as though his dignity had been hurt, as though his trust has been misplaced. "Nobody can cheat at chess." he said. "Simpossible. In chess, everything is open and above the board. The nature of the game of chess is such that cheating is impossible."

That's what I used to think, too," said the man. "But there *is* a way."

"Well, it doesn't surprise me any," put in the bartender. "The first time I laid my eyes on that crummy thing I spotted it for a crook."

"Two rye-and-water," said the man.

"You can't have the whiskey," said the bartender. He glared at the mechanical brain. "How do I know it ain't drunk already?"

"That's simple. Ask it something," said the man.

The customers shifted and stared into the mirror. We were in this thing now, up to our necks. We waited. It was the bartender's move.

"Ask it what? Such as?" said the bartender.

"Makes no difference. Pick a couple of big figures, ask it

to multiply them together. You couldn't multiply big figures together if you were drunk, could you?"

The machine shook slightly, as though making internal preparations.

"Ten thousand eight hundred and sixty-two, multiply it by ninety-nine," said the bartender viciously. We could tell that he was throwing in the two nines to make it hard.

The machine flickered. One of its tubes spat, and a hand changed position, jerkily.

"One million seventy-five thousand three hundred and thirty-eight," said the machine.

Not a glass was raised all along the bar. People just stared gloomily into the mirror; some of us studied our own faces, others took carom shots at the man and the machine.

Finally, a youngish, mathematically minded customer got out a piece of paper and a pencil and went into retirement. "It works out," he reported, after some minutes of calculating. "You can't say the machine is drunk!"

Everyone now glared at the bartender. Reluctantly he poured two shots of rye, drew two glasses of water. The man drank his drink. Then he fed the machine its drink. The machine's light grew fainter. One of its cranky little arms wilted.

For a while the saloon simmered along like a ship at sea in calm weather. Every one of us seemed to be trying to digest the situation, with the help of liquor. Quite a few glasses were refilled. Most of us sought help in the mirror—the court of last appeal.

The fellow with the unbuttoned collar settled his score. He walked stiffly over and stood between the man and the machine. He put one arm around the man, the other around the machine. "Let's get out of here and go to a good place." he said.

The machine glowed slightly. It seemed to be a little drunk now.

"All right," said the man. "That suits me fine. I've got my car outside."

He settled for the drinks and put down a tip. Quietly and a trifle uncertainly he tucked the machine under his arm, and he and his companion of the night walked to the door and out into the street.

The bartender stared fixedly, then resumed his light housekeeping. "So he's got his car outside," he said, with heavy sarcasm. "Now isn't that nice!"

A customer at the end of the bar near the door left his drink, stepped to the window, parted the curtains, and looked out. He watched for a moment, then returned to his place and addressed the bartender. "It's even nicer than you think," he said. "It's a Cadillac. And which one of the three of them d'ya think is doing the driving?"

Interpreter's Notebook

Careful attention must be paid to the character sketches in "The Hour of Letdown." Much of the humor is wrapped up in the incongruity of the bartender's confronting a situation he is not equipped to deal with. He must be gruff, straightforward, and recognizable as a type. Don't forget a special voice for the machine.

EVERYONE SANG
SIEGFRIED SASSOON

Everyone suddenly burst out singing;
And I was filled with such delight
As prisoned birds must find in freedom
Winging wildly across the white
Orchards and dark green fields; on; on;
    and out of sight.

Everyone's voice was suddenly lifted,
And beauty came like the setting sun.
My heart was shaken with tears, and horror
Drifted away. . . . O, but everyone
Was a bird; and the song was wordless; the singing
    will never be done.

EDGE
SYLVIA PLATH

The woman is perfected.
Her dead

Body wears the smile of accomplishment,
The illusion of a Greek necessity

Flows in the scrolls of her toga,
Her bare

Feet seem to be saying:
We have come so far, it is over.

Each dead child coiled, a white serpent,
One at each little

Pitcher of milk, now empty.
She has folded

Them back into her body as petals
Of a rose close when the garden

Stiffens and odours bleed
From the sweet, deep throats of the night flower.

The moon has nothing to be sad about,
Staring from her hood of bone.

She is used to this sort of thing.
Her blacks crackle and drag.

HOW SOON HATH TIME
JOHN MILTON

How soon hath Time, the subtle thief of youth,
   Stol'n on his wing my three and twentieth year!
   My hasting days fly on with full career,
But my late spring no bud or blossom shew'th.
Perhaps my semblance might deceive the truth,
   That I to manhood am arrived so near,
   And inward ripeness doth much less appear,
That some more timely-happy spirits endu'th.
Yet be it less or more, or soon or slow,
   It shall be still in strictest measure ev'n
    To that same lot, however mean, or high,
   Toward which Time leads me, and the will of Heav'n;
All is, if I have grace to use it so,
   As ever in my great task-Master's eye.

Interpreter's Notebook

Although "How Soon Hath Time" is a sonnet, treat it as it it were a soliloquy. Move slowly through the thoughts as if they were occurring to you at the moment you voice them.

THE SLEEPING GIANT
(A Hill, So Named, in Hamden, Connecticut)
DONALD HALL

The whole day long, under the walking sun
That poised an eye on me from its high floor,
Holding my toy beside the clapboard house
I looked for him, the summer I was four.

I was afraid the walking arm would break
From the loose earth and rub against his eyes
A fist of trees, and the whole country tremble
In the exultant labor of his rise;

Then he with giant steps in the small streets
Would stagger, cutting off the sky, to seize
The roofs from house and home because we had
Covered his shape with dirt and planted trees;

And then kneel down and rip with fingernails
A trench to pour the enemy Atlantic
Into our basin, and the water rush,
With the streets full and the voices frantic.

That was the summer I expected him.

Later the high and watchful sun instead
Walked low behind the house, and school began,
And winter pulled a sheet over his head.

TRAVELOGUE IN A SHOOTING-GALLERY
KENNETH FEARING

There is a jungle, there is a jungle, there is a vast,
  wild, wild, marvelous, marvelous, marvelous jungle,
Open to the public during business hours,
A jungle not very far from an Automat, between a hat store
  there, and a radio shop.

There, there, whether it rains, or it snows, or it shines,
Under the hot, blazing, cloudless, tropical neon skies that the
  management always arranges there,
Rows and rows of marching ducks, dozens and dozens and
  dozens of ducks, move steadily along on smoothly-oiled
  ballbearing feet,
Ducks as big as telephone books, slow and fearless and out of
  this world,
While lines and lines of lions, lions, rabbits, panthers,
  elephants, crocodiles, zebras, apes,
Filled with jungle hunger and jungle rage and jungle love,
Stalk their prey on endless, endless rotary belts through never-
  ending forests, and burning desserts, and limitless veldts,
To the sound of tom-toms, equippped with silencers, beaten
  by thousands of savages hidden there.

And there it is that all the big-game hunters go, there the
  traders and the explorers come,
Lean-faced men with windswept eyes who arrive by streetcar,
  auto or subway, taxi or on foot, streetcar or bus,
And they nod, and they say, and they need no more:
"There . . . there . . .
There they come and there they go."
And weighing machines, in this civilized jungle, will read your
  soul like an open book, for a penny at a time, and tell you
  all,
There, there, where smoking is permitted,
In a jungle that lies, like a rainbow's end, at the very end of
  every trail,
There, in the only jungle in the whole wide world where
  ducks are waiting for streetcars,
And hunters can be psychoanalyzed, while they smoke and
  wait for ducks.

Interpreter's Notebook

Both "The Sleeping Giant" and "Travelogue in a Shooting-Gallery" are fantasies which develop out of each poet's response to something real. The Sleeping Giant is a mountain seen through a child's eyes. The poet reflects upon his memory of that mountain, the emotions it stirred in him as a child, and his changing perception of it as he got older. It is a personal story, told through a first-person narrator. Be sure to convey the change of mood which occurs with "That was the summer I expected him."

"Travelogue" is told through a third-person narrator and is more objective. You need to keep up your level of excitement and psychologically justify the many repetitions like ". . . wild, wild, marvelous, marvelous, marvelous jungle."

DEATH, BE NOT PROUD
JOHN DONNE

Death, be not proud, though some have called thee
Mighty and dreadful, for thou are not so;
For those whom thou think'st thou dost overthrow
Die not, poor Death, nor yet canst thou kill me.
From rest and sleep, which but thy pictures be,
Much pleasure; then from thee much more must flow,
And soonest our best men with thee do go,
Rest of their bones, and soul's delivery.
Thou art slave to fate, chance, kings, and desparate men,
And dost with poison, war, and sickness dwell,
And poppy or charms can make us sleep as well
And better than thy stroke; why swell'st thou then?
One short sleep past, we wake eternally
And death shall be no more; Death, thou shalt die.

POEM FOR A REGAL LADY
IRWIN L. MCJUNKINS

YES MISS LADY
I'M HITTIN' ON YOU
BECAUSE

I WANT TO FEEL
THE LYRICS OF YOUR LOVE
RECIPROCATING WITH MINE
BECAUSE
I WANT TO WRITE POEMS
ABOUT ME/YOU
RACING THRU GALAXIES
OF SPRING
FOR THE FIRST TIME

YES WOMAN
I'M HITTIN' ON YOU
BECAUSE
I WANT YOU TO SEE
THE JEWELED HUES
OF MY SOUL
BECAUSE
I WANT YOU TO KNOW
THE PULSATIC RYTHMS
OF A REAL HEART
INSTEAD OF
SOME DIME STORE TOY

YEA BABY
I'M HITTIN' ON YOU
BECAUSE EVEN THO' OUR WORLDS
ARE LIKE COURSES UNCHARTED
I BELIEVE TOGETHER
WE CAN DISCOVER THE LAND
OF SHANGRI-LA
AND REJOICE IN SINGING
LULLABYS OF LOVE
TO EACH OTHER
BECAUSE I SEE YOU
AS A REGAL LADY
DESERVING SOME ROYAL ATTENTION
SO I'M HITTIN' ON YOU MOMMA!

Part Three
The Different Forms of Interpretation

PART THREE consists of four chapters. Chapter 7 discusses the characteristics of poetry and the various types of poetry the interpreter will encounter. Chapter 8 focuses on the narrator as the key element in the interpreter's mastery of the prose form. Chapter 9 covers the basic techniques for the interpretive performance of drama. Chapter 10 introduces the student to ensemble techniques and explores the potential for staging larger shows.

Chapter 7
Reading poetry

KEY CONCEPTS

The characteristics of poetry

Types of poetry

Figurative language

Poetic structure

There are many ways to describe what a poem is. Literary critics have been doing just that ever since the first poem was uttered in a place where others could hear it. Poems can be examined biographically and historically as well as empirically. While such considerations are always important to the study of literature, the interpreter must be primarily concerned with the content of a poem. Again, the process begins with questions. Is this poem primarily a portrayal of human experience? Does it describe something or someone? Does it present a point of view? Is it part of an argument?

One of the marvelous things about poetry, of course, is that it can be any or all of these things. The interpreter must think like the poet, not like the critic. For, in the end, the performance will not explain the poem; it will depict the act of poetic creation.

THE CHARACTERISTICS OF POETRY

In addition to exhibiting wide and varied differences in content, all poems hold many elements in common. Discovering these commonalities is an important part of the interpreter's training.

ORGANIZATION

All poems have organization. The poet has applied some logic, some principle to help attain the desired end. When you can answer the question "Why am I saying these things?" you have discovered the desired end. The poet employs organization to move the content forward to the desired end. The poem may introduce an image and then develop it into a series of related images. It may begin with a wide view of a subject, which, as the poem progresses, may become increasingly narrow; or the reverse can occur. Still another approach may introduce and expand upon an analogy. The poem may state a proposition, and then set out to prove it. Some poems follow a chronological order. Others, particularly descriptive in content, are arranged spatially. *It is **Gottlieb's Eleventh Principle** which states that the essence of the interpreter's power over the audience lies in being the only one who knows what is coming next.*

TECHNIQUE

All poems have technique. Technique refers to the means by which the poet reveals the content; the two main ways in which this is done are *point of view* and *selection*.

POINT OF VIEW

We already know that all literature is presented through a narrator. The type of narrator is determined by the *point of view* selected by the poet. As in prose, there are three basic choices: *first person* (sometimes called present or dramatic point of view), *third person* (sometimes called the witness narrator), and *omniscient*. An extended discussion of the different types of narrators appears in Chapter 8.

Briefly, the first-person narrator reveals the content of the poem as if it were experienced personally. The third-person narrator reveals the content as if it were witnessed or encountered second hand. The omniscient narrator has the same perspective as the third-person narrator, with the added capability of having access to the thoughts and feelings of all the participants in the events of the poem.

SELECTION

In addition to being concerned with the point of view, or, perhaps as an outgrowth of it, the poet must be concerned with *selection*. With the whole vast array of detail available within the context of an experience, the poet must choose what is to be included in the content and what is to be left out. This is called *primary selection*. A further selection occurs among those portions of the idea or experience which have been selected for inclusion. Since everything cannot be given the same emphasis, the poet selects the most important images or arguments for extended treatment, while reserving others for clarification or special effects. This selection within the poem is called *secondary selection*.

Understanding the technique which the poet has applied to the creation of the poem is extremely important to the interpreter. When one sets out to prepare a poem for presentation, one must enter into this process of applying poetic technique. Remember, the interpreter focuses on the act of poetic creation and, therefore, must project the process of selection as if it were taking place at the very moment the poem is being presented. The interpreter continually asks, "What alternative word or image might have been considered, and, at length, rejected in favor of the one selected?" The process of selection does not flow quickly for most poets; therefore it should not be depicted as such. The more the interpreter is able to project to the audience that alternate words and images are being considered and rejected in favor of the ones that are ultimately spoken, the more the performance will appear spontaneous and realistic. In addition, the important words and images will receive a natural emphasis, appearing, as they will, to be the result of the narrator's considered judgment.

Becoming aware of the poet's application of technique will also help the interpreter develop meaningful phrasing patterns. When alternative words and images are being considered, the automatic response is a pause. The beginning interpreter should pay close attention to this principle. *It is* **Gottlieb's Twelfth Principle** *which states that the interpreter pauses for thought, not for effect.* The desired effect will be most readily achieved if the manifestation of technique on the part of the interpreter demonstrates the process through which the poet arrived at the selection of words and images.

Obviously, in most cases, poems are not written in anything approximating the short span of time it takes to perform them. Some poets, like W. B. Yeats, continue to alter their poems even after publication. What we as interpreters strive for is not the re-creation of the moment-by-moment bringing into being of a poem, but rather a clear, condensed *illustration* of the process.

The following poem by Robert Browning is a masterpiece of organization and selection.

MEETING AT NIGHT
ROBERT BROWNING

The gray sea and the long black land;
And the yellow half-moon large and low;
And the startled little waves that leap
In fiery ringlets from their sleep,
As I gain the cove with pushing prow,
And quench its speed in the slushy sand.

Then a mile of warm sea-scented beach;
Three fields to cross till a farm appears;
A tap at the pane, the quick sharp scratch
And the blue spurt of a lighted match,
And a voice less loud, through its joys and fears,
Then the two hearts beating each to each!

If we are to discover something about the organization and selection operating in this poem, we must first *discover the narrator.* In the fifth line we know the point of view.

As *I* gain the cove with pushing prow,

This is first-person narration. We also discover that the events are being described in the present tense, or, more accurately, the *historical present.*

Browning is using the present tense to give a sense of immediacy to the description of these past events. True present tense exists for the interpreter only in drama (see Chapter 9) and in some special ensemble forms, such as Readers Theatre and Chamber Theatre (see Chapter 10).

The organizational pattern is a combination of spatial and chronological order, with the chronology asserting itself as the most important as the poem heads toward its conclusion. This chronological pattern moves skillfully from large segments of time:

> Then a mile of warm sea-scented beach;
> Three fields to cross till a farm appears;

to split seconds:

> A tap at the pane, the quick sharp scratch
> And the blue spurt of a lighted match,

In addition to his very carefully arranged organizational patterns, Browning also employs the art of selection to good purpose. The interpreter reveals the selection process of a poem while doing the extended paraphrase part of the analysis (see Chapter 3). Place yourself within the context of the poem. You are the narrator. What else do you see besides what is being described here? What about your boat? What kind of a boat is it? What color? What season is it? What else do you see on the way? Where did you come from? Has it been a long journey? Are you tired from rowing? Or, did you sail? Were there any sights of interest in those three fields you crossed? What does the farm look like? What do you see first? The barn? The silo? The house? Are there any animal noises?

The answers to all these questions, and many more which could be asked about the details of this experience, are the material left out of the poem through the process of selection. The last two lines illustrate the care taken by Browning to cut away everything but the bare essentials, as he introduces the second character in this drama.

> And a voice less loud, through its joys and fears,
> Than the two hearts beating each to each!

We assume that the narrator is a man and that the "voice" belongs to a woman. We don't know that for a fact, nor do we know anything else about her—what she looks like, how old she is. Through the process of selection, Browning has created *ambiguity*, thereby forcing the members of the audience to bring much of themselves to the understanding of the poem.

The interpreter can do a great deal to enhance ambiguity and create the desired effect through illustrating the process of selection. Let's look at the first line again.

The gray sea and the long black land;

What if after the "and" the narrator thinks of something else first before saying "the long black land"? Maybe the impression was fuller, such as, "The gray sea and the clouds, the oars dipping in and out of the water, the sound of bullfrogs, and the long black land." Try reading this passage aloud. Now, read it again. But this time say aloud only the words that actually exist in the poem. The other choices are heard in your head but not spoken.

The gray sea and (the clouds, the oars dipping in and out of
the water, the sound of bullfrogs) the long black land;

The word "and" appears eight times in this poem. Try this technique each time it occurs. You will begin to hear a difference in your phrasing and emphasis. You have begun to illustrate the process of selection in your delivery.

STYLE

All poems have style. The way in which a poet says something determines not only what is said, but also how it will be received. Entire volumes have been written in various attempts to analyze style in poetry. The more an interpreter knows about poetry, the easier it will be to deal with it. But, without the four basics of *diction, sound, rhythm,* and *figures* of speech, it can't be dealt with at all.

DICTION

The term *diction* means the poet's choice of words. It is a characteristic of all languages to develop synonyms as a natural historical outcome of changes in meaning. Each word in a group of synonyms carries with it a slightly different *connotative* meaning, while generally *denoting* the same thing as the rest of the synonyms. It's not so much what a word *means* as how it *feels* that will determine whether a poet will use it over another possible choice. The words "fasten," "restrain," and "secure" share the same general meaning, but each carries with it a different feeling. The same is true of "lean." Some of its synonyms include "emaciated," "spare," "scraggy," and "rawboned." We often hear the term "rawboned" used to connote strength and firmness and "lean" to connote a generally favorable physical appearance—quite a difference from "spare" and "emaciated."

There are over 200,000 words available in the English language for the poet to use. The words chosen to express a particular thought or feeling must be considered carefully by the interpreter. Always begin with the assumption that the poet has given careful consideration to the connotative effects of the poem. Understanding the choice of words gives the interpreter insight into the impression the poet wants to convey through the attitude of the narrator. The poet's diction is governed by the context of the experience to be conveyed. By careful study of this diction, the interpreter gets closer to the poet's intention. Using Browning's poem as an example, note how his diction in the first stanza creates anticipation and connotes a clandestine sexual encounter.

> The gray sea and the long *black* land;
> And the yellow half-moon large and low;
> And the *startled* little waves that *leap*
> In *fiery ringlets* from their sleep,
> As I gain the *cove* with *pushing prow*,
> And *quench* its speed in the *slushy* sand.

SOUND

The next aspect of style that must be considered is sound. The best statement on the role of sound in literary art comes from Wellek and Warren.

> Every work of literary art is, first of all, a series of sounds out of which arises the meaning. In some literary works, this stratum of sounds is minimized in its importance; and it becomes, so to speak, diaphanous, as in most novels. But even there the phonetic stratus is a necessary precondition of the meaning. . . . In many works of art, including of course prose, the sound-stratum attracts attention and thus constitutes an integral part of the aesthetic effect. This is true of much ornate prose and of all verse, which by definition is an organization of a language's sound-system.[1]

Several complicated studies of sound systems in literature have been done by scholars focusing on rhyme, "orchestration," and sound symbolism.[2]

---

[1] Rene Wellek and Austin Warren, *Theory of Literature,* Harcourt, Brace & World, New York, 1956, p. 158.
[2] The following are some important studies of literary sound systems: W. W. Wimsatt, "One Relation of Rhyme to Reason," *Modern Language Quarterly,* vol. 5, 1944, pp. 323–338. W. J. Bate, *The Stylistic Development of Keats,* Humanities, Atlantic Highlands, N.J., 1945.

It is hard to generalize about the effect of sound patterns, but the interpreter needs to be aware of their function within the poem being prepared for performance. These patterns can be classified according to their type.

Assonance, one type of pattern, occurs when two or more words having the same vowel sounds are placed close together in a poem.

Three fields to cross till a farm appears;

Consonance is the result of placing two or more words with the same consonant sounds close together.

In fiery ringlets from their sleep,

When the repeated consonant sounds are at the beginning of the words, the effect achieved is called *alliteration.*

And quench its speed in the slushy sand.

The effect of assonance and consonance can help set the pace of the poem, as in the case of the long e sound, which suggests a longer time lapse necessary to cross the "three fields." Their effect can also help develop pictures in the listeners' minds, as they experience the sound of "slushy sand." Careful attention to these devices will enrich an interpreter's performance beyond the ordinary. The sound pattern which presents the greatest challenge to the interpreter is, of course, rhyme.

Rhyme also consists of types. However, basic to all rhyme is the repetition of at least one similar-sounding syllable, especially at the ends of two or more lines within the same poem.

If a single syllable serves, it is a *single rhyme* (song-wrong); if two, a *double* (trouble-bubble); if three, a *triple* (piety-anxiety). If the repeated sounds match, it is a *full-rhyme* (love-dove); but if only part of the syllable is repeated, or if the repeated sounds are not precisely alike, then it is a *half-rhyme* (man-sun). A rhyming syllable which coincides with accent is a *masculine rhyme* (alive-derive); one which falls on a slack syllable is a *feminine rhyme* (standing-handing). Repeated final syllables which fall within the line rather than at the end are *internal rhymes.*[3]

---

[3] Norman Friedman and Charles A. McLaughlin, *Poetry: An Introduction to Its Form and Art,* rev. ed., New York, Harper and Row, 1963, p. 137.

Masculine rhymes prevail in English. In fact the use of feminine rhymes and triple rhymes usually produces a comic effect. The opposite is true of other languages; medieval Latin, Italian, and Polish employ feminine rhymes for the most serious subjects.

Rhyme serves as an organizer when it is present in a poem. It signals the end of a line. Groups of rhymes organize the poem into *stanzas*. But, most importantly for the interpreter, rhyme serves a *semantic* function. It links or contrasts words; it gives clues about meaning and emphasis.

As part of the analysis, the interpreter should mark the rhyme scheme using lowercase letters.

AT THE AQUARIUM
MAX EASTMAN

Serene the silver fishes glide,	a
Stern-lipped, and pale, and wonder-eyed!	a
As through the aged deeps of ocean,	b
They glide with wan and wavy motion!	b
They have no pathway where they go.	c
They flow like water to and fro.	c
They watch with never-winking eyes,	d
They watch with staring, cold surprise,	d
The level people in the air,	e
The people peering, peering there:	e
Who also wander to and fro.	f(c)
And know not why or where they go,	f(c)
Yet have a wonder in their eyes,	g(d)
Sometimes a pale and cold surprise.	g(d)

A quick look at the rhyme scheme of this poem will reveal several words which the poet has selected for emphasis. In four lines, he has chosen to repeat rhymes used earlier in the poem. The inversion of the "fro-go" rhyme emphasizes the inversion of perspective.

In the preceding poem the rhymes fall into groups of two and are, therefore, called *couplets*. Groups of three rhyming lines form *triplets* or *tercets:*

From PROVIDE, PROVIDE
ROBERT FROST

The witch that came (the withered hag)	a

To wash the steps with pail and rag,	a
Was once the beauty Abishag,	a
The picture pride of Hollywood.	b
Too many fall from great and good	b
For you to doubt the likelihood.	b

Groups of four are called *quatrains:*

From ODE ON SOLITUDE
ALEXANDER POPE

Happy the man, whose wish and care	a
A few paternal acres bound,	b
Content to breathe his native air,	a
In his own ground.	b

Quatrains will be found arranged in different ways, such as *a b b a* or *a a b a.* Groups of five rhyming lines form *quintains;* of six, *sestets;* and so on.

Certain stanzaic patterns have developed into fixed schemes. The most prominent is the *sonnet.* The sonnet always contains fourteen lines. An *Italian sonnet* rhymes *a b b a a b b a c d e c d e* (with some variation). The *English sonnet* rhymes *a b a b c d c d e f e f g g* (with some variation). Sonnets are further required to be written in iambic pentameter (see discussion of metric patterns below). The sonnet is an excellent proving ground for the interpreter. It contains nearly all the major problems faced by the reader of poetry: prominent rhyme and rhythm schemes, a restriction of fourteen lines within which to express generally strong emotional and intellectual issues, and the placement (as in Shakespearean sonnets) of the material within its proper historical and linguistic context.

Other stanzaic patterns which have become fixed come down to us primarily from medieval and Renaissance French and Italian poetry. Our discussion will not include any detail on these patterns, but the serious student of poetry will want to look into a few, such as the *ballade, villanelle, triolet, sestina, rondel,* and *rondeau.*

In summary, then, the interpreter must analyze the *sound* of the poem if the desired effect is to be achieved. Assonance, consonance, alliteration, and rhyme all create pleasurable sensations for the ear, help pace and organize the material, and enhance emotional and pictorial transmission. These elements of sound, in conjunction with rhythm, form the structure upon which the poem is built.

RHYTHM

Rhythm, as a third component of style, can be looked at in two ways. One view is that it occurs when stressed syllables reoccur in fixed patterns. The other view does not insist on patterned reoccurrences of stressed syllables. It sees all movement, even in prose, as rhythmical. Once again, the interpreter shouldn't become bogged down in an argument which is more important to a literary critic than a performing artist. The interpreter must learn to sense rhythm, to play against it, or allow it to command. **Gottlieb's Thirteenth Principle** *states that the interpreter must control the material, or the material will control the interpreter.* Rhythm is the movement of the poem. We must assert our authority over this movement, or it will sweep us away.

The first view of rhythm, that of patterned stresses, ties it closely with *meter.* Whether you agree with the view or not, as an interpreter you must have a knowledge of meter. The primary characteristic of meter is regularity. *Stressed syllables* appear at the same intervals, set apart by one or two *unstressed* or *slack* syllables. Each group of stressed and unstressed syllables is called a *foot.* When one describes meter, it is in terms of the type of foot used and the number of such feet in each line of poetry. The *iambic* foot contains an unstressed syllable followed by a stressed syllable (desire); *trochaic* is exactly the opposite (happy); the *anapestic* foot contains two unstressed syllables followed by a stressed syllable (renaissance); and its opposite, the *dactylic,* begins with a stressed syllable (tapestry). The number of feet per line are counted this way: One foot per line is *monometer;* two, *dimeter;* three, *trimeter;* four, *tetrameter;* five, *pentameter;* six, *hexameter,* and so on. The following line is *iambic pentameter:*

How soon hath Time the subtle thief of youth,

That is, the iambic foot repeats five times within the line.

The interpreter's problem with meter, more times than not, is how to avoid it. If we follow strictly the pattern of stress produced by the iambic foot, we create a sing-song effect. Being overconscious of meter will rob a performance of its spontaneity and produce a "read" rather than a "spoken" or "conversational" quality. Some readers are so sensitive to metrical patterns that they cannot resist stopping at the end of every line and find it virtually impossible to pause within a line. The meter drives them relentlessly onward. Such readers are being controlled by their material, rather than the other way around. The extended paraphrase and improvisational techniques discussed in Chapter 4 are designed to overcome this problem. Some readers find it helpful to recopy the poem in prose form so that it doesn't appear to be so regular on the page. Remember, the poet who has chosen to encase his material within a particular rhythm scheme is obligated to follow it; the interpreter is under no such obligation.

Apart from the problems it creates, meter is very useful to the interpreter. It provides important clues to meaning and suggests where the poet decided the stress should be placed. Consider the following familiar line:

To be or not to be, that is the question.

Shakespeare has written an essentially iambic pentameter line, even though it ends with an extra unstressed syllable—a feminine ending. If we scan the line normally, we can determine where the natural stresses fall:

To *be* or *not* to *be,* that *is* the *que*stion.

Whether or not the pattern of iambic stress is followed, it is important for the interpreter to know that Shakespeare chose to emphasize certain words over others by virtue of this arrangement. Therefore, unless we have a compelling reason to do otherwise, we will, for example, give more importance to "is" than to "that."

In addition, there are many poems in which meter has a primary function, where part of what is being described in the content involves rhythm itself. Vachel Lindsey's "Congo" is one example that comes immediately to mind. But there are many instances, even within poems not so overtly rhythmical in construction, where the subtle application of rhythmical stress enhances the picturization of the content. The following excerpt from Yeats' "The Second Coming" is an example.

Turning and turning in the widening gyre
The falcon cannot hear the falconer;

These two lines, with minor variation, consist of a series of dactylic feet. When the meter is subtly stressed, it emphasizes the turning motion being described, and makes the picture more vivid.

Metric stress can also be used as a comic device, as in the following excerpt from Gilbert and Sullivan's *The Mikado.*

To sit in solemn silence in a dull, dark dock
In a pestilential prison with a life-long lock,
Awaiting the sensation of a short, sharp shock
From a cheap and chippy chopper on a big black block!

Literature in the oral tradition depends heavily on metrical stress for its powers of incantation. The ancient Greeks, the Anglo-Saxons, the African tribesman, and the American Indian are but a few examples of cultures, both past and present, which depend heavily on the primary role of meter in their poetic experiences.

During the past hundred years, poets have been searching for forms of rhythmic regularity other than metrical. The poet working in *free verse* attempts to avoid obvious meter by setting up patterns based on repetitions and variations in syntax, reoccurring images, and phrases rather than syllables. While the interpreter does not vary the metrical approach in a poem, there is obviously less concern in free verse with meter than with other elements.

In summary, the awareness of meter gives the interpreter substantial clues about the nature of the material being dealt with. Meters can progress slowly or move with great speed, they can produce qualities of heaviness or lightness, and these differences can have direct emotional associations. The poet's patterns of stress help disclose meaning and give insights into the experience as the poet lived it. In many poems, the skillful emphasis of certain stress patterns by the interpreter, without the loss of the essential spontaneous nature of the performance, will elevate that performance above the level of common speech—creating a more pleasurable, memorable, and meaningful experience for the audience.

FIGURES OF SPEECH

The final aspect of style the interpreter needs to consider is a group of literary conventions called *figures of speech*. In a sense, all figures of speech are devices for comparison, which serve different purposes. When a poet employs a figure of speech rather than a literal statement, the purpose is to produce a clearer picture of the subject. Figures also make the impressions more vivid; they involve the senses and establish a common ground between the speaker and his audience.

One such figure is the *simile*. A simile compares two things explicitly through the use of "like" or "as."

My friends forsake me like a memory lost;

The poet is expressing a feeling or, more accurately, making a statement about how his friends are treating him; and at the same time, through the device of the simile, he expresses his feeling.

A *metaphor* compares two things implicitly.

And the startled little waves that leap
In fiery ringlets from their sleep,

Here, the sight of the little waves in the moonlight is compared to little rings of fire. Browning wants us to see the shape and color of what he sees.

Personification endows a nonhuman subject with human qualities. The above example, which contains a metaphor, also personifies the "little waves" with the ability to "sleep" and be awakened. The following stanza from Robert Penn Warren's "Original Sin: A Short Story" demonstrates personification and simile.

Nodding, its great head rattling like a gourd,
And locks like seaweed strung on the stinking stone,
The nightmare stumbles past, and you have heard
It fumble your door before it whimpers and is gone:
It acts like the old hound that used to snuffle your door and
moan.

The preceding stanza also introduces us to another figure, the analogy.

The *analogy* is an extended comparison, which sometimes continues throughout the poem. In the above example, sin is personified in the form of a creature resembling a dog. Actually, this type of analogy is called *allegory:* the personification of an abstraction.

Two final figures which the interpreter needs to know are *synecdoche* and *metonymy*. Synecdoche occurs when a subject is represented by one of its parts, or by an image that describes one of its parts, as in "She wears the pants." This implies that she is dominant or aggressive. *Metonomy* uses the name of one thing in place of a subject which has become synonymous with it; "native tongue" for language, "the Cross" for Christianity.

As with the other poetic elements we have discussed, figures of speech yield important information to the interpreter. The selection of comparisons tells us something very important about the attitude and experiences of the speaker of these words. Figures also provide fertile ground for the growth of physical awareness, which will turn into illustrative action during the performance. The principles for presenting figures are the same as for presenting technique. That is, the interpreter must depict the process of selection. When one thing is being compared to another for the purpose of clarity, vividness, or emphasis, there are alternative images to the one selected. The interpreter must consider these alternatives mentally, and allow the selected image to break freshly and spontaneously on the audience as if it just came to mind. If the interpreter pauses after "like" to consider what comparison to use, the audience will begin to think along with the interpreter. This process of causing the audience to participate in the event helps create *empathy*.

TYPES OF POETRY: LYRIC, NARRATIVE, AND DRAMATIC

While this artificially imposed classification is rapidly passing from the poetry scene (most beginning poetry texts no longer use it), it is still considered doctrine by many teachers of oral interpretation. In fact, there are some useful aspects to such a division for the interpreter. Even though the interpreter will ultimately arrive at the same conclusions about the speaker of the poem by following the methodology outlined in this text, identifying the poem as a member of one of the three general categories may move things along a bit faster.

LYRIC POETRY

Lyric poems are generally defined as being short, personal, and emotional. The narrator may be the poet, but does not have to be portrayed as such. If the content of the poem suggests age or cultural differences from the reader, then characterization is appropriate. Lyric poetry is further identified by its high density of figurative language. In addition, lyrics are traditionally divided into four subcategories: reflective lyric, elegy, ode, and sonnet.

The *reflective lyric* presents the narrator in the act of remembering and reflecting upon a past emotional experience. The *elegy* expresses the grief brought on by the death of someone. The *ode* expresses celebration of some important experience or event, usually in formal language and structure. The *sonnet*, which we have discussed above, generally expresses exalted love or the triumph of the intellect.

DRAMATIC POETRY

In order to have meaning as a category, dramatic poetry must be limited to *verse drama, monologue,* and *soliloquy*. In each case the interpreter is presenting a character (or characters in verse drama) in action: answering a charge, confronting an obstacle, working through a personal problem, having a realization, and the like. The content and given circumstances will determine the characterization for the narrator.

Soliloquys present a special problem for the interpreter. They are specifically designed as a dramatic device to reveal the private thoughts of an individual. Much of the success of the soliloquy depends on the creation of an aura of solitude. A soliloquy should be approached in the same way as any dramatic speech (see Chapter 8), since it is analogous except that there is no other character present.

NARRATIVE POETRY

Narrative poetry, like narrative prose, relates a series of events, generally in chronological order, which ultimately add up to a story. As with all stories, more than one character may be introduced, and, therefore, portrayed by the interpreter. The narrator will fall into one of the three categories, discussed briefly at the beginning of this chapter and at length in Chapter 7: first person, third person, or omniscient. The type of narrator will determine the relationship of the interpreter to both the story and the audience.

Narrative poems can be quite long; Milton's *Paradise Lost* is an example. Ballads also fall into this category, as do many modern song lyrics.

In this chapter an attempt has been made to provide the interpreter with the basic information needed for the presentation of poetry. With practice, interpreters learn how to shape their performances into something more than coherent readings of poems. They become sensitive to the poet's techniques, uses of sound and juxtapositions of sounds, and other devices to produce word colors and dramatic builds within the poem. They learn to use pauses, inflections, and sustained tones to convey these poetic devices to the audience. Above all, interpreters learn that poetry, like all art, has logic, meaning, and reality—that it is not to be feared or revered and held at arm's length, but is to be experienced and responded to. Poetry began with oral interpretation. They belong together.

QUESTIONS FOR STUDY AND DISCUSSION

1
Why must the interpreter think like the poet rather than the critic?

2
Explain the differences between a first-person narrator and a third-person narrator.

3
Explain the differences between a third-person narrator and an omniscient narrator.

4
Why must the interpreter be aware of the poet's application of technique?

5

What is meant by denotation and connotation?

6

How does rhyme help to organize a poem?

7

How does meter help the interpreter determine the meaning of a poem?

SUGGESTED ACTIVITIES

1

Develop an image, such as "a sunrise," and use it as a simile, a metaphor, an analogy, and a personification.

2

Select a poem, and scan it for the metrical pattern.

3

Select a poem which has a rhyme scheme, and mark the rhyming lines with the *a b c* method.

Selections for Analysis and Performance

STRANGE FITS OF PASSION HAVE I KNOWN
WILLIAM WORDSWORTH

Strange fits of passion have I known:
And I will dare to tell,
But in the Lover's ear alone,
What once to me befell.

When she I loved looked every day
Fresh as a rose in June,
I to her cottage bent my way,
Beneath an *evening-moon*.

Upon the *moon* I fixed my eye,
All over the wide lea;
With quickening pace my horse drew nigh
Those paths so dear to me.

And now we reached the orchard-plot;
And, as we climbed the hill,
The *sinking moon* to Lucy's cot
Came near, and nearer still.

In one of those sweet dreams I slept,
Kind Nature's gentlest boon!
And all the while my eyes I kept
On the *descending moon*.

My horse moved on; hoof after hoof
He raised, and never stopped:

When down behind the cottage roof,
At once, the *bright moon dropped.*

What fond and wayward thoughts will slide
Into a Lover's head!
"O mercy!" to myself I cried,
"If Lucy should be dead!"

Interpreter's Notebook

In "Strange Fits of Passion Have I Known" Wordsworth tells a story about how he was once frightened by his imagination. As the narrator of this story, don't recall the details too quickly. Also, be careful of the insistent iambic rhythm, or it will cause you to sound sing-song.

I HAVE NOT LOVED THE WORLD
From CHILDE HAROLD'S PILGRIMAGE
(Canto 3, stanzas 113, 114)
GEORGE GORDON, LORD BYRON

I have not loved the world, nor the world me;
I have not flattered its rank breath, nor bowed
To its idolatries a patient knee,
Nor coined my cheek to smiles, nor cried aloud
In worship of an echo; in the crowd
They could not deem me one of such; I stood

Among them, but not of them; in a shroud
Of thoughts which were not their thoughts, and still could,
Had I not filed my mind, which thus itself subdued.

I have not loved the world, nor the world me,—
But let us part fair foes; I do believe,
Though I have found them not, that there may be
Words which are things, hopes which will not deceive,
And virtues which are merciful, nor weave
Snares for the failing; I would also deem
O'er others' griefs that some sincerely grieve;
That two, or one, are almost what they seem,
That goodness is no name, and happiness no dream.

THE WORLD IS TOO MUCH WITH US
WILLIAM WORDSWORTH

The world is too much with us; late and soon,
Getting and spending, we lay waste our powers:
Little we see in Nature that is ours;
We have given our hearts away, a sordid boon!
This Sea that bares her bosom to the moon;
The winds that will be howling at all hours,
And are up-gathered now like sleeping flowers;
For this, for everything, we are out of tune;
It moves us not.—Great God! I'd rather be
A Pagan suckled in a creed outworn;
So might I, standing in this pleasant lea,
Have glimpses that would make me less forlorn;
Have sight of Proteus rising from the sea;
Or hear old Triton blow his wreathed horn.

THE DAY
THEODORE SPENCER

The day was a year at first
When children ran in the garden;
The day shrank down to a month
When the boys played ball.

The day was a week thereafter
When young men walked in the garden;
The day was itself a day
When love grew tall.

The day shrank down to an hour
When old men limped in the garden;
The day will last forever
When it is nothing at all.

AN EASY DECISION
KENNETH PATCHEN

I had finished my dinner
Gone for a walk

It was fine
Out and I started whistling

It wasn't long before

I met a
Man and his wife riding on
A pony with seven
Kids running along beside them

I said hello and

Went on
Pretty soon I met another
Couple
This time with nineteen
Kids and all of them
Riding on
A big smiling hippopotamus

I invited them home

SNAKE
D. H. LAWRENCE

A snake came to my water-trough
On a hot, hot day, and I in pyjamas for the heat,
To drink there.

In the deep, strange-scented shade of the great dark carob-tree
I came down the steps with my pitcher
And must wait, must stand and wait, for there he was at the
   trough before me.

He reached down from a fissure in the earth-wall in the gloom
And trailed his yellow-brown slackness soft-bellied down, over
   the edge of the stone trough,
And rested his throat upon the stone bottom,
And where the water had dripped from the tap, in a small
   clearness,
He sipped with his straight mouth,

Softly drank through his straight gums, into his slack long
    body,
Silently.

Someone was before me at my water-trough,
And I, like a second comer, waiting.

He lifted his head from his drinking, as cattle do,
And looked at me vaguely, as drinking cattle do,
And flickered his two-forked tongue from his lips, and mused
    a moment,
And stopped and drank a little more,

Being earth-brown, earth-golden from the burning bowels of
    the earth
On the day of Sicilian July, with Etna smoking.
The voice of my education said to me
He must be killed,
For in Sicily the black, black snakes are innocent, the gold are
    venomous.

And voices in me said, If you were a man
You would take a stick and break him now, and finish him off.

But must I confess how I liked him,
How glad I was he had come like a guest in quiet, to drink at
    my water-trough
And depart peaceful, pacified, and thankless,
Into the burning bowels of this earth?

Was it cowardice, that I dared not kill him?
Was it perversity, that I longed to talk to him?
Was it humility, to feel so honoured?
I felt so honoured.

And yet those voices:
If you were not afraid, you would kill him!

And truly I was afraid, I was most afraid,
But even so, honoured still more
That he should seek my hospitality
From out the dark door of the secret earth.

He drank enough
And lifted his head, dreamily, as one who has drunken,
And flickered his tongue like a forked night on the air, so
    black,
Seeming to lick his lips,
And looked around like a god, unseeing, into the air,
And slowly turned his head,
And slowly, very slowly, as if thrice adream,
Proceeded to draw his slow length curing round
And climb again the broken bank of my wall-face
And as he put his head into that dreadful hole,
And as he slowly drew up, snake-easing his shoulders, and
    entered farther,
A sort of horror, a sort of protest against his withdrawing into
    that horrid black hole,
Deliberately going into the blackness, and slowly drawing
    himself after,
Overcame me now his back was turned.

I looked round, I put down my pitcher,
I picked up a clumsy log
And threw it at the water-trough with a clatter.

I think it did not hit him,
But suddenly that part of him that was left behind convulsed
    in undignified haste,
Writhed like lightning, and was gone
Into the black hole, the earth-lipped fissure in the wallfront,
At which, in the intense still noon, I stared with fascination.

And immediately I regretted it.
I thought how paltry, how vulgar, what a mean act!
I despised myself and the voices of my accursed human
    education.

And I thought of the albatross,
And I wished he would come back, my snake.

For he seemed to me again like a king,
Like a king in exile, uncrowned in the underworld,
Now due to be crowned again.

And so, I missed my chance with one of the lords
Of life.
And I have something to expiate:
A pettiness.

POLO GROUNDS
ROLFE HUMPHRIES

Time is of the essence. This is a highly skilled
And beautiful mystery. Three or four seconds only
From the time that Riggs connects till he reaches first,
And in those seconds Jurges goes to his right,
Comes up with the ball, tosses to Witek at second
For the force on Reese, Witek to Mize at first,
In time for the out—a double play.

(Red Barber crescendo. Crowd noises, obbligato;
Scattered staccatos from the peanut boys,
Loud in the lull, as the teams are changing sides) . . .

Hubbell takes the sign, nods, pumps, delivers—
A foul into the stands. Dunn takes a new ball out,
Hands it to Danning, who throws it down to Werber;
Werber takes off his glove, rubs the ball briefly,
Tosses it over to Hub, who goes to the rosin bag,
Takes the sign from Danning, pumps, delivers—
Low, outside, ball three. Danning goes to the mound,
Says something to Hub, Dunn brushes off the plate,
Adams starts throwing in the Giant bullpen,
Hub takes the sign from Danning, pumps, delivers,
Camilli gets hold of it, a *long* fly to the outfield,
Ott goes back, back, back, against the wall, gets under it,
Pounds his glove, and takes it for the out.
That's all for the Dodgers. . . .

Time is of the essence. The rhythms break,
More varied and subtle than any kind of dance;
Movement speeds up or lags. The ball goes out
In sharp and angular drives, or long, slow arcs,
Comes in again controlled and under aim;
The players wheel or spurt, race, stoop, slide, halt,

Shift imperceptibly to new positions,
Watching the signs, according to the batter,
The score, the inning. Time is of the essence.

Time is of the essence. Remember Terry?
Remember Stonewall Jackson, Lindstrom, Frisch,
When they were good? Remember Long George Kelly?
Remember John McGraw and Benny Kauff?
Remember Bridwell, Tenney, Merkle, Youngs,
Chief Myers, Big Jeff Tesreau, Shufflin' Phil?
Remember Matthewson, and Ames, and Donlin,
Buck Ewing, Rusie, Smiling Mickey Welch?
Remember a left-handed catcher named Jack Humphries,
Who sometimes played the outfield, in '83?

Time is of the essence. The shadow moves
From the plate to the box, from the box to second base,
From second to the outfield, to the bleachers.

Time is of the essence. The crowd and players
Are the same age always, but the man in the crowd
Is older every season. Come on, play ball!

Interpreter's Notebook

As the first line of "Polo Grounds" says, "Time is of the essence." The poem begins with "real time" as the play-by-play is reported by the announcer. Then it speeds through generations of ballplayers by invoking their names. It ends by focusing on one lifetime metaphorically represented by the shadow moving across the playing field. Vary your pace to follow the movement of the poem.

NIGHT GAME
ROLFE HUMPHRIES

Only bores are bored,—wrote William Saroyan—
And I was a bore, and so I went to the ball game;
But there was a pest who insisted on going with me.
I thought I could shake him if I bought one ticket,

But he must have come in on a pass. I couldn't see him,
But I knew he was there, back of third, in the row behind me,
His knees in my back, and his breath coming over my
    shoulder,
The loud-mouthed fool, the sickly nervous ego,
Repeating his silly questions, like a child
Or a girl at the first game ever. *Shut up,* I told him,
For Christ's sweet sake, shut up, and watch the ball game.
He didn't want to, but finally subsided,
And my attention found an outward focus,
Visible, pure, objective, inning by inning,
A well-played game, with no particular features,—
Feldman pitched well, and Ott hit a couple of homers.

And after the ninth, with the crowd in the bleachers thinning,
And the lights in the grandstand dimming out behind us,
And a full moon hung before us, over the clubhouse,
I drifted out with the crowd across the diamond,
Over the infield brown and the smooth green outfield,
So wonderful underfoot, so right, so perfect,
That each of us was a player for a moment,
The men my age and the soldiers and the sailors,
Their girls, and the running kids, and the plodding old men,
Taking it easy, the same unhurried tempo,
In the mellow light and air, in the mild cool weather,
Moving together, moving out together,
Oh, this is good, I felt, to be part of this movement,
This mood, this music, part of the human race,
Alike and different, after the game is over,
Streaming away to the exit, and underground.

Interpreter's Notebook

In this second poem "Night Game," Humphries again uses baseball as his metaphor for life. Time again is a factor ("... Taking it easy, the same unhurried tempo, ..."), but not so prominent. This is a more personal poem, using a first-person narrator. Build the story slowly, respond physically to the "... smooth green outfield,/So wonderful underfoot," and be passionate and wistful at the end. What is the "exit"? What is "underground"?

SECRETS
Cj STEVENS

Now that I am old, I will tell you secrets
that were kept from me when I was young.
The scent of flowers is more elusive, but still
as sweet. Wine is more varied to the taste.
Springs still surprise the winter eyes, and falls
still flaunt their hectic colors. Music, now,
has narrowed down and simple has become complex.
Song still can break the heart, love still amaze.

THE WOOD-PILE
ROBERT FROST

Out walking in the frozen swamp one grey day,
I paused and said, "I will turn back from here.
No, I will go on farther—and we shall see."
The hard snow held me, save where now and then
One foot went through. The view was all in lines
Straight up and down of tall slim trees
Too much alike to mark or name a place by
So as to say for certain I was here
Or somewhere else: I was just far from home.
A small bird flew before me. He was careful
To put a tree between us when he lighted,
And say no word to tell me who he was
Who was so foolish as to think what *he* thought.
He thought that I was after him for a feather—
The white one in his tail; like one who takes
Everything said as personal to himself.
One flight out sideways would have undeceived him.
And then there was a pile of wood for which
I forgot him and let his little fear
Carry him off the way I might have gone,
Without so much as wishing him good-night.
He went behind it to make his last stand.
It was a cord of maple, cut and split
And piled—and measured, four by four by eight.
And not another like it could I see.

No runner tracks in this year's snow looped near it.
And it was older sure than this year's cutting,
Or even last year's or the year's before.
The wood was grey and the bark warping off it
And the pile somewhat sunken. Clematis
Had wound strings round and round it like a bundle.
What held it though on one side was a tree
Still growing, and on one a stake and prop,
These latter about to fall. I thought that only
Someone who lived in turning to fresh tasks
Could so forget his handiwork on which
He spent himself, the labor of his axe,
And leave it there far from a useful fireplace
To warm the frozen swamp as best it could
With the slow smokeless burning of decay.

REQUIEM
KENNETH FEARING

Will they stop,
Will they stand there for a moment, perhaps before some shop
    where you have gone so many times
(Stand with the same blue sky above them and the stones, so
    often walked, beneath)

Will it be a day like this—
As though there could be such a day again—
And will their own concerns still be about the same,
And will the feeling still be this that you have felt so many
    times,
Will they meet and stop and speak, one perplexed and one
    aloof,

Saying: Have you heard,
Have you heard,
Have you heard about the death?

Yes, choosing the words, tragic, yes, a shock,
One who had so much of this, they will say, a life so filled
    with that,

Then will one say that the days are growing crisp again, the
other that the leaves are turning,
And will they say good-bye, good-bye, you must look me up
some time, good-bye,
Then turn and go, each of them thinking, and yet, and yet,
Each feeling, if it were I, instead would that be all,
Each wondering, suddenly alone, if that is all, in fact—

And will that be all?
On a day like this, with motors streaming through the fresh
parks, the streets alive with casual people,
And everywhere, on all of it, the brightness of the sun.

KING JUKE
KENNETH FEARING

The jukebox has a big square face,
A majestic face, softly glowing with red and green and purple
lights.
Have you got a face as bright as that?

BUT IT'S A PROVEN FACT, THAT A JUKEBOX HAS NO
EARS.

With its throat of brass, the jukebox eats live nickels raw;
It can turn itself on or shut itself off;
It has no hangovers, knows no regrets, and it never feels the
need for sleep.
Can you do that?
What can you do that a jukebox can't, and do it ten times
better than you?

And it hammers at your nerves, and stabs you through the
heart, and beats upon your soul—
But can you do that to the box?

Its resourceful mind, filled with thoughts that range from love
to grief, from the gutter to the stars, from pole to pole,
Can seize its thoughts between fingers of steel,
Begin them at the start and follow them through in an orderly
fashion to the very end.

Can you do that?
And what can you say that a jukebox can't, and say it in a
  clearer, louder voice than yours?
What have you got, a jukebox hasn't got?

Well, a jukebox has no ears, they say.
The box, it is believed, cannot even hear itself.
IT SIMPLY HAS NO EARS AT ALL.

Interpreter's Notebook

Analyze "King Juke" very carefully. What is a logical setting for someone
to say these words? Be very direct with your audience. Challenge them with
"Can you do that?" and "What have you got, a jukebox hasn't got?"

AT THE AQUARIUM
MAX EASTMAN

Serene the silver fishes glide,
Stern-lipped, and pale, and wonder-eyed!
As through the aged deeps of ocean,
They glide with wan and wavy motion!
They have no pathways where they go.
They flow like water to and fro.
They watch with never-winking eyes,
They watch with staring, cold surprise,
The level people in the air,
The people peering, peering there:
Who also wander to and fro,
And know not why or where they go,
Yet have a wonder in their eyes,
Sometimes a pale and cold surprise.

A VALEDICTION FORBIDDING MOURNING
JOHN DONNE

As virtuous men pass mildly away,
And whisper to their souls to go,

Whilst some of their sad friends do say,
   The breath goes now, and some say, no:

So let us melt, and make no noise,
   No tear-floods, nor sigh-tempests move;
'Twere profanation of our joys
   To tell the laity our love.

Moving of the earth brings harms and fears;
   Men reckon what it did and meant;
But trepidation of the spheres,
   Though greater far, is innocent.

Dull sublunary lovers' love
   (Whose soul is sense) cannot admit
Absence, because it doth remove
   Those things which elemented it.

But we, by a love so much refined
   That ourselves know not what it is,
Inter-assured of the mind,
   Care less, eyes, lips, and hands to miss.

Our two souls, therefore, which are one,
   Though I must go, endure not yet
A breach, but an expansion,
   Like gold to airy thinness beat.

If they be two, they are two so
   As stiff twin compasses are two:
Thy soul, the fixed foot, makes no show
   To move, but doth, if the other do.

And though it in the center sit,
   Yet when the other far doth roam,
It leans and harkens after it,
   And grows erect as that comes home.

Such wilt thou be to me, who must,
   Like the other foot, obliquely run;
Thy firmness makes my circle just,
   And makes me end where I begun.

THE AIR PLANT
Grand Cayman
HART CRANE

This tuft that thrives on saline nothingness,
Inverted octopus with heavenward arms
Thrust parching from a palm-bole hard by the cove—
A bird almost—of almost bird alarms,

Is pulmonary to the wind that jars
Its tentacles, horrific in their lurch.
The lizard's throat, held bloated for a fly,
Balloons but warily from this throbbing perch.

The needles and hack-saws of cactus bleed
A milk of earth when stricken off the stalk;
But this,—defenseless, thornless, sheds no blood,
Almost no shadow—but the air's thin talk.

Angelic Dynamo! Ventriloquist of the Blue!
While beachward creeps the shark-swept Spanish Main
By what conjunctions do the winds appoint
Its apotheosis, at last—the hurricane!

THE CHOICE
HILARY CORKE

I have known one bound to a bed by wrist and ankle,
Scarred by the whips of a wasting ache,
Who, at the point of entering of the needle,
Looked once around to take
The final view, then spoke;
The echo of that terribly witty joke
Pursued the surgeon to his home in Kew,
Deafened a nurse all night, and leaden lay
On the heart of a thick-skinned anesthetist
Long after they'd dispatched his ended clay.

That one lies in Oxford and is its earth.
Also, a bright-eyed woman in Germany,
In a sightless trap, far below ground,

Of which another held the key,
Surveyed without visible alarm
Or twitching of a pinioned arm
The instruments set out upon a table;
Then from her mouth there flowed a resolute
Stream of satire deliciously edged until
The tormentor tormented stopped it with a boot.

She fell as ash, not bones, in Dachau fields.
All brave men breathe her when the wind
Blows east from Danube. And Tom Caine,
When the *Imperial* was mined
And water had flooded all but the wireless room,
Spoke without audible gloom
From fifty fathoms down for fifteen hours
To his messmates on land, told several stories,
Then to a doctor carefully described
Asphyxiation's onset and his doom.

He is grown water and surrounds the pole.
If ever you dip a cup in any sea
Tom Caine is in it somewhere. On the whole
Men die asleep or else disgracefully;
But not all men. Perhaps we are never,
By any average mountain, wood, or river,
More than a heart's breadth from the dust
Of one who laughed with nothing left to lose.
Who saw the joke beneath the mammoth's foot?
And what shall I choose, if I am free to choose?

THE BALLAD OF RUDOLPH REED
GWENDOLYN BROOKS

Rudolph Reed was oaken.
His wife was oaken too.
And his two good girls and his good little man
Oakened as they grew.

"I am not hungry for berries.
I am not hungry for bread.

But hungry hungry for a house
Where at night a man in bed

"May never hear the plaster
Stir as if in pain.
May never hear the roaches
Falling like fat rain.

"Where never wife and children need
Go blinking through the gloom.
Where every room of many rooms
Will be full of room.

"Oh my home may have its east or west
Or north or south behind it.
All I know is I shall know it,
And fight for it when I find it."

It was in a street of bitter white
That he made his application.
For Rudolph Reed was oakener
Than others in the nation.

The agent's steep and steady stare
Corroded to a grain.
Why, you black old, tough old hell of a man,
Move your family in!
Nary a grin grinned Rudolph Reed,
Nary a curse cursed he,
But moved in his House. With his dark little wife,
And his dark little children three.

A neighbor would *look,* with a yawning eye
That squeezed into a slit.
But the Rudolph Reeds and the children three
Were too joyous to notice it.

For were they not firm in a home of their own
With windows everywhere
And a beautiful banistered stair
And a front yard for flowers and a back yard for grass?

The first night, a rock, big as two fists.
The second, a rock big as three.
But nary a curse cursed Rudolph Reed.
(Though oaken as man could be.)

The third night, a silvery ring of glass.
Patience ached to endure.
But he looked, and lo! small Mabel's blood
Was staining her gaze so pure.

Then up did rise our Rudolph Reed
And pressed the hand of his wife,
And went to the door with a thirty-four
And a beastly butcher knife.

He ran like a mad thing into the night.
And the words in his mouth were stinking.
By the time he had hurt his first white man
He was no longer thinking.

By the time he had hurt his fourth white man
Rudolph Reed was dead.
His neighbors gathered and kicked his corpse.
"Nigger—" his neighbors said.

Small Mabel whimpered all night long,
For calling herself the cause.
Her oak-eyed mother did no thing
But change the bloody gauze.

THE CHINESE CHECKER PLAYERS
RICHARD BRAUTIGAN

When I was six years old
I played Chinese checkers with a woman
who was ninety-three years old.
She lived by herself
in an apartment down the hall from ours.
We played Chinese checkers
every Monday and Thursday nights.

While we played she usually talked
about her husband
who had been dead for seventy years,
and we drank tea and ate cookies
and cheated.

MEETING AT NIGHT
ROBERT BROWNING

The gray sea and the long black land;
And the yellow half-moon large and low;
And the startled little waves that leap
In fiery ringlets from their sleep,
As I gain the cove with pushing prow,
And quench its speed in the slushy sand.

Then a mile of warm sea-scented beach;
Three fields to cross till a farm appears;
A tap at the pane, the quick sharp scratch
And blue spurt of a lighted match,
And a voice less loud, through its joys and fears,
Than the two hearts beating each to each!

COME, MY CELIA, LET US PROVE
BEN JONSON

Come, my Celia, let us prove,
While we can, the sports of love;
Time will not be ours for ever,
He, at length, our good will sever.
Spend not then his gifts in vain:
Suns that set may rise again;
But if once we lose this light,
'Tis with us perpetual night.
Why should we defer our joys?
Fame and rumour are but toys.
Cannot we delude the eyes
Of a few poor household spies?
Or his easier ears beguile,

Thus removëd by our wile?
'Tis no sin love's fruits to steal,
But the sweet thefts to reveal;
To be taken, to be seen.
These have crimes accounted been.

Interpreter's Notebook

In "Come, My Celia, Let Us Prove" the attitude of the narrator carries the poem. Have fun with it. You are trying to talk this woman into having an affair. Reassure her that there is no great danger of being caught, which is the only sin.

SKINNY POEM
LOU LIPSITZ

Skinny
poem,
all
your
ribs
showing
even
without
a
deep
breath

thin
legs
rotted
with
disease.

Live
here!
on

this
page,
barely
making
it,
like
the
mass
of
mankind.

THE SECOND COMING
WILLIAM BUTLER YEATS

Turning and turning in the widening gyre
The falcon cannot hear the falconer;
Things fall apart; the centre cannot hold;
Mere anarchy is loosed upon the world,
The blood-dimmed tide is loosed, and everywhere
The ceremony of innocence is drowned;
The best lack all conviction, while the worst
Are full of passionate intensity.

Surely some revelation is at hand;
Surely the Second Coming is at hand.
The Second Coming! Hardly are those words out
When a vast image out of *Spiritus Mundi*
Trouble my sight: somewhere in sands of the desert
A shape with lion body and the head of a man,
A gaze blank and pitiless as the sun,
Is moving its slow thighs, while all about it
Reel shadows of the indignant desert birds.

The darkness drops again; but now I know
That twenty centuries of stony sleep
Were vexed to nightmare by a rocking cradle,
And what rough beast, its hour come round at last,
Slouches towards Bethlehem to be born?

THE DRUNKARD
WILLIAM CARLOS WILLIAMS

You drunken
tottering
bum

by Christ
in spite of all
your filth

and sordidness
I envy
you

It is the very face
of love
itself

abandoned
in that powerless
committal

to despair

SATURDAY POEM
ROBERT VAS DIAS

This poem goes well with ham & swiss
on a hard roll with mustard & draft beer on
a Saturday afternoon, the kind of poem
you don't think about but suddenly
it comes to mind as the idea of a sandwich
so you stop in & find yourself getting into
a discussion with a friend on the terrible state
of American jurisprudence, its subservience
to political expediency, after which there's nothing

more to be said, thinking maybe I will &
why the hell not, ordering the poem
& when it comes, smelling it
surreptitiously before the first bite, not so anyone
would think I thought it bad, but
to savor it, that instance
of an idea I can taste.

THE TIGER
WILLIAM BLAKE

Tiger! Tiger! burning bright,
In the forests of the night:
What immortal hand or eye
Could frame thy fearful symmetry?

In what distant deeps or skies
Burnt the fire of thine eyes?
On what wings dare he aspire?
What the hand dare seize the fire?

And what shoulder, & what art,
Could twist the sinews of thy heart?
And when thy heart began to beat,
What dread hand? & what dread feet?

What the hammer? what the chain?
In what furnace was thy brain?
What the anvil? what dread grasp,
Dare its deadly terrors clasp?

When the stars threw down their spears
And watered heaven with their tears:
Did he smile his work to see?
Did he who made the Lamb make thee?

Tiger! Tiger! burning bright,
In the forests of the night:

What immortal hand or eye,
Dare frame thy fearful symmetry?

Interpreter's Notebook

The trochaic rhythm of "The Tiger" is very pronounced. It is effective to let it show through at some points, as in the first and last stanzas. However, it must be subdued for most of the poem. Otherwise you will sound as if you are jumping rope. Blake very effectively employs this rhythm to convey childlike innocence. Trochees are found in many children's verses: "London Bridge is falling down . . ."; "Twinkle, twinkle little star . . ."

EFFORT AT SPEECH BETWEEN TWO PEOPLE
MURIEL RUKEYSER

Speak to me.   Take my hand.   What are you now?
I will tell you all.   I will conceal nothing.
When I was three, a little child read a story about a rabbit
who died, in the story, and I crawled under a chair:

a pink rabbit;   it was my birthday, and a candle
burnt a sore spot on my finger, and I was told to be happy.

Oh, grow to know me.   I am not happy.   I will be
    open:
Now I am thinking of white sails against a sky like music,
like glad horns blowing, and birds tilting, and an arm about
    me.
There was one I loved, who wanted to live, sailing.

Speak to me.   Take my hand.   What are you now?
When I was nine, I was fruitily sentimental,
fluid: and my widowed aunt played Chopin,
and I bent my head on the painted woodwork, and wept.
I want now to be close to you.   I would
link the minutes of my days close, somehow, to your days.

I am not happy.   I will be open.

I have liked lamps in evening corners, and quiet poems.
There has been fear in my life.   Sometimes I speculate
On what a tragedy his life was, really.

Take my hand.   Fist my mind in your hand.   What are
   you now?
When I was fourteen, I had dreams of suicide,
and I stood at a steep window, at sunset, hoping toward
   death:
if the light had not melted clouds and plains to beauty,
if light had not transformed that day, I would have leapt.
I am unhappy.   I am lonely.   Speak to me.

I will be open.   I think he never loved me:
he loved the bright beaches, the little lips of foam
that ride small waves, he loved the veer of gulls:
he said with a gay mouth: I love you.   Grow to know me.

What are you now?   If we could touch one another,
if these our separate entities could come to grips,
clenched like a Chinese puzzle . . . yesterday
I stood in a crowded street that was live with people,
and no one spoke a word, and the morning shone.
Everyone silent, moving. . . . Take my hand.   Speak to me.

Interpreter's Notebook

Don't let the title "Effort at Speech Between Two People" confuse you. There is only one person speaking in the poem. Treat your audience as the other person. Coax them to speak to you. Note the wide spaces the author has placed between some of the sense units. What does she want you to do?

HOW SOON HATH TIME
JOHN MILTON

How soon hath Time, the subtle thief of youth,
   Stolen on his wing my three and twentieth year!
   My hasting days fly on with full career,
   But my late spring no bud or blossom show'th.
Perhaps my semblance might deceive the truth,

That I to manhood am arrived so near,
And inward ripeness doth much less appear,
That some more timely-happy spirits endu'th.
Yet be it less or more, or soon or slow,
It shall be still in strictest measure even
To that same lot, however mean or high,
Toward which Time leads me, and the will of heaven;
All is, if I have grace to use it so,
As ever in my great Taskmaster's eye.

WHAT YOU SEE AIN'T WHAT YOU GOT
REGINALD LOCKETT

it would've been a real real
groove   when i moved thru those
years of discovery after
discovery   wonder after
wonder   to sit before the
toxic beam of the tv set & see
black bart hijack wells fargo
gold shipments on old calif. roads or
wish i was there when my
ace boon john threw a wang-dang
-doodle in the big house after the
massa & the missus went away to
some place good home folks call
philly-me-jinks*
it would've been real
nice to sit in front of the
tv set & watch big bad
shango streak across the
sky on seven bolts of lightning or dig
mighty horus put another
whipping on some
square name seth
it would've been outta sight & pure
delight to just know that
marie laveau was hiding somewhere in my

---

* From the Afro-American folktale, ''Massa Takes a Trip.''

bedroom walls   came out at
night when everybody slept   told me
strange & wonderful things &
gave me a gris-gris bag all my verh own
it would've been great to
imagine riding with the
divine horsemen of the heavens & be real
tight with old slick legba &
ogoun the warrior god
it would've been mighty
fine to see all of this in the
cold & hateful stare of the
tv set   but
it was even
finer & warmer
nicer & sweeter   to
listen to my
grandma   mamafromwaydownhome
tell me how brer rabbit put one or
two over on brer fox & brer bear   sing
songs & tell more
tales of real folks/heroes that
moved thru her days
/thru her years   her
life

MR. FLOOD'S PARTY
EDWIN ARLINGTON ROBINSON

Old Eben Flood, climbing alone one night
Over the hill between the town below
And the forsaken upland hermitage
That held as much as he should ever know
On earth again of home, paused warily.
The road was his with not a native near;
And Eben, having leisure, said aloud,
For no man else in Tilbury Town to hear:

"Well, Mr. Flood, we have the harvest moon
Again, and we may not have many more;
The bird is on the wing, the poet says,

And you and I have said it here before.
Drink to the bird." He raised up to the light
The jug that he had gone so far to fill,
And answered huskily: "Well, Mr. Flood,
Since you propose it, I believe I will."

Alone, as if enduring to the end
A valiant armor of scarred hopes outworn,
He stood there in the middle of the road
Like Roland's ghost winding a silent horn.
Below him, in the town among the trees,
Where friends of other days had honored him,
A phantom salutation of the dead
Rang thinly till old Eben's eyes were dim.

Then, as a mother lays her sleeping child
Down tenderly, fearing it may awake,
He set the jug down slowly at his feet
With trembling care, knowing that most things break;
And only when assured that on firm earth
It stood, as the uncertain lives of men
Assuredly did not, he paced away,
And with his hand extended paused again:

"Well, Mr. Flood, we have not met like this
In a long time; and many a change has come
To both of us, I fear, since last it was
We had a drop together. Welcome home!"
Convivially returning with himself,
Again he raised the jug up to the light;
And with an acquiescent quaver said:
"Well, Mr. Flood, if you insist, I might.

"Only a very little, Mr. Flood—
For auld lang syne. No more, sir; that will do."
So, for the time, apparently it did,
And Eben evidently thought so too;
For soon amid the silver loneliness
Of night he lifted up his voice and sang,
Secure, with only two moons listening,
Until the whole harmonious landscape rang—

"For auld lang syne." The weary throat gave out,
The last word wavered; and the song being done,
He raised again the jug regretfully
And shook his head, and was again alone.
There was not much that was ahead of him,
And there was nothing in the town below—
Where strangers would have shut the many doors
That many friends had opened long ago.

CHANSON INNOCENTE

e. e. cummings

in Just-
spring   when the world is mud-
luscious the little
lame balloonman

whistles   far   and wee

and eddieandbill come
running from marbles and
piracies and it's
spring

when the world is puddle-wonderful

the queer
old balloonman whistles
far   and   wee
and bettyandisabel come dancing

from hop-scotch and jump-rope and

it's
spring
and
    the

       goat-footed

balloonMan   whistles
far
and
wee

LONDON
WILLIAM BLAKE

I wander thro' each chartered street,
Near where the chartered Thames does flow,
And mark in every face I meet
Marks of weakness, marks of woe.

In every cry of every man,
In every infant's cry of fear,
In every voice, in every ban,
The mind-forged manacles I hear.

How the chimney-sweeper's cry
Every black'ning church appalls;
And the hapless soldier's sigh
Runs in blood down palace walls.

But most through midnight streets I hear
How the youthful harlot's curse
Blasts the new born infant's tear,
And blights with plagues the marriage hearse.

Chapter 8
Reading prose

KEY CONCEPTS

Types of prose

The narrator

Sustaining performance

Sketching technique

Cutting

The prose author draws from the same resources as the poet. It is the treatment of these resources—thought, perception, and experience—which distinguishes the writer of prose from the poet. Language, like all media of expression, is self-limiting. The painter can mix infinite varieties of color but, ultimately, must put the paint on something with some method or tool in order for it to have meaning. The sculptor can mold an infinite number of shapes with clay but cannot make it accomplish what paint does. The writer can juxtapose words in an infinite variety of ways but always operates within the restrictions imposed by language.

Prose is the ordinary form of spoken or written language, without metrical pattern. While it occurs in short bursts, it is most often found in longer pieces than poetry. In its written form, it is easily recognized by the way in which it is presented on the page: sentences instead of lines, paragraphs instead of stanzas.

The interpreter must begin with the notion that there is no difference between poetry and prose. Or, more accurately, there are no differences which will require an alternation of approach. For the interpreter, the essential characteristic of prose is its length. It is **Gottlieb's Fourteenth Principle** that *excellent prose reading requires the sustaining of performance.*

Most interpreters, particularly those who have already worked with poetry, will find that, aside from considerations of length, prose is easier to handle. While there are many exceptions, the language of prose is generally less compressed, less ambiguous, and more speechlike in its syntax. The author of prose employs the same tools of *organization, technique,* and *style* as the poet. However, the duration of the prose performance allows time for the audience to focus on certain aspects of technique which are not as prominent in a performance of poetry. This chapter will explore the concept of the narrator in great detail. In addition, the various subdivisions of prose—description, exposition, narration—will be defined from the perspective of the interpreter.

POINT OF VIEW

Interpretation, like all art forms, is a complex process of organizing experiences, sensory impressions, and the tools of communication into a logical composition. Because of its complexity, it is difficult to single out one aspect as the most important. However, an interpreter cannot even begin an intelligent consideration of a performance of prose without attending to the point of view.

Point of view is precisely what it says: the point from which the teller of the story views the objects, characters, and events being described. There are three basic points of view: *first person, third person,* and *omniscient.* For the interpreter, each of these points of view is identified with a particular type of narrator.

FIRST-PERSON NARRATION

We speak of the *first-person narrator* as a teller or speaker who has experienced the content firsthand. The ideas that are being expressed are the speaker's ideas. The events being described happened to the speaker, who was there and remembers the experience as it happened. All speeches, essays, letters, diaries, and much of what is called narrative prose use this type of narration. Many first-person narrators speak impersonally or use third-person forms of the language, as I do when I say "the interpreter" instead of addressing you directly. But the key factor is that I am generating the content; I am not reporting what someone else thinks. In narrative prose, the first-person narrator can be either the central character or a minor character. We experience the content as the character experiences it.

> You have heard this story before? No matter, I will tell it again because it points to a moral, and better than that, to a state of mind.

This passage from the beginning of Calderon's "The Lottery Ticket" illustrates clearly that the story is going to be told from the point of view of the first-person narrator. The speaker addresses us directly in the opening sentence and follows with the personal pronoun "I" in the second sentence. The details provided throughout the story are so specific that one must believe that the narrator was actually present at the incident described.

THIRD-PERSON NARRATION

The *third-person narrator* does not actually play a part in the events being related, but instead exists outside of the action and views it from a distance. Or the narrator has come by the information secondhand; someone has related the incident to the narrator, who is now passing it along to the audience. This point of view does not limit the narrator's response to the emotional content of the experience, but the feelings take on a different character. If you witness an accident, say an automobile turns a corner and strikes someone in a crosswalk only a half block ahead of you, you might experience a number of strong emotions. When you tell what you saw— maybe to a policeman—you will probably express concern, anger, fear, and, perhaps, relief that it wasn't you. You may even have a clearer picture of the events leading up to and following the accident than the person who actually got hit. But in no way have you had the same experience.

Narrative prose employs this point of view quite often, and journalistic prose uses it almost exclusively. Your friendly television anchorman is continually speaking to you in the third person. The following sentences from the opening of Erskine Caldwell's "Daughter" illustrate the use of the third-person narrator.

> At sunrise a Negro on his way to the big house to feed the mules had taken the word to Colonel Henry Maxwell, and Colonel Henry phoned the sheriff. The sheriff had hustled Jim into town and locked him up in the jail, and then he went home and ate breakfast.

Here, the narrator reports a series of events, and as far as we can tell, remains outside of them. Three characters are mentioned, the sheriff, Jim, and Colonel Henry Maxwell, but we are not introduced to the narrator. Of course, in a third-person narration, this perspective must be maintained throughout the story. It is not enough for the interpreter to read one paragraph and decide on the point of view. In the above example, the third-person point of view is consistently maintained throughout the story.

The essential difference, then, between first-person and third-person point of view is your perspective as the narrator. Are you a part of the story? Even a minor character, like Ishmael in *Moby Dick*? Will one of the characters in the story ever say something to you or do something which will affect you directly? If the answer to any of these questions is yes, then you are a first-person narrator. If the answer to all of them is no, then you are a third-person narrator.

OMNISCIENT NARRATION

There is one type of narrator who does not exist outside of fiction—either poetry or prose—because such a narrator cannot actually exist. This is the *omniscient narrator*. At first glance, the omniscient narrator appears to be like any other third-person narrator; he or she exists outside of the action. But the omniscient narrator has one characteristic not found in a regular third-person narrator, the ability to see into people's minds. The omniscient narrator knows, and can tell us, when one of the characters experiences doubt, fear, pain, or any of the whole wide range of human feelings. In addition, through the device of omniscience, a whole monologue of internal thought progression can be revealed without the character's speaking one word. Through the use of omniscience, the author asserts the greatest possible control over the material. By providing for the reader all the internal as well as the external information, the author leaves little room for speculation or doubt about the motives and sensibilities of the characters.

> Then he crossed the street, went back, saw that he had gone out of his way, returned past the Tuileries, saw again he had made a mistake, crossed the Seine, went back to the Champs-Elysées without a single clear notion in his head. He forced himself to think. His wife could not possibly have purchased such valuable jewelry. Absolutely not! Well then? A present? A present! From whom? For what?

The preceding paragraph from "The Jewels of M. Lantin" by Guy De Maupassant skillfully demonstrates the omniscient perspective as it moves between external and internal events. The omniscient narrator is a godlike force from which nothing is hidden. As might be imagined, the omniscient narrator presents the interpreter with his greatest challenge in the reading of prose.

DEVELOPING THE NARRATOR

Once the interpreter has determined what type of narrator is operating in a given piece of literature, the next problem is the portrayal of that narrator.

FIRST-PERSON NARRATOR

If you are to be a first-person narrator, you will, of course, relate the events of the story as if you were a part of those events, even if only a small part. Remember, you were there, you saw, felt, heard whatever was going on. You may have even instigated most of the action, or have been the object of it. Approach the piece as if it were a monologue. Determine what kind of character this narrator is. When first-person narration fails, it is generally due to the fact that the interpreter has not created the proper character to go with the story. In many cases it may be safe to assume that the narrator is someone very much like yourself. However, when an author selects a first-person narrator to tell the story, there may be other devices at work as well. Note where the story takes place. What country? What part of the country? Are there any references, word choices, or syntactical arrangements which suggest regionalisms? Is your first-person narrator contemporary, or from another time? Remember Gottlieb's principle about detail being the key to quality performance.

The audience must accept the narrator before they will believe the performance. While this applies to any narrator, it applies particularly to the first-person narrator. After all, it's your story, so it should sound comfortable coming from your mouth.

THIRD-PERSON NARRATOR

The third-person narrator presents the interpreter with some different problems. First of all, this type of narrator stands outside the mainstream of events in the story. In developing this narrator, the interpreter must first resolve how these events came to be known. Were you eavesdropping? Were you just in the vicinity when you were confronted with this incident? Did someone else tell you the story? The interpreter's attention to these details will show in the final performance in the form of greater reality.

If you have difficulty developing the proper perspective for your third-person narration, get two of your friends to help you in a little experiment. Have one of your friends tell you a short incident, perhaps something which happened on the way to class, or at lunch. Then, turn to the second friend and retell the story as it happened to your first friend. This exercise demonstrates the essential differences between the first- and third-person narrators. When the first friend told the story, it was evident that the events had happened around him or her. The first friend was directly involved in the experience. If it was an embarrassing incident, he or she recalled some of the embarrassment while telling the story. When you retold the story to the second friend, you probably maintained the details and the order of events, but you described the first friend's embarrassment—*you did not directly feel it yourself.*

You might relate to the embarrassment of your first friend empathically. That is, the experience might remind you of one of your own, and you might reexperience your own embarrassment; you might feel sorry that your friend was embarrassed, but you might also feel (since it didn't happen to you) that it was a bit funny. *It is* **Gottlieb's Fifteenth Principle** *that as a third-person narrator you feel like yourself, not like the characters you portray.*

Along with the third-person perspective comes another problem for the interpreter: *dialogue.* Because as a third-person narrator you exist outside the mainstream of events, you are able to watch, overhear, and report on the characters of the story as they interact with one another. Again, there are certainly examples to the contrary, but the general rule is that dialogue appears more frequently in third-person narrations. When there is a great deal of dialogue, there is difficulty maintaining the identity of the narrator. The following passage, also from Caldwell's "Daughter," points up some of the difficulties.

Jim's long face looked as if it would come through the bars. The sheriff came up to the window to see if everything was all right.

"Now, just take it easy, Jim boy," he said.

The man who had asked Jim to tell what had happened elbowed the sheriff out of the way. The other men crowded closer.

"How come, Jim?" the man said. "Was it an accident?"

"No," Jim said, his fingers twisting about the bars. "I picked up my shotgun and done it."

The sheriff pushed towards the window again.

"Go on, Jim, and tell us what it's all about."

"Daughter said she was hungry, and I just couldn't stand it no longer. I just couldn't stand to hear her say it."

Some interpreters find it tempting to cut out the "he said" parts of a passage such as this. We will be discussing the problem of cutting in a later part of this chapter, but, unless there is a compelling reason to do so, do not remove any "he saids" or "she saids." To do so tends to make the story into something it isn't—it is not a play. Also, in many instances, the "he saids" and "she saids" are all the audience has to maintain contact with the narrator.

If you are a keen observer of human behavior, you are probably already aware of the natural tendency to look away from people when you are portraying a character. Perhaps you overheard an interesting discussion on the bus, or between two people in front of you in a movie theater before the picture began, and you want to relate the incident to a group of your friends. Without even thinking about it, you will automatically begin using separate voices for each of the participants in the overheard discussion because it is the way you heard it, and because it helps you keep the characters in the incident separate for your audience. In addition, while you are portraying one or the other of the characters in the discussion, you will tend to look away from your audience for a combination of reasons. You are trying to remember the words, tone, and pace of the dialogue, so you don't want any distractions from your audience. It is a natural result of concentration to lower the level of sensory input when you are trying to think of something. Since the dialogue took place between two people who aren't present, you want to be as descriptive as possible by illustrating postures, mannerisms, gestures, and the way they looked at one another. Each step of the way, after doing a complete coherent segment, you will check back with your audience to make sure that you are creating the desired effect, and to indicate a shift in characters or some other kind of transition. It is at such moments that you cease illustrating the characters and become yourself for a moment, looking directly at your audience, probing for sensory feedback. Depending on what you experience when you check in with your audience, you may provide more description, employ exposition to move the events along, reaffirm who has just been speaking, or introduce the character who speaks next; and at this juncture the "he said" and "she said" play an important part in the communication process.

In the same manner that the interpreter would relate a personal incident to a group of freinds, so should the interpreter relate the events of the text as a third-person narrator. When the dialogue takes place between only two characters in the story, it is possible to enhance their separation by shifting slightly for each role the direction the interpreter looks in. This *projective technique* is covered in detail in the next chapter, but, briefly, the interpreter pretends to be standing at the apex of an equilateral triangle. Each of the two characters being presented are imagined to be on the back wall just at the points where the sides of the angle meet the wall to form the triangle. As the dialogue progresses, the interpreter shifts position to speak to the character being spoken to. Or, to put it another way, the interpreter always faces the silent character. In this way, the interpreter sends a signal to the audience which is easily recognized as a character shift. Carefully done, the projective technique can be used for as many as three characters by placing one character in the center. Beyond three, the system breaks down. While this is a very effective means of indicating character shift, the interpreter should begin to depend on other means to telegraph character change. Changes in voice, posture, gesture, and attitude will also do the job and will add substantially to the quality of the performance as well.

In summary, the third-person narrator tells the story from the perspective of someone outside the action. The events being described have had an effect on the narrator, and the narrator is compelled to pass the events along to the audience. In order for the full effect to be achieved, the author of a third-person narration usually depends on a great deal of descriptive detail and person-to-person dialogue. The interpreter uses projective technique and voice and body changes to keep the characters separate and to bring a sense of reality to the presentation. It is not usually necessary to develop a character for a third-person narrator. The interpreter should concentrate on maintaining contact with the audience as a narrator and on experiencing the events of the story as if outside the action, rather than as the characters experience them.

OMNISCIENT NARRATOR

The *omniscient narrator* is a fascinating supernatural creature who can look directly into people's minds, experience their feelings as they experience them, and span continents and time barriers in pursuit of the action and events of the narrative. In the following passage from "The Sniper," the author, Liam O'Flaherty, through his omniscient narrator, describes heroism and pain.

> Suddenly from the opposite roof a shot rang out and the sniper dropped his rifle with a curse. The rifle clattered to the roof. The sniper thought the noise would wake the dead. He stooped to pick the rifle up. He couldn't lift it. His forearm was dead.
>
> "Christ," he muttered, "I'm hit."
>
> Dropping flat onto the roof he crawled back to the parapet. With his left hand he felt the injured right forearm. There was no pain—just a deadened sensation, as if the arm had been cut off.
>
> Quickly he drew his knife from his pocket, opened it on the breast-work of the parapet, and ripped open the sleeve. There was a small hole where the bullet had entered. On the other side there was no hole. The bullet had lodged in the bone. It must have fractured it. He bent the arm below the wound. The arm bent back easily. He ground his teeth to overcome the pain.
>
> Then taking out the field dressing, he ripped open the packet with his knife. He broke the neck of the iodine bottle and let the bitter fluid drip into the wound. A paroxysm of pain swept through him. He placed the cotton wadding over the wound and wrapped the dressing over it. He tied the ends with his teeth.

The first two sentences read like straight third-person narration. It's the third line that introduces the omniscience: "The sniper *thought* the noise would wake the dead." Later on in the passage we see another example. First comes a sentence without omniscience: "With his left hand he felt the injured right forearm." Then the narrator darts into the brain of the sniper: "*There was no pain—just a deadened sensation,* as if the arm had been cut off."

The interpreter of an omniscient narration must begin with the same approach as that used for third-person narration. The narrator is speaking in the third person: note phrases like "the sniper," and the extensive use of "he" and "his" in the preceding passage. The problem is that, though appearing to have third-person perspective, the narrator also exists within the narrative by virtue of having access to everyone's brain. Therefore, the omniscient narrator also exhibits characteristics of a first-person narrator.

As the events and feelings are recalled,. the omniscient narrator experiences them as if they had been personally experienced before. The pain in the arm is felt and projected to the audience as personal pain. Then the narrator pulls back and delivers a description of a dialogue from a conventional third-person perspective.

As with the third-person narrator, the omniscient narrator rarely requires characterization. The interpreter concentrates on illustrating the characters who appear in the story.

Omniscience is usually not all-encompassing. That is, the reader is not given access to the thoughts and feelings of every character in a story. In some narratives, the omniscient narrator has access to only one main character, as in the example of "The Sniper." When this occurs, it is termed *limited omniscience*. In limited omniscience, the narrator experiences the events of the story through the thoughts, feelings, and reactions of the central character as he or she interacts with the circumstances and characters of the story.

In summary, the omniscient narrator tells the story in the third person, but, where appropriate, responds to the material as if it were a first-person narration. As in third-person narration, the interpreter can expect a large amount of dialogue in some cases. Where it occurs, it should be handled the same way as dialogue in any third-person narration: the characters should be illustrated as clearly as possible. Omniscient narration is the most difficult point of view for the interpreter to present because of its mixed perspective. However, when done well, it can provide a very exciting and enriching experience for both the interpreter and the audience.

TYPES OF PROSE

There are three principal types of prose: *exposition, description,* and *narration.* The type of prose which an author employs is always determined by the purpose of the piece. In many cases more than one type of prose is used in the same piece of material. For example, most narratives use both exposition and description in the course of relating the events of the story. However, it is useful for the interpreter to recognize the problems that each type presents in order to produce an effective performance.

DESCRIPTION

Rarely will the interpreter encounter a prose selection which is descriptive from beginning to end. More often, description is used as a supporting device. Through the use of description, the author tries to project images, moods, and sensations, instead of facts or events. This can be done in one of two ways: through a realistic view or an impressionistic view.

The *realistic* approach to description focuses the attention of the reader on the subject in much the same way that a camera does. While the camera sees only what it's pointed at, its end product is detailed and objective. This approach is exemplified in the short story "A Game of Billiards" by Alphonse Daudet, which describes the serenity of the French headquarters prior to battle.

> And yet it is only a short distance to headquarters, to that beautiful Louis XIII chateau whose red brick walls, washed by the rain, are seen half way up the hill, glistening through the thickets. Truly a princely dwelling, well worthy of bearing the banner of a Marshal of France. Upon an artificial pond which sparkles like a mirror, swans are swimming, and under the pagoda-shaped roof of a large aviary, peacocks and golden pheasants strut about, spreading their wings and sending the shrill cries through the foliage. Though the owners of the house have departed, nowhere is there is preceptible sign of that ruin and desolation which war brings in its train; not the smallest flower dotting the lawn has been destroyed and it is indescribably charming to observe. Such evenly trimmed shrubbery, such silent avenues of shade; yet so near the battlefield! The scene is peaceful. Were it not for the flag floating from the top of the roof, and the sight of two sentinels before the gate, one would never believe headquarters were here.

By establishing the scene with realistic detail, Daudet prepares the reader for the contrast which occurs when the destruction of war reaches the peaceful chateau.

> Already shells are falling in the park. One has burst in the pond. The glassy sheen reddens, and a terrified swan is seen swimming amid a whirl of bloody plumage.

The *impressionistic* approach to description focuses the reader's attention on the subjective responses to sensory impressions. Unlike a photograph, the product of an impressionistic view does not scientifically record the details of the subject. Rather, the details are interpreted through someone's consciousness. The impressionistic approach is illustrated by Herbert Goldstone, in this excerpt from his short story "Virtuoso," which describes what the Maestro experiences when he discovers that his household robot has learned how to play the piano.

> The Maestro snapped erect, threw the covers aside.
> He sat on the edge of the bed, listening.

He groped for his robe in the darkness, shoved bony feet into his slippers.

He crept, trembling uncontrollably, to the door of his studio and stood there, thin and brittle in the robe.

The light over the music rack was an eerie island in the brown shadows of the studio. Rollo sat at the keyboard, prim, inhuman, rigid, twin lenses focused somewhere off into the shadows.

The massive feet working the pedals, arms and hands flashing and glinting—they were living entities, separate, somehow, from the machined perfection of his body.

The music rack was empty.

A copy of Beethoven's "Appassionata" lay closed on the bench. It had been, the Maestro remembered, in a pile of sheet music on the piano.

Rollo was playing it.

He was creating it, breathing it, drawing it through silver flame.

Time became meaningless, suspended in midair.

The Maestro didn't realize he was weeping until Rollo finished the sonata.

The robot turned to look at the Maestro. "The sounds," he droned. "They pleased you?"

In some cases, distinguishing the two types of description is a difficult task. There is no such thing as purely realistic or purely impressionistic description; most selections will exhibit qualities of both types. The interpreter needs to get a "feel" for which type dominates in a passage. Impressionism employs much more figurative language than realism, and the presence of similes, metaphors, alliteration, and personification should signal to the interpreter the author's intent.

The interpreter's response to a descriptive passage must reflect the author's intent. Obviously, the two passages used as examples above could not be approached in the same way. The realistic passage requires coolness, distance, detachment, while the impressionistic passage demands active response, subjectivity, involvement. To a large extent, the type of description is determined by the point of view of the narrator. Third-person narrators, positioned as they are outside the action, use realistic description. Omniscient and first-person narrators, because of their involvement in the action, are more likely to use impressionistic description.

From the standpoint of developing descriptive passages for performance, the interpretor should view the differences described above as differences of degree rather than kind. The approach to performance is basically the same. Identify your narrator: First person? Third person?

Omniscient? How does this descriptive passage affect your narrator? What senses are being appealed to? Sight? Smell? Taste? Touch? Hearing? Does the passage describe movement or physical tension which the narrator can illustrate with body responses?

Remember that the images requiring response in the passage are called fourth from memory; they are not being experienced in the here and now. As such, they can retain a high degree of vividness, but they are at least once removed from the direct stimulus. It is the nature of memory to stimulate the senses in the same way as the actual experience, but very rarely with the same intensity. Remember Gottlieb's Fifth Principle: Thought precedes verbalization. We can add a corollary to this principle that reads: *Response precedes verbalization.* If the image being recalled stimulates a visual sensation, see it before you put it into words. If it stimulates an auditory sensation, hear it yourself before you tell the audience what it is. If the image calls forth a physical sensation, like heat or cold, again, experience the sensation first, then use the words. As a general rule, do not try to convey sensory impressions with inflection, as this is what critics call "ham." That is, don't try to convey the sensation of cold by making the word shiver—c-c-cold. Rather, if the intensity of the stimulus justifies a shiver, shiver as you recall the image, then simply say the words that describe the situation. **Gottlieb's Sixteenth Principle** states: *The interpreter only uses the words when all other means for communicating the experience have been exhausted.*

In sum, we began with a discussion of description because description is present in all forms of prose. It sets the scene, introduces character, and illuminates events. The interpreter must develop an ability to respond to descriptive images and convey them to the audience in such a way that the audience will experience them as well. In preparing a descriptive passage, the interpreter should let the images play in the mind until they elicit a response. We all have a storehouse of sense impressions. We have all felt cold or warm, we have all experienced fear, we have all smelled freshly cut grass or something baking in the oven. The interpreter connects the sensory experience in the descriptive passage with a real-life experience, and, as is always the aim in oral interpretation, creates a new reality for the audience to experience.

EXPOSITION

Exposition is the most commonly encountered form of writing. It is concerned with the setting forth of facts or ideas. Most of the reading that students do is expository: history, psychology, science, any subject which provides information or instruction. What you are reading at this moment is exposition.

There are three principal types of expository writing: process or "how to," analysis, and definition.

The interpreter generally encounters this form of writing if the choice for presentation is an essay, an editorial, or a speech. In such instances, the approach is to develop the appropriate first-person narrator, relate the selection to a logical set of given circumstances—in answer to the question "Why am I saying these things?"—and present it to the audience with as much spontaneity and purpose as possible.

Essays, editorials, and speeches are not always constructed of bloodless facts and propositions. Some essays, like Swift's "A Modest Proposal," can be bitingly satirical and politically powerful. Likewise, speeches such as Martin Luther King's "I Have a Dream" can be psychologically motivating, largely descriptive, and emotionally appealing—much the same kind of qualities one might ascribe to a short story or a novel. Editorials span a wide range of styles as well. They are also an example of argumentative or didactic prose. However, they can be humorous and employ narrative techniques; for example, Art Buchwald frequently employs satiric humor and dialogue in his weekly newspaper column.

Exposition is also used as a narrative device. When an author feels the necessity to set the scene, give background, explain, define, or demonstrate something, the narrator, or one of the characters, steps outside the action and delivers the expository material. Herman Melville frequently uses exposition to describe the process of hunting, killing, and slaughtering whales in *Moby Dick;* such an expository passage from the novel is included in the readings at the end of this chapter.

When confronted with an essay, speech, or editorial, the interpreter does not change the basic work plan. The author of such material is always speaking from a personal view and is, therefore, a first-person narrator. The biggest problem encountered is to determine the attitude of the narrator toward the subject matter. Once again we begin with questions. Is the narrator presenting factual information? Or is the material essentially personal reflections? Does it describe an experience? Is it poking fun at someone or something? Is the author trying to persuade or move us in some way? Does the material instruct, examine, amuse, or simply entertain?

Of course it is possible that, to achieve a particular purpose, the author may develop more than one approach. The interpreter's sensitivity to subtle shifts within the composition will add greatly to the creation of spontaneity and reality, which are the marks of good performance in every case.

The interpreter must choose expository material very carefully. Nothing will destroy a good interpretive effort more quickly than a selection with banal or trite subject matter and a style that lacks artistry. The amount of expository material available to the interpreter is enormous; a new load is pumped out through the pulp magazines each month. Most of it is just plain bad. A safer resource for the beginning interpreter would be anthologized material, the assumption being that the selections have been chosen for purposes other than their topical nature, shock value, or selling power.

NARRATION

It seems almost an innate quality of human beings to desire narrative—to surround themselves with stories. We use narrative for every conceivable purpose: to define our position in the universe, to explain our relationship with a Supreme Being and with our fellow beings, to educate and civilize our children, to entertain and purge ourselves, to feed our souls. In its diversity, narrative encompasses story poems and ballads, historical accounts, short stories, fables, parables, letters, diaries, autobiographies, novels, and fairy tales. The common denominator in all these forms, however, is their attention to events. It is the focus on events which marks a selection as primarily narrative in form.

As a result of this attention to events, narration is usually chronological. All stories have a beginning, a middle, and an end. When an author relates the events of the narrative, a decision must be made as to how these events are going to be ordered. Many times, the story simply begins at the beginning. In other cases, the story begins at a point further on—perhaps to create interest—and later the preceding events are filled in.

A typical narrative begins by explaining the situation to the reader describing the setting, and introducing the characters and the conflicting elements. The reader also picks up the tone of the selection early in the narrative. The *tone* of a narrative reveals the author's attitude toward the subject, and, in some cases, toward the audience. The characters may be presented sympathetically, or they may be held up for ridicule. The author may feel in concert with the audience, or express a tone of anger and chastisement. Through the choice of words and the way the action is moved forward, the author also reveals subjective emotional responses to the events being described. These emotional responses of the author are sometimes termed the *mood* of the selection. As concepts for the interpreter, tone and mood are inseparable. They must be incorporated into the performance as one organic whole. If the interpreter does not reflect the correct tone and mood of a selection, the performance will fail, because the attitude and emotional responses of the narrator will conflict with the words and the progression of the narrative.

The middle part of a narrative develops the event or events being described. Characters interact with each other and with the circumstances they encounter. Subplots, where they exist, are introduced and developed.

The tension builds. As events change, mood is likely to shift as well. It is possible for the interpreter to be called upon to produce joy, anger, depression, indignation—the whole range of human emotions—within the context of one narrative selection. The interpreter must remain alert, take time, and respond accurately to each shift in mood, no matter how subtle. When performances of narrative go wrong, it is usually in the middle section. After the initial assault on the beginning part of the narrative, some interpreters tire from the need to sustain performance for a long period of time. They become less alert. Their energy sags, and the performance loses its crispness and its reality.

The end part of a narrative brings the events to a logical conclusion. In nonfiction, this conclusion may present the author's view, opinion, or interpretation of the events, as with history or biography. In fiction, the conclusion resolves the conflicts established at the beginning and developed in the middle section. The subplots are also resolved, and their relationship to the main theme is revealed. Even in fiction, an author may make use of some time at the end to moralize or generalize, and instruct the reader. The interpreter may find it helpful to slow the pace toward the end. This tactic helps to telegraph to the audience that the end is coming, and, if the resolutions are complicated, the audience will be more readily able to sort everything out. Remember that the audience does not have a copy of the text and cannot re-read a passage if the meaning is unclear.

In sum, the engagement with narration can be a rich and rewarding experience for both the interpreter and the audience. The interpreter has the opportunity to become immersed in circumstances, events, and feelings which are usually quite unlike what he or she normally experiences. This *vicarious experience*, besides being exciting, can broaden the interpreter's understanding of the world and the human condition. One simply does not experience great literature from the inside and walk away unaffected. A good interpretive performance of narrative has a strong effect on the audience as well. It transcends the simple telling of events. It sparks the audience's imagination, heightens interest, and provokes a feeling of satisfaction which grows from the realization that the events have meaning and significance beyond the story level.

INDICATING CHARACTER

In order to successfully indicate character, the interpreter must develop a *sketching technique. It is **Gottlieb's Seventeenth Principle** which states: The interpreter depicts character by means of a sketch rather than a full-blown painting.* In the theater, the actresses and actors can immerse themselves totally in the presentation of character. With only one part to play, with makeup, lights, costumes, scenery, furniture, and props, they can paint character extensively in both vivid and subtle detail. The interpreter, under normal circumstances, is faced with a different set of given circumstances. There are no costumes, props, etc., to help with the portrayal. Besides that, the interpreter is most often called upon to depict more than one character in the same selection. Full characterization is not only impossible in most instances, it would be totally unacceptable to the audience. Clearly, no audience is ever going to believe that you are both Hamlet and Ophelia, but this is precisely the kind of situation you will find yourself in most of the time.

The interpreter sketches character. In the same way that an artist develops an idea by first penciling in proportion, shape, line, and relationship, the interpreter selects a few essential elements of each character and sketches them in for the audience. You should have a very clear notion of what you want to project about each character. Begin again with questions: Is the character male or female? How old? What does the voice sound like? What individualized gestures does the character use? What about the spine? Is the character stiff and straight? Loose and assertive? Bent and cowering?

It is sometimes helpful to use picture resources, such as books or magazines. If you are located near a park that is heavily used, you can find an example of every character you will ever need by spending an hour or so sitting on a bench and observing. Another excellent way to proceed is to decide what kind of animal your character would be if he or she had not turned out to be human. Then take yourself to the zoo and note carefully the way your animal stands, walks, peers around, and relates to the other animals. It is useful for the interpreter to develop a storehouse of animal imitations which can be called upon at any point to sketch character.

Once the essential characteristics of body and voice have been determined, rehearse the selection with them in place. Character sketching must begin early in the process of developing a selection for performance. It can never be added as an afterthought with a few quick rehearsals just before the performance. The elements of character which the interpreter sketches must appear to be as natural and spontaneous as the other elements of the performance.

One final note of caution: Don't allow one character in your selection to become dominant. Interpreters naturally respond in varying degrees to the people who exist in narrative; we may be sympathetic to some and loathe others. But all the characters depicted in the narrative selection must be sketched with the same degree of professionalism.

There is only one character in the interpretive performance who is fully developed—the narrator. The narrator, whether male or female, first, third, or omniscient, is the person who is actually present before the audience. All other characters are presented through the narrator's depiction of them.

CUTTING

The selections in this text were chosen because of type, style, and excellence. However, one additional factor in the choice was length. If selections for performance are chosen exclusively from this text, there should be no need for cutting. In some cases, though, it may be both necessary and beneficial for the interpreter to select material from outside this single resource. If such an outside selection is too long for presentation in its entirety, as in the case of a novel, cutting is necessary. There are two types of cutting: editing and abridgment.

Editing refers to the process of removing material—phrases, sentences, paragraphs—from designated points throughout the selection. Editing must be carefully done so as not to destroy the meaning and flow of the narrative. Long descriptive passages or philosophizing on the part of the author provide the best opportunities for editing. In some instances, short descriptive phrases which refer to some action of one of the characters can be eliminated, since the narrator can portray certain actions, such as, "John smiled before he spoke. . . ." Editing can be equated with surgery. Cut what is necessary without killing the patient.

Abridgment refers to the process of removing whole chunks of a narrative intact and replacing them with a synopsis of the events. For example, an interpreter can "read" an entire novel by selecting an hour's worth of material consisting of the key chapters, and filling in the missing parts with some bridge material which keeps the audience abreast of the events.

It is sometimes desirable to abridge long poems. Some poems, like Milton's *Paradise Lost,* lend themselves to abridgment because they are divided into "books." However, the interpreter never edits poetry. To do so would be the same as deciding you didn't like the smile on the Mona Lisa's face, and taking a brush and some paint and changing it.

Many of the concepts put forth in this chapter are also applicable to drama, which is covered in the following chapter. If the interpreter understands the process of sketching character and the relationship of the narrator to the audience in narrative prose, the basic tools for the reading of drama will have already been acquired.

QUESTIONS FOR STUDY AND DISCUSSION

1

How does prose differ from other forms of literature?

2

What are the three basic points of view? How do they differ?

3

How does the point of view affect the narrator?

4

Why is dialogue more likely to appear in third-person narration?

5

What are the three principal types of prose? What are the requirements each type sets down for the interpreter?

6

What is meant by "response precedes verbalization"?

7

What is the difference between sketching and characterization?

SUGGESTED ACTIVITIES

1

Make up a story, and tell it from all three points of view.

Selections for Analysis and Performance

CUTTING IN
From MOBY DICK
HERMAN MELVILLE

It was a Saturday night, and such a Sabbath as followed! Ex officio professors of Sabbath breaking are all whalemen. The ivory Pequod was turned into what seemed a shamble; every sailor a butcher. You would have thought we were offering up ten thousand red oxen to the sea gods.

In the first place, the enormous cutting tackles, among other ponderous things comprising a cluster of blocks generally painted green, and which no single man can possibly lift—this vast bunch of grapes was swayed up to the main-top and firmly lashed to the lower mast-head, the strongest point anywhere above a ship's deck. The end of the hawser-like rope winding through these intricacies, was then conducted to the windlass, and the huge lower block of the tackles was swung over the whale; to this block the great blubber hook, weighing some one hundred pounds, was attached. And now suspended in stages over the side, Starbuck and Stubb, the mates, armed with this long spades, began cutting a hole in the body for the insertion of the hook just above the nearest of the two side-fins. This done, a broad, semicircular line is cut round the hole, the hook is inserted, and the main body of the crew striking up a wild chorus, now commence heaving in one dense crowd at the windlass. When instantly, the entire ship careens over on her side; every bolt in her starts like the nail-heads of an old house in frosty weather; she trembles, quivers, and nods her frighted mast-heads to the sky. More and more she leans over to the whale, while every gasping heave of the windlass is answered by a helping heave from the billows; till at last, a swift, startling snap is heard; with a great swash the ship rolls upwards and backwards from the whale, and the triumphant tackle rises into sight dragging after it the disengaged semicircular end of the first strip of blubber. Now as the blubber envelops the whale precisely as the rind does an orange, so is it stripped off from the body precisely as an orange is sometimes stripped by spiralizing it. For the strain constantly kept up by the windlass continually keeps the whale rolling over and over in the water, and as the blubber in one strip uniformly peels off along the line called the "scarf," simultaneously cut by the spades of Starbuck and Stubb, the mates; and just as fast as it is thus peeled off, and indeed by that very act itself, it is all the time being hoisted higher and higher aloft till its upper end grazes the main-top; the men at the windlass then cease heaving, and for a moment or two the prodigious blood-dripping mass sways to and fro as if let down from the sky, and every one present must take good heed to dodge it when it swings, else it may box his ears and pitch him headlong overboard.

One of the attending harpooners now advances with a long, keen weapon called a boarding-sword, and watching his chance he dexterously slices out a considerable hole in the lower part of the swaying mass. Into this hole, the end of the second alternating great tackle is then hooked so as to retain a hold upon the blubber, in order to prepare for what follows. Whereupon, this accomplished swordsman, warning all hands to stand off, once more makes a scientific dash at the mass, and with a few sidelong, desperate, lunging slices, severs it completely in twain; so that while the short lower part is still fast, the long upper strip, called a blanket-piece, swings clear, and is all ready for lowering. The heavers forward now resume their song, and while the one tackle is peeling and hoisting a second strip from the whale, the other is slowly slackened away, and down goes the first strip through the main hatchway right beneath, into an unfurnished parlor called the blubber-room. Into this twilight apartment sundry nimble hands keep coiling away the long blanket-piece as if it were a great live mass of plaited serpents. And thus the work proceeds; the two tackles hoisting and lowering simultaneously; both whale and windlass heaving, the heavers singing, the blubber-room gentlemen coiling, the mates scarfing, the ship straining, and all hands swearing occasionally, by way of assuaging the general friction.

VIRTUOSO
HERBERT GOLDSTONE

"Sir?"

The Maestro continued to play, not looking up from the keys.

"Yes, Rollo?"

"Sir, I was wondering if you would explain this apparatus to me."

The Maestro stopped playing, his thin body stiffly relaxed on the bench. His long supple fingers floated off the keyboard.

"Apparatus?" He turned and smiled at the robot. "Do you mean the piano, Rollo?"

"This machine that produces varying sounds. I would like some information about it, its operation and purpose. It is not included in my reference data."

The Maestro lit a cigarette. He preferred to do it himself. One of his first orders to Rollo when the robot was delivered two days before had been to disregard his built-in instructions on the subject.

"I'd hardly call a piano a machine, Rollo," he smiled, "although technically you are correct. It is actually, I suppose, a machine designed to produce sounds of graduated pitch and tone, singly or in groups."

"I assimilated that much by observation," Rollo replied in a brassy baritone which no longer sent tiny tremors up the Maestro's spine. "Wires of different thickness and tautness struck by felt-covered hammers activated by manually opered levers arranged in a horizontal panel."

"A very cold-blooded description of one of man's nobler works," the Maestro remarked dryly. "You make Mozart and Chopin mere laboratory technicians."

"Mozart? Chopin?" The duralloy sphere that was Rollo's head shone stark and featureless, its immediate surface unbroken but for twin vision lenses. "The terms are not included in my memory banks."

"No, not yours, Rollo," the Maestro said softly. "Mozart and Chopin are not for vacuum tubes and fuses and copper wire. They are for flesh and blood and human tears."

"I do not understand," Rollo droned.

"Well," the Maestro said, smoke curling lazily from his nostrils, "they are two of the humans who compose, or design successions of notes—varying sounds, that is, produced by the piano or by other instruments, machines that produce other types of sounds of fixed pitch and tone.

"Sometimes these instruments, as we call them, are played, or operated, individually: sometimes in groups—orchestras, as we refer to them—and the sounds blend together, they harmonize. That is, they have an orderly, mathematical relationship to each other which results in . . ."

The Maestro threw up his hands.

"I never imagined," he chuckled, "that I would some day struggle so mightily, and so futilely, to explain music to a robot!"

"Music?"

"Yes, Rollo. The sounds produced by this machine and others of the same category are called music."

"What is the purpose of music, sir?"

"Purpose?"

The Maestro crushed the cigarette in an ash tray. He turned to the keyboard of the concert grand and flexed his fingers briefly.

"Listen, Rollo."

The wraithlike fingers glided and wove the opening bars of "Clair de Lune," slender and delicate as spider silk. Rollo stood rigid, the fluorescent light over the music rack casting a bluish jeweled sheen over his towering bulk, shimmering in the amber vision lenses.

The Maestro drew his hands back from the keys and the subtle thread of melody melted reluctantly into silence.

"Claude Debussy," the Maestro said. "One of our mechanics of an era long past. He designed that succession of tones many years ago. What do you think of it?"

Rollo did not answer at once.

"The sounds were well formed," he replied finally. "They did not jar my auditory senses as some do."

The Maestro laughed. "Rollo, you may not realize it, but you're a wonderful critic."

"This music, then," Rollo droned. "Its purpose is to give pleasure to humans?"

"Exactly," the Maestro said. "Sounds well formed, that do not jar the auditory senses as some do. Marvelous! It should be carved in marble over the entrance of New Carnegie Hall."

"I do not understand. Why should my definition—?"

The Maestro waved a hand. "No matter, Rollo. No matter."

"Sir?"

"Yes, Rollo?"

"Those sheets of paper you sometimes place before you on the piano. They are the plans of the composer indicating which sounds are to be produced by the piano and in what order?"

"Just so. We call each sound a note; combinations of notes we call chords."

"Each dot, then, indicates a sound to be made?"

"Perfectly correct, my man of metal."

Rollo stared straight ahead. The Maestro felt a peculiar sense of wheels turning within that impregnable sphere.

"Sir, I have scanned my memory banks and find no specific or implied instructions against it. I should like to be taught how to produce these notes on the piano. I request that you feed the correlation between those dots and the levers of the panel into my memory banks."

The Maestro peered at him, amazed. A slow grin traveled across his face.

"Done!" he exclaimed. "It's been many years since pupils helped gray these ancient locks, but I have the feeling that you, Rollo, will prove a most fascinating student. To instill the Muse into metal and machinery . . . I accept the challenge gladly!"

He rose, touched the cool latent power of Rollo's arm.

"Sit down here, my Rolleindex Personal Robot, Model M-e. We shall start Beethoven spinning in his grave—or make musical history."

More than an hour later the Maestro yawned and looked at his watch.

"It's late," he spoke into the end of the yawn. "These old eyes are not tireless like yours, my friend." He touched Rollo's shoulder. "You have the complete fundamentals of musical notation in your memory banks, Rollo. That's a good night's lesson, particularly when I recall how long it took me to acquire the same amount of information. Tomorrow we'll attempt to put those awesome fingers of yours to work."

He stretched. "I'm going to bed," he said. "Will you lock up and put out the lights?"

Rollo rose from the bench. "Yes, sir," he droned. "I have a request."

"What can I do for my star pupil?"

"May I attempt to create some sounds with the keyboard tonight? I will do so very softly so as not to disturb you."

"Tonight? Aren't you—?" Then the Maestro smiled. "You must pardon me, Rollo. It's still a bit difficult for me to realize that sleep has no meaning for you."

He hesitated, rubbing his chin. "Well, I suppose a good teacher should not discourage impatience to learn. All right, Rollo, but please be careful." He patted the polished mahogany. "This piano and I have been together for many years. I'd hate to see its teeth knocked out by those sledgehammer digits of yours. Lightly, my friend, very lightly."

"Yes, sir."

The Maestro fell asleep with a faint smile on his lips, dimly aware of the shy, tentative notes that Rollo was coaxing forth.

Then gray fog closed in and he was in that half-world where reality is dreamlike and dreams are real. It was soft and feathery and lavender clouds and sounds were rolling and washing across his mind in flowing waves.

Where? The mist drew back a bit and he was in red velvet and deep and the music swelled and broke over him.

He smiled.

My recording. Thank you, thank you, thank—

The Maestro snapped erect, threw the covers aside.

He sat on the edge of the bed, listening.

He groped for his robe in the darkness, shoved bony feet into his slippers.

He crept, trembling uncontrollably, to the door of his studio and stood there, thin and brittle in the robe.

The light over the music rack was an eerie island in the brown shadows of the studio. Rollo sat at the keyboard, prim inhuman, rigid, twin lenses focused somewhere off into the shadows.

The massive feet working the pedals, arms and hands flashing and glinting—they were living entities, separate, somehow, from the machined perfection of his body.

The music rack was empty.

A copy of Beethoven's "Appassionata" lay closed on the bench. It had been, the Maestro remembered, in a pile of sheet music on the piano.

Rollo was playing it.

He was creating it, breathing it, drawing it through silver flame.

Time became meaningless, suspended in midair.

The Maestro didn't realize he was weeping until Rollo finished the sonata.

The robot turned to look at the Maestro. "The sounds," he droned. "They pleased you?"

The Maestro's lips quivered. "Yes, Rollo," he replied at last. "They pleased me." He fought the lump in his throat.

He picked up the music in fingers that shook.

"This," he murmured. "Already?"

"It has been added to my store of data," Rollo replied. "I applied the principles you explained to me to these plans. It was not very difficult."

The Maestro swallowed as he tried to speak. "It was not very difficult . . ." he repeated softly.

The old man sank down slowly onto the bench next to

Rollo, stared silently at the robot as though seeing him for the first time.

Rollo got to his feet.

The Maestro let his fingers rest on the keys, strangely foreign now.

"Music!" he breathed. "I may have heard it that way in my soul. I know Beethoven did!"

He looked up at the robot, a growing excitement in his face.

"Rollo," he said, his voice straining to remain calm. "You and I have some work to do tomorrow on your memory banks."

Sleep did not come again that night.

He strode briskly into the studio the next morning. Rollo was vacuuming the carpet. The Maestro preferred carpets to the new dust-free plastics, which felt somehow profane to his feet.

The Maestro's house was, in fact, an oasis of anachronisms in a desert of contemporary antiseptic efficiency.

"Well, are you ready for work, Rollo?" he asked. "We have a lot to do, you and I. I have such plans for you, Rollo—great plans!"

Rollo, for once, did not reply.

"I have asked them all to come here this afternoon," the Maestro went on. "Conductors, concert pianists, composers, my manager. All the giants of music, Rollo. Wait until they hear you play."

Rollo switched off the vacuum and stood quietly.

"You'll play for them right here this afternoon." The Maestro's voice was high-pitched, breathless. "The 'Appassionata' again, I think. Yes, that's it. I must see their faces!

"Then we'll arrange a recital to introduce you to the public and the critics and then a major concerto with one of the big orchestras. We'll have it telecast around the world, Rollo. It can be arranged.

"Think of it, Rollo, just think of it! The greatest piano virtuoso of all time . . . a robot! It's completely fantastic and completely wonderful. I feel like an explorer at the edge of a new world."

He walked feverishly back and forth.

"Then recordings, of course. My entire repertoire, Rollo, and more. So much more!"

"Sir?"

The Maestro's face shone as he looked up at him. "Yes, Rollo?"

"In my built-in instructions, I have the option of rejecting any action which I consider harmful to my owner," the robot's words were precise, carefully selected. "Last night you wept.

That is one of the indications I am instructed to consider in making my decisions.''

The Maestro gripped Rollo's thick, superbly molded arm.

"Rollo, you don't understand. That was for the moment. It was petty of me, childish!''

"I beg your pardon, sir, but I must refuse to approach the piano again.''

The Maestro stared at him, unbelieving, pleading.

"Rollo, you can't! The world must hear you!''

"No, sir.'' The amber lenses almost seemed to soften.

"The piano is not a machine,'' that powerful inhuman voice droned. "To me, yes. I can translate the notes into sounds at a glance. From only a few I am able to grasp at once the composer's conception. It is easy for me.''

Rollo towered magnificently over the Maestro's bent form.

"I can also grasp,'' the brassy monotone rolled through the studio, "that this . . . music is not for robots. It is for man. To me it is easy, yes. . . . It was not meant to be easy.''

THE JEWELS OF M. LANTIN
GUY DE MAUPASSANT

M. Lantin, having met this young lady at a party given by his immediate superior, was literally enmeshed by love.

She was the daughter of a provincial tax collector who had died a few years previously. With her mother, she had come to Paris. Her mother became friendly with several middle-class families of the neighborhood in hopes of marrying off the young lady. Mother and daughter were poor, honorable, quiet, and gentle. The girl seemed to be the typical dream woman into whose hands any young man would yearn to entrust his entire life. Her modest beauty had an angelic quality, and the imperceptible smile which constantly graced her lips, seemed a reflection of her heart.

Everyone sang her praises; everyone who knew her repeated incessantly: "It will be a lucky fellow who wins her. You couldn't find a better catch!''

M. Lantin, now chief clerk of the Minister of the Interior, at a salary of 3500 francs, asked and received her hand in marriage.

He was unbelievably happy. She managed the house with such skill that their life was one of luxury. There was no delicacy, no whim of her husband's which she did not secure and satisfy; and her personal charm was such that, six years after their first meeting, he loved her even more than he had initially.

He begrudged her only two traits—her love of the theater and her passion for artificial jewels.

Her friends (she knew the wives of several minor functionaries) were always getting her seats for the fashionable plays, sometimes even for first nights; and she dragged her poor husband, willy-nilly, to these entertainments which completely wore him out, tired as he was after a hard day's work. He begged her to agree to go to the theater with some lady friend of her who would accompany her home. She took a long time to decide, claiming this a most inconvenient arrangement. At last, however, she agreed, and he was profoundly grateful to her.

Now, this taste for the theater naturally stirred in her the need to primp. Her toilette remained simple, to be sure—always modest but in good taste; and her gentle grace, her irresistible, humble, smiling grace seemed to acquire a new savor from the simplicity of her dress, but she became accustomed to wearing two huge rhinestone earrings, which looked like diamonds; and she had strings of artificial pearls around her neck, and wore bracelets of similar gems.

Her husband, who somewhat scorned this love of garish display, said, "Dearest, when you haven't the means to wear real jewelry, you should show yourself adorned only with your own grace and beauty; these are the true pearls."

But she, smiling quietly, would insist, "Can I help it? I love it so. This is my vice. I know, my dear, how absolutely right you are; but I can't really remake myself, can I? I think I would just idolize real jewelry."

And she would roll the pearls in her fingers. "See how perfect," she'd say. "You'd swear they were real."

Sometimes, during the evening, while they sat before the fire, she would bring out her jewel chest, put it on the tea table, and commence to examine the contents with passionate attention, as though there were some subtle and profound secret delight in this pursuit. She persisted in draping strings of pearls around her husband's neck; then she would laugh merrily, crying, "How silly you look, my darling!" And she would throw herself into his arms and kiss him wildly.

One wintry evening, when she had been at the opera, she came home shivering with cold. The next day she was coughing wretchedly. A week later she died.

Lantin nearly followed her into the tomb. His despair was such that, in a month's time, his hair turned completely white. He wept incessantly, his very soul seared by unbearable suffering, haunted by the memory, the smile, the voice—by the over-whelming beauty of his deceased wife.

Even the passage oftime failed to stem his grief. Frequently, at his office, while his colleagues were chatting idly, his cheeks would tremble and his eyes would fill with tears; he would grimace horribly and commence to sob.

He kept his wife's room intact, and sealed himself in every day to meditate. All her furniture and even her dresses remained just where they had been on the fatal day.

Living became difficult for him. His income which, under his wife's management, amply supplied the needs of both, now became insufficient for him alone. Dazed, he wondered how she had been able to purchase the superb wines and delicacies which he could no longer afford.

He fell into debt and began to scurry around for money as does anyone suddenly plunged into poverty. One fine morning, finding himself penniless a full week before payday, he thought about selling something. Suddenly the idea swept over him of taking a look at his wife's treasure trove, because, if the truth be told, he had always harbored some resentment towards this store of brilliants. The mere sight of them slightly tarnished the memory of his beloved.

It was a difficult business, searching through the case of jewels, because, even up to the very last days of her life, his wife had shopped stubbornly, bringing home some new bauble practically every night. He finally chose the magnificent necklace she seemed to have preferred, which, he figured, was worth six or seven francs, because, for artificial gems, it was really a masterpiece of craftsmanship.

With the jewels in his pocket he walekd towards the Ministry, looking for a reliable jeweler.

Spotting a store, he entered—somewhat chagrined to be making this public display of his poverty and ashamed at attempting to sell so worthless an object.

He approached the merchant. "Excuse me. I wonder what value you would place on this piece."

The man took the necklace, examined it, turned it over, weighed it, called to his partner, talked to him in low tones, placed the necklace on the counter and scrutinized it carefully from a distance as though judging the effect.

M. Lantin, overwhelmed by this process, opened his mouth to protest: "Oh! I know that piece isn't worth anything," but just at that moment the storekeeper said:

"Monsieur, this piece is worth between twelve and fifteen thousand francs, but I cannot buy it until I learn exactly how you came into possession of it."

Lantin stared, wide-eyed, silent—uncomprehending. He finally stammered, "What? You are absolutely sure?"

The gentleman seemed offended by his attitude, and said wryly, "You may go elsewhere if you think you can do better. To me that is worth fifteen thousand at the very most. If you find no better offer, you may come back here."

M. Lantin, stupified, took the necklace and left, feeling a curious urge to be alone and undisturbed.

But, before he had gone far, he was seized with an impulse to laugh, and he thought, "Imbecile! What a fool! What if I had taken him at his word! What a jeweler—not to know the difference between real gems and fakes!"

And he entered another jewelry store on the Rue de la Paix. As soon as he saw the jewel, the dealer cried, "Of course! I know this necklace well; I sold it!"

Deeply disturbed, M. Lantin asked, "How much is it worth?"

"Sir—I sold it for twenty-five thousand francs. I'm ready to take it back for eighteen thousand, if you will tell me—the law, you know—how you happened to receive it."

This time Lantin sat paralyzed with astonishment. He stuttered. "But—but—examine it very closely, sir. I have always thought it was—artificial."

The jeweler asked, "Would you please tell me your name, sir?"

"Of course. I'm Lantin. I work at the Ministry of the Interior, and I live at 16 Rue des Martyrs."

The merchant opened his ledger, looked through it, and said, "This necklace was sent to Mme. Lantin, 16 Rue des Martyrs, on the twentieth of July, 1876."

And the two men stared at each other, the clerk dumbfounded; the jeweler scenting a robber.

The merchant said, "Would you mind letting me have this for a day? Naturally, I'll give you a receipt."

M. Lantin blurted out, "Of course!" And he left, folding the paper into his pocket.

Then he crossed the street, went back, saw that he had gone out of his way, returned past the Tuileries, saw again he had made a mistake, crossed the Seine, went back to the Champs-Elysées without a single clear notion in his head. He forced himself to think. His wife could not possibly have purchased such valuable jewelry. Absolutely not! Well then? A present? A present! From whom? For what?

He was brought up short, and he stood stock still—there in the middle of the street. A horrible thought flashed across his mind. She? But all those other jewels were also gifts! He felt the earth shiver; a tree just before him seemed to crush him. He threw out his arms and fell, senseless, to the ground.

He regained consciousness in a nearby pharmacy to which passers-by had carried him. He asked that he be taken home, and he locked himself in.

He wept bitterly until nightfall—stuffing a handkerchief into his mouth to stifle his cries. Then he staggered to bed, wrung out with fatigue and chagrin, and he slept heavily.

A ray of sunshine woke him, and he got up slowly to go to his office. After such a blow, it would be hard to carry on with his work. He felt that he could be excused, and he wrote his superior a note. Then he thought that he ought to go back to the jeweler; and he crimsoned with shame. He could not possibly leave the necklace with that man. He dressed hurriedly and went out.

As he walked along, Lantin said to himself, "How easy it is to be happy when you're rich! With money you can even shake off your sorrows; you can go or stay as you please! You can travel and amuse yourself. If only I were really rich!"

Then he became aware of the fact that he was hungry, not having eaten since the previous evening. But his pockets were empty, and he reminded himself of the necklace. Eighteen thousand francs! Eighteen thousand francs! What a fortune!

He reached the Rue de la Paix, and he began pacing up and down opposite the shop. Eighteen thousand francs! More than twenty times he started to enter; but shame always halted him.

He was still hungry—famished—and without a sou. He finally made up his mind, raced across the street so as not to give himself time to think, and burst into the store.

As soon as he saw him, the merchant greeted him royally, offered him a chair with smiling courtesy. The partners then came in and sat down near Lantin, happiness beaming from their eyes and their lips.

The jeweler declared, "I am satisfied, Monsieur, and if you feel as you did yesterday, I am ready to pay you the sum agreed upon."

"Certainly," stammered Lantin.

The merchant took eighteen large notes from a drawer, counted them, gave them to Lantin, who signed a receipt and, with trembling hand, stuffed the money into his pocket.

Then, just as he was going out, he turned back towards the grinning shopkeeper, and lowering his eyes, murmured, "I—I have some other gems—which came to me in the same way. Would you be willing to buy those from me?"

The jeweler nodded, "Of course, Monsieur."

One of the partners barely stifled a laugh, while the other was forced to leave the room to hide his mirth.

Lantin, impassive and stern, said, "I'll bring them to you."

When he returned to the store, an hour later, he had still not eaten. They set about examining the jewels piece by piece, assessing each one. Then they all went back to Lantin's house.

Now Lantin entered into the spirit of the business, arguing, insisting that they show him the bills of sale, and getting more and more excited as the values rose.

The magnificent earrings were worth twenty thousand francs; the bracelets, thirty-five thousand. The brooches, pins and medallions, sixteen thousand. The whole collection was valued at one hundred ninety-six thousand francs.

The merchant boomed out in a jolly voice, "That's what happens when you put your money into jewelry."

Lantin said solemnly, "That's one way to invest your money!" Then he left, after having agreed with the purchaser to have a second expert appraisal the following day.

When he was out in the street, he looked up at the Vendôme Column. He felt like leaping up to the top. He felt light enough to play leapfrog with the statue of the Emperor perched up there in the clouds.

He went into an elegant restaurant to eat, and he drank wine at twenty francs a bottle.

Then he took a cab and rode around the Bois de Boulogne. He looked at the gleaming carriages, suppressing a desire to cry out, "I'm rich, too! I have two hundred thousand francs!"

He thought of his office. He drove up, entered his Chief's office solemnly, and announced, "Sir—I'm tendering my resignation! I've just inherited three hundred thousand francs!" He went around shaking hands with his colleagues, and telling them all about his plans for the future. Then he went out to dinner at the Café Anglais.

Finding himself seated alongside a distinguished-looking gentleman, he couldn't resist whispering to him, a little archly, that he had just inherited four hundred thousand francs.

For the first time in his life he enjoyed the theater and he spent the night carousing.

Six months later he remarried. His second wife was a most worthy woman, but rather difficult. She made his life unbearable.

Interpreter's Notebook

De Maupassant uses an omniscient narrator in "The Jewels of M. Lantin" to tell this little tale of surprise and reversal. Remember that the omniscient narrator has some of the characteristics of the first-person narrator; let some of M. Lantin's internal responses show through. A line like "He was unbelievably happy" needs to be rendered so that not only are we informed as to M. Lantin's state of mind but we also see him in his happiness.

Take plenty of time for M. Lantin's realization, particularly during the dialogue sequences with the jewelers. As always, keep in touch with your narrator's attitude toward the characters and events of the story.

MY SIXTH CHRISTMAS
From HOMECOMING
FLOYD DELL

That fall, before it was discovered that the soles of both my shoes were worn clear through, I still went to Sunday school. And one time the Sunday-school superintendent made a speech to all the classes. He said that these were very hard times, and that many poor children weren't getting enough to eat. It was the first that I had heard about it. He asked everybody to bring some food for the poor children next Sunday. I felt very sorry for the poor children.

Also, little envelopes were distributed to all the classes. Each little boy and girl was to bring money for the poor, next Sunday. The pretty Sunday-school teacher explained that we were to write our names, or have our parents write them, up in the left-hand corner of the little envelopes. . . . I told my mother all about it when I came home. And my mother gave me, the next Sunday, a small bag of potatoes to carry to Sunday school. I supposed the poor children's mothers would make potato soup out of them. . . . Potato soup was good. My father, who was quite a joker, would always say, as if he were surprised, "Ah! I see we have some nourishing potato soup today!" It was so good that we had it every day. My father was at home all day long and every day, now; and I liked that, even if he was grumpy as he sat reading Grant's "Memoirs." I had my parents all to myself, too; the others were away. My oldest brother was in Quincy, and memory does not reveal where the others were: perhaps with relatives in the country.

Taking my small bag of potatoes to Sunday school, I looked around for the poor children; I was disappointed not to see them. I had heard about poor children in stories. But I was told just to put my contribution with the others on the big table in the side room.

I had brought with me the little yellow envelope, with some money in it for the poor children. My mother had put the money in it and sealed it up. She wouldn't even tell me how much money she had put in it, but it felt like several dimes. Only she wouldn't let me write my name on the envelope. I had learned to write my name, and I was proud of being able to do it. But my mother said firmly, no, I must not write my name on the envelope; she didn't tell me why. On the way to Sunday school I had pressed the envelope against the coins until I could tell what they were; they weren't dimes but pennies.

When I handed in my envelope, my Sunday-school teacher noticed that my name wasn't on it, and she gave me a pencil; I could write my own name, she said. So I did. But I was confused because my mother had said not to; and when I came home, I confessed what I had done. She looked distressed. "I told you not to!" she said. But she didn't explain why. . . .

I didn't go back to school that fall. My mother said it was because I was sick. I did have a cold the week that school opened; I had been playing in the gutters and had got my feet wet, because there were holes in my shoes. My father cut insoles out of cardboard, and I wore those in my shoes. As long as I had to stay in the house anyway, they were all right.

I stayed cooped up in the house, without any companionship. We didn't take a Sunday paper any more, but the Barry *Adage* came every week in the mails; and though I did not read small print, I could see the Santa Clauses and holly wreaths in the advertisements.

There was a calendar in the kitchen. The red days were Sundays and holidays; and that red 25 was Christmas. (It was on a Monday, and the two red figures would come right together in 1893; but this represents research in the World Almanac, not memory.) I knew when Sunday was, because I could look out of the window and see the neighbor's children, all dressed up, going to Sunday school. I knew just when Christmas was going to be.

But there was something queer! My father and mother didn't say a word about Christmas. And once, when I spoke of it, there was a strange, embarrassed silence; so I didn't say anything more about it. But I wondered, and was troubled. Why didn't they say anything about it? Was what I had said I wanted (memory refused to supply that detail) too expensive?

I wasn't arrogant and talkative now. I was silent and frigntened. What was the matter? Why didn't my father and mother say anything about Christmas? As the day approached, my chest grew tighter with anxiety.

Now it was the day before Christmas. I couldn't be mistaken.

But not a word about it from my father and mother. I waited in painful bewilderment all day. I had supper with them, and was allowed to sit up for an hour. I was waiting for them to say something. "It's time for you to go to bed," my mother said gently. I had to say something.

"This is Christmas Eve, isn't it?" I asked, as if I didn't know.

My father and mother looked at one another. Then my mother looked away. Her face was pale and stony. My father cleared his throat, and his face took on a joking look. He pretended he hadn't known it was Christmas Eve, because he hadn't been reading the papers. He said he would go downtown and find out.

My mother got up and walked out of the room. I didn't want my father to have to keep on being funny about it, so I got up and went to bed. I went by myself without having a light. I undressed in the dark and crawled into bed.

I was numb. As if I had been hit by something. It was hard to breathe. I ached all through. I was stunned—with finding out the truth.

My body knew before my mind quite did. In a minute, when I could think, my mind would know. And as the pain in my body ebbed, the pain in my mind began. I knew. I couldn't put it into words yet. But I knew why I had taken only a little bag of potatoes to Sunday school that fall. I knew why there had been only pennies in my little yellow envelope. I knew why I hadn't gone to school that fall—why I hadn't any new shoes— why we had been living on potato soup all winter. All these things, and others, many others, fitted themselves together in my mind, and meant something.

Then the words came into my mind and I whispered them into the darkness:

"We're poor!"

That was it. I was one of those poor children I had been sorry for, when I heard about them in Sunday school. My mother hadn't told me. My father was out of work, and we hadn't any money. That was why there wasn't going to be any Christmas at our house.

Then I remembered something that made me squirm with shame—a boast. (Memory will not yield this up. Had I said to some Nice little boy, "I'm going to be President of the United States"? Or to a Nice little girl: "I'll marry you when I grow up."? It was some boast as horribly shameful to remember.)

"We're poor." There in bed in the dark, I whispered it over and over to myself. I was making myself get used to it. (Or—just torturing myself, as one presses the tongue against a sore tooth? No, memory says not like that—but to keep myself from ever

being such a fool again: suffering now, to keep this awful thing
from ever happening again. Memory is clear on that; it was more
like pulling the tooth, to get it over with—never mind the pain,
this will be the end!)

It wasn't so bad, now that I knew. I just hadn't known! I
had thought all sorts of foolish things: that I was going to Ann
Arbor—going to be a lawyer—going to make speeches in the
Square, going to be President. Now I knew better.

I had wanted (something) for Christmas. I didn't want it,
now. I didn't want any thing.

I lay there in the dark, feeling the cold emotion of
renunciation. (The tendrils of desire unfold their clasp on the
outer world of objects, withdraw, shrivel up. Wishes shrivel up,
turn black, die. It is like that.)

It hurt. But nothing would ever hurt again. I would never
let myself want anything again.

I lay there stretched out straight and stiff in the dark, my
fists clenched hard upon Nothing. . . .

In the morning it has been like a nightmare that is not clearly
remembered—that one wishes to forget. Though I hadn't hung
up any stocking, there was one hanging at the foot of my bed.
A bag of popcorn, and a lead pencil, for me. They had done the
best they could, now they realized that I knew about Christmas.
But they needn't have thought they had to. I didn't want anything.

THE CHASER
JOHN COLLIER

Alan Austen, as nervous as a kitten, went up certain dark and
creaky stairs in the neighborhood of Pell Street, and peered about
for a long time on the dim landing before he found the name
he wanted written obscurely on one of the doors.

He pushed open this door, as he had been told to do, and
found himself in a tiny room, which contained no furniture but
a plain kitchen table, a rocking-chair, and an ordinary chair. On
one of the dirty buff-colored walls were a couple of shelves,
containing in all perhaps a dozen bottles and jars.

An old man sat in the rocking-chair, reading a newspaper.
Alan, without a word, handed him the card he had been given.
"Sit down, Mr. Austen," said the old man very politely. "I am
glad to make your acquaintance."

"Is it true," asked Alan, "that you have a certain mixture that has—er—quite extraordinary effects?"

"My dear sir," replied the old man, "my stock in trade is not very large—I don't deal in laxatives and teething mixtures—but such as it is, it is varied. I think nothing I sell has effects which could be precisely described as ordinary."

"Well, the fact is . . ." began Alan.

"Here, for example," interrrupted the old man, reaching for a bottle from the shelf. "Here is a liquid as colourless as water, almost tasteless, quite imperceptible in coffee, wine, or any other beverage. It is also quite imperceptible to any known method of autopsy."

"Do you mean it is a poison?" cried Alan, very much horrified.

"Call it a glove-cleaner if you like," said the old man indifferently. "Maybe it will clean gloves. I have never tried. One might call it a life-cleaner. Lives need cleaning sometimes."

"I want nothing of that sort," said Alan.

"Probably it is just as well," said the old man. "Do you know the price of this? For one teaspoonful, which is sufficient, I ask five thousand dollars. Never less. Not a penny less."

"I hope all your mixtures are not as expensive," said Alan apprehensively.

"Oh dear, no," said the old man. "It would be no good charging that sort of price for a love potion, for example. Young people who need a love potion very seldom have five thousand dollars. Otherwise they would not need a love potion."

"I am glad to hear that," said Alan.

"I look at it like this," said the old man. "Please a customer with one article, and he will come back when he needs another. Even if it is *is* more costly. He will save up for it, if necessary."

"So," said Alan, "you really do sell love potions?"

"If I did not sell love potions," said the old man, reaching for another bottle, "I should not have mentioned the other matter to you. It is only when one is in a position to oblige that one can afford to be so confidential."

"And these potions," said Alan. "They are not just—just—er—"

"Oh, no," said the old man. "Their effects are permanent, and extend far beyond the mere casual impulse. But they include it. Oh, yes, they include it. Bountifully, insistently. Everlastingly."

"Dear me!" said Alan, attempting a look of scientific detachment. "How very interesting!"

"But consider the spiritual side, ' said the old man.

"I do indeed," said Alan.

"For indifference," said the old man, "they substitute

devotion. For scorn, adoration. Give one tiny measure of this to the young lady—its flavour is imperceptible in orange juice, soup, or cocktails—and however gay and giddy she is, she will change altogether. She will want nothing but solitude and you."

"I can hardly believe it," said Alan. "She is so fond of parties."

"She will not like them any more," said the old man. "She will be afraid of the pretty girls you may meet."

"She will actually be jealous?" cried Alan in a rapture. "Of me?"

"Yes, she will want to be everything to you."

"She is, already. Only she doesn't care about it."

"She will, when she has taken this. She will care intensely. You will be her sole interest in life."

"Wonderful!" cried Alan.

"She will want to know all you do," said the old man. "All that has happened to you during the day. Every word of it. She will want to know what you are thinking about, why you smile suddenly, why you are looking sad."

"That is love!" cried Alan.

"Yes," said the old man. "How carefully she will look after you! She will never allow you to be tired, to sit in a draught, to neglect your food. If you are an hour late, she will be terrified. She will think you are killed, or that some siren has caught you."

"I can hardly imagine Diana like that!" cried Alan, overwhelmed with joy.

"You will not have to use your imagination," said the old man. "And, by the way, since there are always sirens, if by any chance you *should*, later on, slip a little, you need not worry. She will forgive you, in the end. She will be terribly hurt, of course, but she will forgive you—in the end."

"That will not happen," said Alan fervently.

"Of course not," said the old man. "But, if it did, you need not worry. She would never divorce you. Oh, no! And, of course, she will never give you the least, the very least, grounds for—uneasiness."

"And how much," said Alan, "Is this wonderful mixture?"

"It is not as dear," said the old man, "as the glove-cleaner, or life-cleaner, as I sometimes call it. No. That is five thousand dollars, never a penny less. One has to be older than you are, to indulge in that sort of thing. One has to save up for it."

"But the love potion?" said Alan.

"Oh, that?" said the old man, opening the drawer in the kitchen table, and taking out a tiny, rather dirty-looking phial. "That is just a dollar."

"I can't tell you how grateful I am," said Alan, watching him fill it.

"I like to oblige," said the old man. "Then customers come back, later in life, when they are better off, and want more expensive things. Here you are. You will find it very effective."

"Thank you again," said Alan. "Good-bye."

"Au revoir," said the old man.

Interpreter's Notebook

The key for unlocking the humor in "The Chaser" is characterization. The two characters, Alan and the old man, must have contrast in voice, attitude, and physical action.

There is a great deal of dialogue within this third-person narration, but resist the temptation to delete too many of the "said Alan" and "said the old man" constructions. These are the words of the narrator, who must also have a distinct personality. Ask yourself, "As the narrator what is my attitude toward these people? This incident?"

A WICKED BOY
ANTON CHEKHOV

Ivan Ivanych Lapkin, a young man of nice appearance, and Anna Semionovna Zamblitskaia, a young girl with a little turned-up nose, went down the steep bank and sat down on a small bench. The bench stood right by the water among some thick young osier bushes. What a wonderful little place! Once you'd sat down, you were hidden from the world—only the fish saw you, and the water-tigers, running like lightning over the water. The young people were armed with rods, nets, cans of worms, and other fishing equipment. Having sat down, they started fishing right away.

"I'm glad we're alone at last," Lapkin began, looking around. "I have to tell you a lot of things, Anna Semionovna . . . an awful lot . . . when I saw you the first time. . . . You've got a bite . . . then I understood what I'm living for, understood where my idol was—to whom I must devote my honest, active life . . . that must be a big one that's biting. . . . Seeing you, I feel in love for the first time, feel passionately in love! Wait before you give it a jerk . . . let it bite harder. . . . Tell me, my darling,

I adjure you, may I count on—not on reciprocity, no! I'm not worthy of that, I dare not even think of that—may I count on. . . . Pull!"

Anna Semionovna raised her hand with the rod in it, yanked, and cried out. A little silvery-green fish shimmered in the air.

"My Lord, a perch! Ah, ah. . . . Quickly! It's getting-free!"

The perch got free of the hook, flopped through the grass toward its native element . . . and plopped into the water!

In pursuit of the fish, Lapkin somehow inadvertently grabbed Anna Semionovna's hand instead of the fish, inadvertently pressed it to his lips. . . . She quickly drew it back, but it was already too late; their mouths inadvertently merged in a kiss. It happened somehow inadvertently. Another kiss followed the first, then vows and protestations . . . What happy minutes! However, in this earthly life there is no absolute happiness. Happiness usually carries a poison in itself, or else is poisoned by something from outside. So this time, too. As the young people were kissing, a laugh suddenly rang out. They glanced at the river and were stupefied: a naked boy was standing in the water up to his waist. This was Kolia, a schoolboy, Anna Semionovna's brother. He was standing in the water, staring at the young people, and laughing maliciously.

"Ah-ah-ah . . . you're kissing?" he said. "That's great! I'll tell Mama."

"I hope that you, as an honest man, . . ." muttered Lapkin, blushing. "It's low-down to spy, and to tell tales is foul and detestable . . . I assume that you, as an honest and noble young man . . ."

"Give me a ruble and then I won't tell!" said the noble young man. "Or else I will."

Lapkin pulled a ruble out of his pocket and gave it to Kolia. Kolia squeezed the ruble in his wet fist, whistled, and swam off. And the young people didn't kiss any more that time.

The next day Lapkin brought Kolia some paints and a ball from town, and his sister gave him all her empty pill-boxes. After that they had to give him some cuff-links with dogs' heads on them. The wicked boy obviously liked all the things very much and, in order to get still more, he started keeping his eye on them. Wherever Lapkin and Anna Semionovna went, he went, too. He didn't leave them alone for a minute.

"The bastard!" Lapkin gnashed his teeth. "So little, and already such a real bastard! What's he going to be like later?!"

All through June, Kolia made life impossible for the poor lovers. He threatened to tell on them, kept his eye on them, and demanded presents; it all wasn't enough for him, and he finally started talking about a pocket watch. And what then? They had to promise the watch.

One time at dinner, when the waffle cookies were being passed, he suddenly burst out in a gaffaw, winked an eye, and asked Lapkin:

"Shall I tell? Huh?"

Lapkin blushed terribly and started eating his napkin instead of the cookie. Anna Semionovna jumped up from the table and ran into the other room.

And the young people found themselves in this position until the end of August, until the very day when, at last, Lapkin proposed to Anna Semionovna. Oh, what a happy day that was! Having talked to the parents of his bride, and having received their consent, Lapkin first of all ran out into the garden and started looking for Kolia. Once he had found him, he almost sobbed from delight and seized the wicked boy by the ear. Anna Semionovna, who had also been looking for Kolia, ran up, and seized him by the other ear. And you really ought to have seen what joy was written all over the lovers' faces as Kolia cried and begged them:

"Dearest, darling, angels, I'll never do it again! Ow, ow! Forgive me!"

And afterwards they both admitted that during the whole time they had been in love with each other they had never once felt such happiness, such breath-taking bliss as during those moments when they were pulling the wicked boy's ears.

Interpreter's Notebook

Chekhov employs a third-person narrator for this delightful story of "A Wicked Boy." Aside from the names, the one big trouble spot is the second paragraph. The reader must make clear, through voice change and physical action, that it is Lapkin who is both making protestations of love and worrying about the fish on Anna's line.

A Russian accent is effective, but not essential.

DAUGHTER
ERSKINE CALDWELL

At sunrise a Negro on his way to the big house to feed the mules had taken the word to Colonel Henry Maxwell, and Colonel Henry phoned the sheriff. The sheriff had hustled Jim into town and locked him up in the jail, and then he went home and ate breakfast.

Jim walked around the empty cellroom while he was buttoning his shirt, and after that he sat down on the bunk and tied his shoelaces. Everything that morning had taken place so quickly that he had not even had time to get a drink of water. He got up and went to the water bucket near the door, but the sheriff had forgotten to put water into it.

By that time there were several men standing in the jailyard. Jim went to the window and looked out when he heard them talking. Just then another automobile drove up, and six or seven men got out. Other men were coming towards the jail from both directions of the street.

"What was the trouble out at your place this morning, Jim?" somebody said.

Jim stuck his chin between the bars and looked at the faces in the crowd. He knew everyone there.

While he was trying to figure out how everybody in town had heard about his being there, somebody else spoke to him.

"It must have been an accident, wasn't it, Jim?"

A colored boy hauling a load of cotton to the gin drove up the street. When the wagon got in front of the jail, the boy whipped up the mules with the ends of the reins and made them trot.

"I hate to see the State have a grudge against you, Jim," somebody said.

The sheriff came down the street swinging a tin dinner pail in his hand. He pushed through the crowd, unlocked the door, and set the pail inside.

Several men came up behind the sheriff and looked over his shoulder into the jail.

"Here's your breakfast my wife fixed up for you, Jim. You'd better eat a little, Jim boy."

Jim looked at the pail, at the sheriff, at the open jail door, and he shook his head.

"I don't feel hungry," he said. "Daughter's been hungry, though—awful hungry."

The sheriff backed out the door, his hand going to the handle of his pistol. He backed out so quickly that he stepped on the toes of the men behind him.

"Now, don't you get careless, Jim boy," he said. "Just sit and calm yourself."

He shut the door and locked it. After he had gone a few steps towards the street, he stopped and looked into the chamber of his pistol to make sure it had been loaded.

The crowd outside the window pressed in closer. Some of the men rapped on the bars until Jim came and looked out. When he saw them, he stuck his chin between the iron and gripped his hands around it.

"How come it to happen, Jim?" somebody asked. "It must have been an accident, wasn't it?"

Jim's long thin face looked as if it would come through the bars. The sheriff came up to the window to see if everything was all right.

"Now, just take it easy, Jim boy," he said.

The man who had asked Jim to tell what had happened elbowed the sheriff out of the way. The other men crowded closer.

"How come, Jim?" the man said. "Was it an accident?"

"No," Jim said, his fingers twisting about the bars. "I picked up my shotgun and done it."

The sheriff pushed towards the window again.

"Go on, Jim, and tell us what it's all about."

Jim's face squeezed between the bars until it looked as though only his ears kept his head from coming through.

"Daughter said she was hungry, and I just couldn't stand it no longer. I just couldn't stand to hear her say it."

"Don't get all excited now, Jim boy," the sheriff said, pushing forward one moment and being elbowed away the next.

"She waked up in the middle of the night again and said she was hungry. I just couldn't stand to hear her say it."

Somebody pushed all the way through the crowd until he got to the window.

"Why, Jim, you could have come and asked me for something for her to eat, and you know I'd have given you all I got in the world."

The sheriff pushed forward once more.

"That wasn't the right thing to do," Jim said. "I've been working all year and I made enough for all of us to eat."

He stopped and looked down into the faces on the other side of the bars.

"I made enough working on shares, but they came and took it all away from me. I couldn't go around begging after I'd made enough to keep us. They just came and took it all off. Then Daughter woke up again this morning saying she was hungry, and I just couldn't stand it no longer."

"You'd better go and get on the bunk now, Jim boy," the sheriff said.

"It don't seem right that the little girl ought to be shot like that," somebody said.

"Daughter said she was hungry," Jim said. "She'd been saying that for all of the past month. Daughter'd wake up in the middle of the night and say it. I just couldn't stand it no longer."

"You ought to have sent her over to my house, Jim. Me and my wife could have fed her something, somehow. It don't look right to kill a little girl like her."

"I'd made enough for all of us," Jim said. "I just couldn't stand it no longer. Daughter'd been hungry all the past month."

"Take it easy, Jim boy," the sheriff said, trying to push forward.

The crowd swayed from side to side.

"And so you picked up the gun this morning and shot her?" somebody asked.

"When she woke up this morning saying she was hungry, I just couldn't stand it."

The crowd pushed closer. Men were coming towards the jail from all directions, and those who were then arriving pushed forward to hear what Jim had to say.

"The State has got a grudge against you now, Jim," somebody said, "but somehow it don't seem right."

"I can't help it," Jim said. "Daughter woke up again this morning that way."

The jailyard, the street, and the vacant lot on the other side were filled with men and boys. All of them were pushing forward to hear Jim. Word had spread all over town by that time that Jim Carlisle had shot and killed his eight-year-old daughter, Clara.

"Who does Jim share-crop for?" somebody asked.

"Colonel Henry Maxwell," a man in the crowd said. "Colonel Henry has had Jim out there about nine or ten years."

"Henry Maxwell didn't have no business coming and taking all the shares. He's got plenty of his own. It ain't right for Henry Maxwell to come and take Jim's, too."

The sheriff was pushing forward once more.

"The State's got a grudge against Jim now," somebody said. "Somehow it don't seem right, though."

The sheriff pushed his shoulder into the crowd of men and worked his way in closer.

A man shoved the sheriff away.

"Why did Henry Maxwell come and take your share of the crop, Jim?"

"He said I owed it to him because one of his mules died about a month ago."

The sheriff got in front of the barred window.

"You ought to go to the bunk now and rest some, Jim boy," he said. "Take off your shoes and stretch out, Jim boy."

He was elbowed out of the way.

"You didn't kill the mule, did you, Jim?"

"The mule dropped dead in the barn," Jim said. "I wasn't nowhere around it. It just dropped dead."

The crowd was pushing harder. The men in front were jammed against the jail, and the men behind were trying to get within earshot. Those in the middle wree squeezed against each other so tightly they could not move in any direction. Everyone was talking louder.

Jim's face pressed between the bars and his fingers gripped the iron until the knuckles were white.

The milling crowd was moving across the street to the vacant lot. Somebody was shouting. He climbed up on an automobile and began swearing at the top of his lungs.

A man in the middle of the crowd pushed his way out and went to his automobile. He got in and drove off alone.

Jim stood holding to the bars and looking through the window. The sheriff had his back to the crowd, and he was saying something to Jim. Jim did not hear what he said.

A man on his way to the gin with a load of cotton stopped to find out what the trouble was. He looked at the crowd in the vacant lot for a moment, and then he turned around and looked at Jim behind the bars. The shouting across the street was growing louder.

"What's the trouble, Jim?"

Somebody on the other side of the street came to the wagon. He put his foot on a spoke in the wagon wheel and looked up at the man on the cotton while he talked.

"Daughter woke up this morning again saying she was hungry," Jim said.

The sheriff was the only person who heard him.

The man on the load of cotton jumped to the ground, tied the reins to the wagon wheel, and pushed through the crowd to the car where all the shouting and swearing was being done. After listening for a while, he came back to the street, called a Negro who was standing with several other Negroes on the corner, and handed him the reins. The Negro drove off with the cotton towards the gin, and the man went back into the crowd.

Just then the man who had driven off alone in his car came back. He sat for a moment behind the steering wheel, and then he jumped to the ground. He opened the rear door and took out a crowbar that was as long as he was tall.

"Pry that jail door open and let Jim out," somebody said. "It ain't right for him to be in there."

The crowd in the vacant lot was moving again. The man who had been standing on top of the automobile jumped to the ground, and the men moved towards the street in the direction of the jail.

The first man to reach it jerked the six-foot crowbar out of the soft earth where it had been jabbed.

The sheriff backed off.

"Now, take it easy, Jim boy," he said.

He turned and started walking rapidly up the street towards his house.

Interpreter's Notebook

In "Daughter" the narrator is third person, affording the interpreter a wide range of possibilities of age, sex, and personality. From the detail and the large amounts of dialogue, our narrator must have been present at the incident—the story is being told firsthand.

The story makes two primary demands of an interpreter. First, the pieces of dialogue must be separated by different sounding voices, which can be accomplished by varying the rate of delivery as well as pitch and tone. Also, the dialogue calls for a southern accent, although the accent is optional for the narrator. Second, since much of the texture of this story is carried in the physical action, the interpreter must employ descriptive movement to convey the important moments.

THE LOTTERY TICKET
VENTURA GARCIA CALDERÓN

You have heard this story before? No matter, I will tell it again because it points to a moral, and, better than that, to a state of mind. Also it is not without present-day interest.

The dancer, whom we will call Cielito, was the loveliest Spanish "bailadora" of about fifteen years ago, though not in the fashion of Madrid, where the taste in women at that time was Turkish—for fat all over. She was the Medici Venus, not the Milo—which measures three feet eleven inches around the hips.

You remember Cielito's version of the rumba, with a pink-tipped finger pointing to Heaven; and how the public used to roar for one more look; and how she allowed it, just for one second, smiling like an angel fallen in the worst Gomorrah? If you have not seen Cielito dance the rumba, you do not know tropical love. In her dancing she played instinctively the cruel game of rousing lust and leaving it. Like the Persian butterfly, she was always playing with fire without ever getting burnt.

Cielito learned to dance in the West Indies, where this story takes place. The "danse du ventre" is a bourgeois family spectacle beside the swinging of the breasts. Breasts fit to be molded into beautiful cups, or like coupled doves to be caressed. The impish wanton shawl follows the swinging game, and at last, for a too brief unforgettable instant, is thrown aside.

One loses his head when one speaks of Cielito; which would hardly surprise her, for there is not a woman in the world who knows more about men than she does.

Once when she was touring in South America, she drove the men so mad that they had to have a lottery for her. Yes, a singular idea, but not really so strange in Cuba, where we leave everything to chance, even the pretty women. Well, in this distant town of the island of sugar cane and honey, the spectators were able one night to buy with their theater tickets the chance of taking Cielito away with them after the performance. Only one spectator could win, of course, but in the crowds at the booking-office every man was Don Juan looking with hatred at his possible rival, the neighbor who was also buying the right to be the happiest of men.

Even Cielito was a little moved when the evening came, and there was something almost chaste in her languorous glances at the audience who riotously refused any other music-hall items. They only wanted Cielito with her shuffling false-Negro steps and very soft Creole words "arza columpiate." But there were no passionate encores, no one asked Cielito to carry her perversity any further. Everyone was in too great a hurry for the draw, which was very correctly carried out, like a family lottery, on the stage itself.

A top hat was filled with numbered place-slips, and the draw was presided over by the theater manager; rather pale and nervous, for any suspicion of trickery would have been punished on the spot, and there's no knowing what may happen when a lot of violent men are after the same girl. Believe me, it was more than mere lust for a beautiful woman; you have no idea how much magic and romance is attached to any European actress by South Americans dreaming of Montmartre and Andalusia. A Frenchwoman is all Paris to them, a Spaniard is Seville or Granada with the chirrup of grasshoppers in the sunshine. These phantasies are a sort of feverish mental stimulant to our people, and a beautiful body does not help to lessen the fever.

At exactly midnight the winning number, 213, was called by a man in evening dress who had turned his back on the hat and unhesitatingly drawn a slip of paper.

The whole room looked for the winner, some mocking

voices called for him to go up on the stage so that everyone could see him before he went into the wings with Cielito.

No one answered, and there was an expectant silence. A spectator who had come very near success jogged the elbow of his neighbor in seat 213, almost forcing him to rise.

He was a fine-looking Negro, "a bit of ebony" the conquistadores would have called him; "black as sin" the old women say even now. He rose slowly with the charming comic solemnity of the colored people, whose vain smile fitly answers the amused glances of the crowd. With deliberate slowness he looked through his note-case for the ticket, found it at last in a greasy envelope, and tore it up into very small pieces which he threw in the air like confetti before the astounded audience.

That ample gesture ought to have made his refusal clear enough. But the people could not believe he was rejecting Cielito, the finest flower of Spain. So he shook his head, looking grave and sulky, but enjoying very much the displeasure he was causing.

All the bitterness of the subject races was in him, all the misery of his ancestors who had died as slaves among the sugar cane. The hot joy of revenge burned on his obstinate coal-black face as he disdained what so many white men had dreamed about with longing. Then with a shrug of his shoulders, very dignified and sure of his importance, he prepared to leave the theater, while from the stage Cielito with her hands on her hips in a truly Spanish fury spat out at him her shame and her disgust.

But there was no need of a word from her. The whole audience rushed on the black man and began to beat him. So he did not want the flower of Spain—he was disgusted with the darling of Andalusia—they would show him—they would finish him.

It was a most unlooked-for lynching, unknown no doubt in the United States where they don't yet punish the abstemious Negro who refuses to "outrage" a white woman.

Half an hour afterwards they sent the dying man to hospital; and as they have given up drawing lots for Cielito, I will not bother you with the address of the theater.

Interpreter's Notebook

"The Lottery Ticket" can be very suspenseful when done well. The narrator is first person and of indeterminate age. It is probably safe to assume a person of mature years, since the event described seems to have taken place sometime in the fairly distant past. The narrator is probably a man, but a woman could be very effective.

Particular attention should be paid to the development of this narrator's personality. There should be some trace of Spanish accent, but not caricature. Also, our narrator has a good mind for detail, is in no hurry, and is, as the first lines suggest, quite authoritative. The interpreter must enjoy describing Cielito and the reactions to her. Treat this like "soft-core" pornography.

Chapter 9. Reading Drama

KEY CONCEPTS

Character projection

Reading stage directions

Moving the characters around

The successful reading of drama is one of the great satisfactions encountered by the interpreter. Of the three basic genres or types of literature, drama is the most clearly designed for performance. As with all things developed for a specific purpose, this design for performance creates problems as well as opportunities. Most playwrights write with the theater in mind. That is, they imagine how the finished product will look in performance. They reveal their conception in their stage directions and other materials which accompany the play.

Playwrights have basically the same purposes as other writers. They feel that they have something worth expressing: a point of view, an emotion, an observation. As their means of expression they choose language, and as their medium of expression they choose drama. To get a clear grasp of the problems which will need solving, the interpreter must ask some questions. What are the essential differences between drama and the other forms of literature—poetry and prose? What are the differences between theatrical performance and interpretive performance? And then there is the question which invariably comes up, even though it is somewhat counterproductive: How does the interpreter differ from the actor?

Of course, these questions cannot really be handled separately. The answers to all of them are interrelated and flow from the same basic concepts. Some of the differences between drama and the other forms of literature are quite obvious. For example, in drama there is a total dependence on dialogue to reveal the circumstances and events of the story. Another obvious distinction is the absence in drama of a narrative voice, at least in most theatrical presentations.

There are some obvious similarities as well. Because of the attention to events, drama is narrative in character, and it is also generally chronological. Much of what was discussed in the preceding chapter concerning narrative prose is applicable to drama. In fact, the interpreter should be firmly grounded in narrative prose before attempting drama.

The essential conceptual difference between drama and other forms of literature lies in its relationship with the audience. Drama is an eavesdropping medium. It is designed in such a way that the audience comes to know the circumstances and events of the story because the audience is endowed, through theatrical convention, with the uncanny supernatural ability to peer, undetected, through one wall in a four-walled room, or to be present on the periphery of an outdoor scene without being heard or seen. Drama places its audience in the position of a third-person narrator, viewing the events from the outside without taking part in them.

When drama is performed in the conventional way, several support mechanisms—lights, scenery, costumes, makeup—are brought into play in order to create an illusion of reality. Each character in the play is represented by a separate performer, whose task it is to portray that character as completely as possible. For the duration of the play the audience must believe that the performer *is* the character, and should not see the performer at all.

An interpreter, faced with the prospect of performing a dramatic scene, does not have at his or her disposal any of the support mechanisms necessary to produce the conventional effects. Moreover, the interpreter lacks not only the conventional lights, scenery, costumes, props, and makeup, but also the company of other performers. When there is dialogue between two or more characters, the interpreter must say all the lines. Since we as interpreters cannot reproduce the effects dictated by normal theatrical conventions, we abandon them.

The interpreter replaces the abandoned theatrical conventions with new ones—interpretive conventions. These interpretive conventions produce an effect quite unlike what is usually seen on the stage, but certainly no less interesting or effective. In the interpretive performance, the audience has the opportunity to examine a play in detail. Free of distractions which might cover flaws, the language of the drama is laid bare, and thus rises or falls of its own accord. An explanation of these interpretive conventions will be given later in this chapter.

In the same way that we abandon the conventions because they won't work for our purposes, we also abandon the actor. Many actors are fine interpreters, and vice versa. In order to be a successful performer of either type, one has to be grounded in the same basic training. Both actors and interpreters must be able to use their voices and bodies effectively; they must develop emotional storehouses which can be called upon to give the proper reality to the words they say. But actors never tell a story. They live in the present tense and are always part of the story. While conscious of their audience, they rarely address them directly. They sense them somewhere in the blackness and shape the nuances of their performance to please them. The actor becomes a character who relates only to other characters who inhabit the make-believe world which has been created on the stage.

Interpreters always tell a story. They live primarily in the past tense. The circumstances and events laid out before the audience come from memory and reflection. Most often, interpreters are not a part of the story; and when they are, as in a first-person narration, it is a story which has been played out sometime in the past. They are not only conscious of their audience, but also confront them directly, visibly, and interact with them. The interpreter becomes a narrator in the real world, who describes characters and events as they filter through his or her consciousness. There are no other characters to relate to; the interpreter relates to the audience alone.

STRUCTURE

Plays follow the same basic structural plan as narrative prose. There is a beginning which is generally expository, introduces characters, and sets up the given circumstances. The middle develops the relationships between the characters and plays out the conflicts. In the classical sense, this middle part is termed the *rising action*. This rising action ultimately reaches a peak, called the *climax*, and then heads downward as the conflicts are resolved.

When plays are performed on a stage in the conventional manner, they have a rhythm and tempo which grows out of the variations of conflict, tension, and the interaction of the characters. The interpreter cannot produce this same tempo. The interpretive reading must be paced differently from the staged version. More time is needed to set the scene and to move from character to character. The way to accomplish the right pace will be discussed further on in the chapter, when we focus on technique.

While similar in structure to narrative, plays have some unique features as well. The average play takes only around 2 hours to perform from beginning to end. Yet, most plays leave the audience with the feeling that they have had a much fuller experience. This impression is accomplished, in part, by frequently changing scene and continually juxtaposing the characters in different arrangements. The interpreter looking for a cut version to use for performance should understand the structural element called the *french scene*. The beginning and ending of a french scene is determined by the raising and lowering of the curtain (or the lights), the entrance or exit of a character, or the occurrence of some extraordinary effect. A single french scene is generally the right length for classroom presentation, and has a logical beginning and ending. Several examples of french scenes are included in the selections at the end of this chapter.

Perhaps the difference in the presentation of a stage production and interpretive drama can be summarized in this way. In the normal stage performance, the drama is played out in total in front of the audience. The characters, the scenery, the action—these are all provided. Thus, the experience of an audience with a stage production is shaped almost entirely by the actor's, director's, and designer's conception of the play.

In the interpretive performance, the actual visualization of the drama takes place in the audience's imagination. The characters, scenery, and action which they experience are only set in motion by the interpretive artist. Each member of the audience brings a great deal of himself or herself to the performance. This high degree of involvement on the part of the audience makes the characters and events more personal and allows each member of the audience to shape the experience uniquely.

BASIC TECHNIQUES

The two essential problems of technique which the interpreter of drama faces at the outset are the projection of scene and the projection of character. These elements of drama must be handled very differently than in a conventional stage production.

PROJECTION OF SCENE

As we noted above, the interpreter does not enjoy the support of costumes, scenery, props, and lights to set the stage and orient the audience to the physical life of the scene. Nonetheless, the audience must have not only a clear conception of what the scene looks like but also the historical context in which the scene occurs. Since the interpreter cannot show these things, they must be told to the audience. The voice that sets the scene and fills the audience in on events and action which they cannot see is the voice of the *dramatic narrator.*

As in all other forms of interpretation, the narrator is physically present in the interpretation of drama. The difference between this type of narrator and others lies in the fact that the interpreter of drama must, in a sense, participate in the creation of the narrative material to accompany the dramatic performance. For example, if the scene chosen comes from a portion of the play which follows several other important scenes, the interpreter must create a synopsis of the preceding events and deliver it to the audience as part of the introduction. The audience must be mentally prepared to enter the action at the point the interpreter picks it up.

In addition, the scenery (which is not present) must be described, as well as all important props. The more carefully the interpreter sets the scene, the more able the audience becomes to visualize the scene taking place. The scenic elements of a play are extremely important in setting the mood and tone. By using good descriptive language and sound technique, the interpreter can enhance the audience's perception. This introductory material should not be treated as if it were just something tacked onto the scene, but rather as an integral part of the performance. Remember, you are performing as soon as you come into view, so make the most of it.

If the historical context of the play is important to its understanding, this also must be conveyed before the scene begins. At the very least, the audience must be told what the characters are wearing.

Another function of the dramatic narrator is to read the *stage directions*. The amount of stage directions that are present in a scene varies widely. However, when they do occur, they almost always describe an action that is essential to the audience's understanding of what is happening. The interpreter must present this material as a good third-person or omniscient narrator would: with directness, spontaneity, and realism.

The manner in which stage directions are printed in most scripts requires that the interpreter expand them for presentation. Publishers tend to save ink and space when it comes to stage directions, so they leave out all but the essential words: "Moves left, puts hat on table, sits." No interpreter, no matter how skillful, could read such directions without sounding like a grade B Hollywood version of an Indian. The directions might be expanded as follows: "George moves across the room to the left. He places his hat on the dining room table and sits in one of the chairs."

In summary, when reading drama, the interpreter also becomes, in part, a writer. The materials which would normally be seen by the audience, and, therefore, taken for granted by the playwright, are missing. The careful construction of essential introductory materials, along with the expansion and thoughtful presentation of the stage directions, will project the scene into the audience's imagination.

PROJECTION OF CHARACTER

In Chapter 7, the technique of *character sketching* was introduced. Those basic ideas will be expanded upon here in relation to presenting drama. Drama, most simply defined, is the interaction of characters in a given set of circumstances. The interpreter does not have many narrative elements to present which help in the description of character. Some delineation of character can be done in the introduction, and some stage directions are helpful. But the problem of presenting character is primarily one of *doing* character rather than *talking about* character.

We should already be aware of the limitations placed on the interpreter who is *doing* character. The lack of sets, props, and other performers to interact with creates a unique situation. First, if there are two characters in your scene, you have to play them both. Second, it is quite possible that at least one of your characters will not be the same sex that you are. Third, one or more of the characters could be older or younger than you. Age, which is difficult enough for young actors to project with the aid of costumes and makeup, becomes even more difficult for the interpreter, who must work without such things.

The interpreter should approach the problem of characterization in drama in precisely the same way as when it occurs in narrative prose—as a sketch rather than a full characterization. Although it is not obvious, the interpreter remains a narrator telling a story, rather than *becoming* two or more characters.

When reading drama, the interpreter becomes an omniscient narrator; the scene becomes narrative. The performance begins, as do all narratives, with the narrator setting the scene and introducing the characters. Then the narrator presents the two or more characters and demonstrates how they interact. Periodically, a stage direction will cause the narrator to suspend the demonstration and return to direct contact with the audience. *It is* **Gottlieb's Eighteenth Principle** *that states: The oral interpreter of drama never loses his identity as a narrator.*

As the narrator of events, then, the interpreter depicts the interplay of the characters and keeps them separate one from the other by sketching a spearate character for each. The sketch is accomplished by selecting a few specific traits of voice, posture, and accent which are appropriate for the character, and which will project that character to the audience—make that character immediately identifiable.

The dramatic narrator never has to worry about the sex of the characters conflicting with the sex of the reader, since the reader and the characters maintain separate identities. If you are a woman, and you witness an interesting dialogue which takes place between two men, and you repeat that dialogue at a subsequent time to a group of your friends, giving as much character to the men as you can in order to bring the scene to life, no one will say that you shouldn't tell that story because you're the wrong sex.

THE PROJECTIVE TECHNIQUE

The interpreter must apply technique in order to keep the narrative elements separate from the dialogue, and to aid in keeping the characters separate and distinguishable from one another. The key to effective projection of character relationships is to make it appear as if the characters are really addressing each other.

When we sketch characters for each other, as we do all the time in relating events from our own lives, it is natural to turn our eyes away from each other. If you monitor yourself carefully (as any creative artist should), you will notice that when you relate an incident to your friends that involves dialogue, you won't deliver that dialogue to your friends, but rather somewhere off to the side. You do this for a variety of reasons. First, the material is coming from memory, and any distractions could make you forget. Second, you unconsciously want to create theatrical or aesthetic distance—to put your friends in the position of being objective observers. Third, whatever action there is takes place between the characters being described, and any interaction with the audience would be inappropriate. However, prior to the dialogue, and intermittently throughout, you will probably reestablish direct contact with your friends in order to amplify or comment on the dialogue, or to receive feedback. This model is precisely what the interpreter follows when reading drama, with the application of some specific techniques.

First of all, the interpreter views performance space differently from the way it is normally conceptualized in the theatre. The diagram here illustrates the interpreter's perspective.

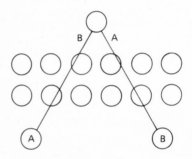

The interpreter here is reading a two-character scene and is positioned in front of the audience in normal fashion. The two characters in the scene are placed behind the audience. When Character A speaks to Character B, the interpreter faces Character B and projects the characteristics of A. When B responds, the interpreter shifts and looks at A, this time projecting the characteristics of B. This shifting technique can be extraordinarily effective for two-character scenes, since it bolsters the impression that the characters are really speaking to one another. However, the system breaks down when more characters are added. With more than two characters, the shifts become random, and the interpreter has to depend more on actual character elements—voice, posture, accent—to keep the characters separate in the audience's mind.

The key factors in character shifting are these. Always play through the audience at or about eye level. Always appear as though you are speaking to someone that the audience can't see. Make the shifts as crisp as possible. One of the by-products of an interpretive performance of drama is that the audience gets to watch a metamorphosis as one character is dropped by the narrator and another picked up.

The effect of the character shift can be enhanced by allowing the newly assumed character a split-second reaction to what the dropped character just said. Don't pace the scene too rapidly. It cannot be played out at the same tempo as in a stage production. Besides, the audience has much to watch and adjust to, so while it may seem slow to you, it is moving fast enough for them.

SKETCHING PHYSICAL ACTION

Like all good storytellers, the interpreter will want to prompt the audience's visualization of a scene through the use of physical action. Gestures and other body language which are appropriate in the sketching of character are always desirable. They add dimension and animation to a performance which otherwise might appear stiff and wordy, no matter how well thought out. However, the interpreter is without props. A sword cannot be drawn. A gun cannot be pointed. The interpreter is also without other performers. So there is no hand to shake, face to slap, or cheek to stroke. To act these things out, as in pantomime, is always a failure. Never try to substitute a complete action for something that will have greater impact if left to the audience's imagination. *It is* **Gottlieb's Nineteenth Principle** *that states: Never place anything within the sight line of the audience which cannot actually be seen.*

The interpreter sketches physical action. When one of the characters pulls a gun, the interpreter makes a sudden move with his hand toward an imaginary holster. This move is never completed. A stage direction, or the next line, will serve to complete the information that the gun has been pulled. The initiating movement will set the audience's imagination in motion, and they will experience the complete action even though it has not actually taken place. In the meantime, the interpreter has returned hand and arm to a neutral position, prepared for the next action.

It will require some practice until the sketching of action becomes comfortable. But, the interpreter must think of this technique as one of those circumstances where less is more. As interpreters, we are working on the audience members' minds, not their eyes.

One prop which the interpreter always has can be used effectively in some circumstances. In the hands of a skilled interpreter, the book, which contains the text being presented, can represent many things. It can be knocked upon as a door. It can be a mirror for admiring one's reflection. It can be a wall to be peered over. I can remember watching with awe, as an undergraduate, while my coach, Alvina Kraus, cradled and rocked a book in her arms, and in my imagination brought it to life as a baby.

Such techniques can become gimmickly if overused. But, the skillful weaving of the text into the action of the performance will make it less intrusive.

CHARACTER MOVEMENT

There are times in the performance of drama when it is effective to have one or more of the characters change position. For example, one character may be pursuing the other. Movement is accomplished in two ways. One way is to have the speaking character move toward the silent character who is placed at the back of the room. Then, when the characters shift, the pursued character moves backward, as if to get away. These must be small moves, however, since the interpreter is only suggesting the action of the scene. Besides, large moves of this type would soon remove you from the performance area. The other way to sketch movement involves moving the silent character. While one character speaks to the other, the interpreter's eyes follow an imaginary line along the wall. In this way, the audience members will be able to keep the various character positions sorted out in their minds.

In sum, the reading of drama requires a great deal from the interpreter. Expository materials must be created by the interpreter in order to set the scene and bring the audience to the proper moment in the movements of events. Stage directions, where they occur, must be developed into pieces of narrative prose. Characters must be carefully sketched and kept separate in the audience's mind.

The beginning interpreter should usually not attempt scenes with more than two characters. However, scenes where there is a third character with a small but distinctive role can be accomplished with great effort. It is not recommended that interpreters at any level of competence attempt scenes with more than three characters. Such multicharacter scenes simply deteriorate into a circus; and, even if the interpreter is successful in differentiating four or five characters, the virtuosity of the performance would remove all attention from the text—an undesirable end.

There are forms of interpretation which allow for the presentation of many characters through the use of more than one interpreter. Most commonly called *Readers Theatre,* this technique is discussed in the next chapter.

QUESTIONS FOR STUDY AND DISCUSSION

1

What are the essential differences between drama and the other forms of literature?

2

How does the interpreter differ from the actor?

3

What are the two essential problems which the interpreter faces
when reading drama?

4

Why does the interpreter read the stage directions?

5

What is meant by "As interpreters, we are working on the
audience members' minds, not their eyes."

SUGGESTED ACTIVITIES

1

Relate an experience to the class from your own life which
involves a conversation between two people other than yourself.

2

Practice your projective technique by taping pictures or other
representations of characters to the back wall, and reading
directly and specifically to the appropriate character.

Selections for Analysis and Performance

From ELECTRA
SOPHOCLES

Electra and Chrysothemis are the daughters of Agamemnon. When he returned from the Trojan War, Agamemnon was slain by his wife, Clytemnestra, and her lover, Aegisthos, who now rule as king and queen.

Electra has hopes that her brother, Orestes, will return and avenge his father's death. She nurses her anger and hatred toward Clytemnestra and Aegisthos, and spends her days openly denouncing them.

Crysothemis is younger and does not possess Electra's strength of purpose. She has capitulated and is satisfied to live well and leave things as they are. In this scene she comes to Electra and warns her what will happen if she doesn't restrain her hatred.

It is important to keep the contrast between the two women clear throughout. Also, the Chorus Leader must be separated either through voice or positioning. Don't neglect Chrysothemis: she is as important as Electra in this scene.

LEADER

Tell me, is Aegisthos near? Or has he left the house?

ELECTRA

He has left, of course. How should I be out,
If he were near?

LEADER

If he is away, then,
I may speak further with you?

ELECTRA

Yes, you may speak.

LEADER

Let me enquire about your brother.
Is he coming? Delaying? I must know.

ELECTRA

He says he is coming but does not come.

LEADER

A man with a great work likes to delay.

ELECTRA

When I saved him I did not delay.

LEADER

Take courage. He is the man to help those he loves.

ELECTRA

I trust him, or I should not still be alive.

LEADER

Hush for now, hush.
Chrysothemis is at the door, your own sister.
She is bringing offerings for the gods of the dead.

[*Enter* Chrysothemis *with offerings. She comes from the palace.*]

CHRYSOTHEMIS

Sister, what are you proclaiming out here at the door?
Won't you learn, after all this time
Not to pamper a helpless anger?
And you must know that I too suffer
And that if I had the strength
I too should show them what I think of them.
But in foul weather I lower my sails,
I never threaten when I am helpless.
If you would only do the same! . . . Well,
What I say is immoral, of course,
And you are right. And yet, if I am to breathe freely,
I must listen to what *they* say.

ELECTRA

Horrible; the own child of such a father

231

And you forget him for that mother!
Your moralizing of course is from her,
None of it yours. Well, choose: either be foolish,
Or else be very prudent, and forget
Those who have been dear to you. Consider:
You say you'd show your hatred if you had the strength,
But you give me no help, though I am given
Completely to the cause of vengeance; you dissuade me even.
So we must be cowards too in our misery?
But tell me, what should I gain by silence?
Or I'll tell you. Have I life now? Little;
And yet enough, for I harrow them
To the honor of the dead, if the dead know honor;
While you are a hater in word only,
Living in deed with your father's killers.
I would not yield so—
If they offered me everything that you enjoy,
I would not so yield. For you
Let the tables of life be richly spread,
Let them overflow. For my sole pasturage
I would be unoffending, I do not crave
Your honors—nor would you, if you were wise.
You might have been your father's: be your mother's:
Belong to her who everyone knows is evil,
The betrayer of your dying father and your own kin!

LEADER

By the fear of the gods, no anger!
If you will learn from her, and she from you,
You may still profit from these words.

CHRYSOTHEMIS

I am accustomed to what she says, my friends,
And I should never have approached her now,
Had I not heard of a greater misfortune coming
To end her mourning.

ELECTRA

What? Tell me of a greater
And I say no more.

CHRYSOTHEMIS

I'll tell you all I heard.
Unless you stop wailing, they will send you in
Where you can not see the light of the sun:
Far away and under a low roof
You shall sing your sorrows. Think, therefore;
Do not blame me later, when you suffer,
But think in time.

ELECTRA

And this they really plan?

CHRYSOTHEMIS

At once; as soon as Aegisthos returns.

ELECTRA

Well then, let him come soon.

CHRYSOTHEMIS

What, are you mad?

ELECTRA

If that's what he intends, let him come soon!

CHRYSOTHEMIS

To bring you suffering? What are you thinking of?

ELECTRA

Of escaping you all.

CHRYSOTHEMIS

Your life here
Means nothing to you?

ELECTRA

How beautiful it is!

CHRYSOTHEMIS

It might have been if you had learned wisdom.

ELECTRA

Teach me no treachery to those I love.

CHRYSOTHEMIS

I don't. I teach you to yield to the strong.

ELECTRA

Go. Fawn. Fawn on the strong. I can not.

CHRYSOTHEMIS

Still, it would be well not to fall through *folly*.

ELECTRA

I will fall—if I must, to honor my father.

CHRYSOTHEMIS

But you know that our father understands.

ELECTRA

That's what traitors say.

CHRYSOTHEMIS

Then you will not listen
To what *I* say?

ELECTRA

No. I have my wits still.

CHRYSOTHEMIS

Then I shall go about my own business.

ELECTRA

Where are you going? For whom are those offerings?

CHRYSOTHEMIS

My mother sent me with them to our father's grave.

ELECTRA

What, to the grave of her mortal enemy?

CHRYSOTHEMIS

Of the man she slaughtered, as you like to say.

ELECTRA

From whom or what did that inspiration come?

CHRYSOTHEMIS

From something she saw in the night, I think.

ELECTRA

O fathergods! Come! Help!

CHRYSOTHEMIS

Do you take courage
From her fear?

ELECTRA

If you would tell me what she saw,
I should answer that.

CHRYSOTHEMIS

I know very little to tell.

ELECTRA

But tell me, tell! It is the little things
By which we rise or fall.

CHRYSOTHEMIS

They say
She saw our father with her in the light of day.
On the hearth he was, planting his sceptre
Which Aegisthos holds now. From the sceptre grew
A swelling branch which brought at last
The whole land of Mycenae under its shadow.
This I heard
From one who heard her tell her dream to the sun.
It is all I know
Except that it was in fear she sent me.

Now, by the gods I beg you, listen! Don't fall through folly!
It will be the worse for you if you push me away!

ELECTRA

Sister, let none of these things touch his tomb.
It is against piety, against wisdom,
To offer our father gifts from that woman.
Give them to the wind, or bury them deep in the dust
Where they can never reach our father's bed;

When she is dead, there let her find them.
Only a woman of brass, an iron woman,
Would offer her murder-victim gifts.
Do you suppose the dead man would receive them gladly?
From her who killed him in dishonor and cruelty,
After mutilation washing the blood-stained head
To cleanse herself of murder? No! throw them away,
And cut a lock of hair from your head and one from mine,
And give him also this poor thing, all I have,
This plain and unembroidered belt; then fall on your knees
And pray that a helper may rise for us
Out of the earth, against our enemies: pray
That the young Orestes may come in his strength
To trample them underfoot, so that with fuller hands than these
We may make offering. I think, I think
It was he who sent this dream, prophetic of evil.
There help yourself in this, my sister,
And me, and him, the dearest mortal:
Our father lying underground.

LEADER

This girl speaks wisely. You, my friend,
If you are prudent, will do as she requests.

CHRYSOTHEMIS

I will. For it is right to join for action,
Not wrangle back and forth. But in the name of the gods,
Let there be silence among you, friends,
While I make this effort! If my mother hears
I shall have bitter things to endure.

[*Exit* CHRYSOTHEMIS.]

From CYRANO DE BERGERAC
EDMOND ROSTAND

Cyrano is the greatest swordsman of his time. He also has an extraordinarily large nose. He doesn't like remarks about his nose and has killed many men who have insulted him. Cyrano is in love with his beautiful cousin, Roxane. However, Roxane has told him she is in love with a young cadet named Christian.

In this scene Cyrano and Christian meet for the first time. Christian insults Cyrano by making fun of his nose. But Cyrano, not wanting to offend Roxane by killing her lover, is placed in a difficult situation.

The scene lends itself to physical illustration. Be active and keep the level of tension high. Enjoy saying the combinations of words.

(They all draw up their stools and group themselves around Cyrano, eagerly. Cyrano *places himself astride of a chair, his arms on the back of it.)*
I marched on, all alone
To meet those devils. Overhead, the moon
Hung like a gold watch at the fob of heaven,
Till suddenly some Angel rubbed a cloud,
As it might be his handkerchief, across
The shining crystal, and—the night came down.
No lamps in those back streets—It was so dark—
Mordious! You could not see beyond—

CHRISTIAN

Your nose.
(Silence. Every man slowly rises to his feet. They look at Cyrano *almost with terror. He has stopped short, utterly astonished. Pause.)*

CYRANO

Who is that man there?

A CADET

(In a low voice)

A recruit—arrived

This morning.

CYRANO
(Takes a step toward Christian.*)*

A recruit—

CARBON

(In a low voice)

His name is Christian

De Neuvil—

CYRANO

(Suddenly motionless)

Oh . . .

(He turns pale, flushes, makes a movement as if to throw himself upon CHRISTIAN.)
                    I—

    (Controls himself, and goes on in a choking voice.)
                                        I see. Very well,
As I was saying—

            (With a sudden burst of rage)
                        Mordious! . . .

(He goes on in a natural tone.)

                                        It grew dark,
You could not see your hand before your eyes.
I marched on, thinking how, all for the sake
Of one old souse

(They slowly sit down, watching him.)

                            who wrote a bawdy song
Whenever he took—

                    CHRISTIAN
                A noseful—

(Everyone rises. CHRISTIAN *balances himself on two legs of his chair.)*

                        CYRANO
(Half strangled)

                                    —Took a notion.

Whenever he took a notion— For his sake,
I might antagonize some dangerous man,
One powerful enough to make me pay—

                        CHRISTIAN
Through the nose—

                        CYRANO
(Wipes the sweat from his forehead.)

                            —Pay the Piper. After all,
I thought, why am I putting in my—

                        CHRISTIAN
                                    Nose—

                        CYRANO
—My oar . . . Why am I putting in my oar?

The quarrel's none of mine. However—now
I am here, I may as well go through with it.
Come Gascon—do your duty!—Suddenly
A sword flashed in the dark. I caught it fair—

CHRISTIAN

On the nose—

CYRANO

On my blade. Before I knew it,
There I was—

CHRISTIAN

Rubbing noses—

CYRANO

(Pale and smiling)

Crossing swords
With half a score at once. I handed one—

CHRISTIAN

A nosegay—

CYRANO

(Leaping at him)

Ventre-Saint-Gris! . . .

*(The Gascons tumble over each other to get a good view. Arrived in front
of* CHRISTIAN, *who has not moved an inch,* CYRANO *masters himself again,
and continues.)*

He went down;
The rest gave way; I charged—

CHRISTIAN

Nose in the air—

CYRANO

I skewered two of them—disarmed a third—
Another lunged— Paf! And I countered—

CHRISTIAN

Pif!

CYRANO

(Bellowing)

TONNERRE! Out of here!—All of you!
(All the Cadets rush for the door.)

FIRST CADET

At last—

The old lion wakes!

CYRANO

All of you! Leave me here
Alone with that man!
(The lines following are heard brokenly in the confusion of getting through the door.)

SECOND CADET

Bigre! He'll have the fellow
Chopped into sausage—

RAGUENEAU

Sausage?—

THIRD CADET

Mince-meat, then—

One of your pies!—

RAGUENEAU

Am I pale? You look white
As a fresh napkin—

CARBON

(At the door)

Come!

FOURTH CADET

He'll never leave
Enough of him to—

FIFTH CADET

Why, it frightens me
To think of what will—

SIXTH CADET

(Closing the door)

                            Something horrible
Beyond imagination . . .

(They are all gone: some through the street door, some by the inner doors to right and left. A few disappear up the staircase. CYRANO *and* CHRISTIAN *stand face to face a moment, and look at each other.)*

CYRANO

        To my arms!

CHRISTIAN

Sir? . . .

CYRANO

     You have courage!

CHRISTIAN

                     Oh, that! . . .

CYRANO

                     You are brave—
That pleases me.

CHRISTIAN

     You mean? . . .

CYRANO

                    Do you not know
I am her brother? Come!

CHRISTIAN

               Whose?—

CYRANO

               Hers—Roxane!

CHRISTIAN

Her . . . brother? You? *(Hurries to him.)*

CYRANO

              Her cousin. Much the same.

CHRISTIAN

And she has told you? . . .

CYRANO

Everything.

CHRISTIAN

She loves me?

CYRANO

Perhaps.

CHRISTIAN

(Takes both his hands.)

My dear sir—more than I can say,
I am honored—

CYRANO

This is rather sudden.

CHRISTIAN

Please

Forgive me—

CYRANO

(Holds him at arm's length, looking at him.)

Why, he is a handsome devil.
This fellow!

CHRISTIAN

On my honor—if you knew
How much I have admired—

CYRANO

Yes, yes—and all

Those Noses which—

CHRISTIAN

Please! I apologize.

CYRANO

(Change of tone)

Roxane expects a letter—

CHRISTIAN

Not from me?—

CYRANO

Yes. Why not?

CHRISTIAN

Once I write, that ruins all!

CYRANO

And why?

CHRISTIAN

Because . . . because I am a fool!
Stupid enough to hang myself!

CYRANO

But no—

You are no fool; you call yourself a fool,
There's proof enough in that. Besides, you did not
Attack me like a fool.

CHRISTIAN

Bah! Any one

Can pick a quarrel. Yes, I have a sort
Of rough and ready soldier's tongue. I know
That. But with any woman—paralyzed,
Speechless, dumb. I can only look at them.
Yet sometimes, when I go away, their eyes . . .

CYRANO

Why not their hearts, if you should wait and see?

CHRISTIAN

No. I am one of those— I know—those men
Who never can make love.

CYRANO

Strange. . . . Now it seems

I, if I gave my mind to it, I might

Perhaps make love well.

CHRISTIAN

                                              Oh, if I had words

To say what I have here!

CYRANO

                                              If I could be

A handsome little Musketeer with eyes!—

CHRISTIAN

Besides—you know Roxane—how sensitive—
One rough word, and the sweet illusion—gone!

CYRANO

I wish you might be my interpreter.

CHRISTIAN

I wish I had your wit—

CYRANO

                                              Borrow it, then!—

Your beautiful young manhood—lend me that,
And we two make one hero of romance!

CHRISTIAN

What?

CYRANO

                      Would you dare repeat to her the words

I gave you, day by day?

CHRISTIAN

                      You mean?

CYRANO

                                                          I mean

Roxane shall have no disillusionment!
Come, shall we win her both together? Take
The soul within this learthern jack of mine,
And breathe it into you?

(Touches him on the breast.)

So—there's my heart

Under your velvet, now!

                    CHRISTIAN

                              But— Cyrano!—

            CYRANO

But— Christian, why not?

            CHRISTIAN

                              I am afraid—

            CYRANO

                                   I know—

Afraid that when you have her all alone,
You lose all. Have no fear. It is yourself
She loves—give her yourself put into words—
My words, upon your lips!

            CHRISTIAN

                    But . . . but your eyes! . . .

They burn like—

            CYRANO

            Will you? . . . Will you?

            CHRISTIAN

                              Does it mean

So much to you?

        CYRANO *(Beside himself)*

            It means—

(Recovers, changes tone.)

                    A Comedy,

A situation for a poet! Come.
Shall we collaborate? I'll be your cloak
Of darkness, your enchanted sword, your ring
To charm the fairy Princess!

            CHRISTIAN

                    But the letter—

I cannot write—

CYRANO

Oh yes, the letter.

(He takes from his pocket the letter which he has written.)

Here.

CHRISTIAN

What is this?

CYRANO

All there; all but the address.

CHRISTIAN

I—

CYRANO

Oh, you may send it. It will serve.

CHRISTIAN

But why

Have you done this?

CYRANO

I have amused myself

As we all do, we poets—writing vows
To Chloris, Phyllis—any pretty name—
You might have had a pocketful of them!
Take it, and turn to facts my fantasies—
I loosed these loves like doves into the air;
Give them a habitation and a home.
Here, take it— You will find me all the more
Eloquent, being insincere! Come!

CHRISTIAN

First,

There must be a few changes here and there—
Written at random, can it fit Roxane?

CYRANO

Like her own glove.

CHRISTIAN

No, but—

CYRANO

My son, have faith—

Faith in the love of women for themselves—

Roxane will know this letter for her own!

CHRISTIAN

(Throws himself into the arms of CYRANO. *They stand embraced.)*

My friend!

(The door up stage opens a little. A Cadet steals in.)

THE CADET

Nothing. A silence like the tomb . . .

I hardly dare look— *(He sees the two.)*

Wha-at?

(The other Cadets crowd in behind him and see.)

THE CADETS

No!—No!

SECOND CADET

Mon dieu!

THE MUSKETEER

(Slaps his knee.)

Well, well, well!

CARBON

Here's our devil . . . Christianized!

Offend one nostril, and he turns the other.

THE MUSKETEER

Now we are allowed to talk about his nose! *(Calls)*

Hey, Lise! Come here— *(Affectedly)*

Snf! What a horrid smell!

What is it? . . .

(Plants himself in front of CYRANO, *and looks at his nose in an impolite manner.)*

You ought to know about such things;

What seems to have died around here?

CYRANO

(Knocks him backward over a bench.)

Cabbage-heads!

(Joy. The Cadets have found their old CYRANO *again. General disturbance.)*

(Curtain)

From A VIEW FROM THE BRIDGE
ARTHUR MILLER

Catherine is an orphan living with her aunt and uncle. Over the years Eddie Carbone, the uncle, has developed a more than natural attachment to her. Catherine has been going out with a young illegal alien whom Eddie and Beatrice, his wife, have given refuge in their home. Just before this scene begins, Eddie tells Catherine that Rudolpho, the young immigrant, is trying to marry her just to get his papers and stay in the United States. Beatrice is concerned about Eddie's attachment to Catherine and confronts her in this scene.

BEATRICE

Listen, Catherine.

*(*CATHERINE *halts, turns to her sheepishly.)*

What are you going to do with yourself?

CATHERINE

I don't know.

BEATRICE

Don't tell me you don't know; you're not a baby any more, what are you going to do with yourself?

CATHERINE

He won't listen to me.

BEATRICE

I don't understand this. He's not your father, Catherine. I don't understand what's going on here.

CATHERINE

(as one who herself is trying to rationalize a buried impulse) What am I going to do, just kick him in the face with it?

BEATRICE

Look, honey, you wanna get married, or don't you wanna get married? What are you worried about, Katie?

CATHERINE

(*quietly, trembling*) I don't know B. It just seems wrong if he's against it so much.

BEATRICE

(*never losing her aroused alarm*) Sit down, honey, I want to tell you something. Here, sit down. Was there ever any fella he liked for you? There wasn't, was there?

CATHERINE

But he says Rodolpho's just after his papers.

BEATRICE

Look, he'll say anything. What does he care what he says? If it was a prince came here for you it would be no different. You know that, don't you?

CATHERINE

Yeah, I guess.

BEATRICE

So what does that mean?

CATHERINE

(*slowly turns her head to* BEATRICE) What?

BEATRICE

It means you gotta be your own self more. You still think you're a little girl, honey. But nobody else can make up your mind for you any more, you understand? You gotta give him to understand that he can't give you orders no more.

CATHERINE

Yeah, but how am I going to do that? He thinks I'm a baby.

BEATRICE

Because *you* think you're a baby. I told you fifty times already, you can't act the way you act. You still walk around in front of him in your slip—

CATHERINE

Well I forgot.

BEATRICE

Well you can't do it. Or like you sit on the edge of the bathtub talkin' to him when he's shavin' in his underwear.

CATHERINE

When'd I do that?

BEATRICE

I seen you in there this morning.

CATHERINE

Oh . . . well, I wanted to tell him something and I—

BEATRICE

I know, honey, But if you act like a baby and he be treatin' you like a baby. Like when he comes home sometimes you throw yourself at him like when you was twelve years old.

CATHERINE

Well I like to see him and I'm happy so I—

BEATRICE

Look, I'm not tellin' you what to do honey, but—

CATHERINE

No, you could tell me, B.! Gee, I'm all mixed up. See, I—He looks so sad now and it hurts me.

BEATRICE

Well look Katie, if it's goin' to hurt you so much you're gonna end up an old maid here.

CATHERINE

No!

BEATRICE

I'm tellin' you, I'm not makin' a joke. I tried to tell you a couple of times in the last year or so. That's why I was so happy you were going to go out and get work, you wouldn't be here so much, you'd be a little more independent. I mean it. It's wonderful for a whole family to love each other, but you're a grown woman and you're in the same house with a grown man. So you'll act different now, heh?

CATHERINE

Yeah, I will. I'll remember.

BEATRICE

Because it ain't only up to him, Katie, you understand? I told him the same thing already.

CATHERINE

(quickly) What?

BEATRICE

That he should let you go. But, you see, if only I tell him, he thinks I'm just bawlin' him out, or maybe I'm jealous or somethin', you know?

CATHERINE

(astonished) He said you was jealous?

BEATRICE

No, I'm just sayin' maybe that's what he thinks. *(She reaches over to* CATHERINE'S *hand; with a strained smile.)* You think I'm jealous of you honey?

CATHERINE

No! It's the first I thought of it.

BEATRICE

(with a quiet sad laugh) Well you should have thought of it before . . . but I'm not. We'll be all right. Just give him to understand; you don't have to fight, you're just—You're a woman, that's all, and you got a nice boy, and now the time came when you said good-by. All right?

CATHERINE

(strangely moved at the prospect) All right . . . If I can.

BEATRICE

Honey . . . you gotta.

*(*CATHERINE, *sensing now an imperious demand, turns with some fear, with*

a discovery, to BEATRICE. *She is at the edge of tears, as though a familiar world had shattered.)*

CATHERINE

Okay.

From PYGMALION
GEORGE BERNARD SHAW

This is a play about transformation. Henry Higgins, on a bet, takes a common flower girl from the street and, by correcting her speech and manners, is able to pass her off as a duchess to the polite society of the period.

This scene takes place at the very end of the play. Higgins has won his bet, and the question is, what becomes of Eliza now? Shaw's characters duel with words. Keep the language crisp and pointed. Try an English accent.

ELIZA *goes out on the balcony to avoid being alone with* HIGGINS. *He rises and joins her there. She immediately comes back into the room and makes for the door; but he goes along the balcony and get his back to the door before she reaches it.*

HIGGINS

Well, Eliza, youve had a bit of your own back, as you call it. Have you had enough? and are you going to be reasonable? Or do you want any more?

LIZA

You want me back only to pick up your slippers and put up with your tempers and fetch and carry for you.

HIGGINS

I havent said I wanted you back at all.

LIZA

Oh, indeed. Then what are we talking about?

HIGGINS

About you, not about me. If you come back I shall treat you just as I have always treated you. I cant change my nature; and I dont intend to change my manners. My manners are exactly the same as Colonel Pickering's.

LIZA

Thats not true. He treats a flower girl as if she was a duchess.

HIGGINS

And I treat a duchess as if she was a flower girl.

LIZA

I see [*She turns away composedly, and sits on the ottoman, facing the window*]. The same to everybody.

HIGGINS

Just so.

LIZA

Like father.

HIGGINS

[*grinning, a little taken down*] Without accepting the comparison at all points, Eliza, its quite true that your father is not a snob, and that he will be quite at home in any station of life to which his eccentric destiny may call him. [*Seriously*] The great secret, Eliza, is not having bad manners or good manners or any other particular sort of manners, but having the same manner for all human souls: in short, behaving as if you were in Heaven, where there are no third-class carriages, and one soul is as good as another.

LIZA

Amen. You are a born preacher.

HIGGINS

[*irritated*] The question is not whether I treat you rudely, but whether you ever heard me treat anyone else better.

LIZA

[*with sudden sincerity*] I dont care how you treat me. I dont mind your swearing at me. I shouldnt mind a black eye. Ive had one before this. But [*standing up and facing him*] I wont be passed over.

HIGGINS

Then get out of my way; for I wont stop for you. You talk about me as if I were a motor bus.

LIZA

So you are a motor bus: all bounce and go, and no consideration for anyone. But I can do without you: dont think I cant.

HIGGINS

I know you can. I told you you could.

LIZA

[*wounded, getting away from him to the other side of the ottoman with her face to the hearth*] I know you did, you brute. You wanted to get rid of me.

HIGGINS

Liar.

LIZA

Thank you. [*She sits down with dignity*]

HIGGINS

You never asked yourself, I suppose, whether *I* could do without you.

LIZA

[*earnestly*] Dont you try to get round me. Youll have to do without me.

HIGGINS

[*arrogant*] I can do without anybody. I have my own soul: my own spark of divine fire. But [*with sudden humility*] I shall miss you, Eliza. [*He sits down near her on the ottoman*] I have learnt something from your idiotic notions: I confess that humbly and gratefully. And I have grown accustomed to your voice and appearance. I like them, rather.

LIZA

Well, you have both of them on your gramophone and in your book of photographs. When you feel lonely without me, you can turn the machine on. It's got no feelings to hurt.

HIGGINS

I cant turn your soul on. Leave me those feelings; and you can take away the voice and the face. They are not you.

LIZA

Oh, you are a devil. You can twist the heart in a girl as easy as some could

---

twist her arms to hurt her. Mrs Pearce warned me. Time and again she has wanted to leave you; and you always got round her at the last minute. And you dont care a bit for her. And you dont care a bit for me.

HIGGINS

I care for life, for humanity; and you are a part of it that has come my way and been built into my house. What more can you or anyone ask?

LIZA

I wont care for anybody that doesnt care for me.

HIGGINS

Commercial principles, Eliza. Like [*reproducing her Covent Garden pronunciation with professional exactness*] s'yollin voylets [*selling violets*], isnt it?

LIZA

Dont sneer at me. It's mean to sneer at me.

HIGGINS

I have never sneered in my life. Sneering doesnt become either the human face or the human soul. I am expressing my righteous contempt for Commercialism. I dont and wont trade in affection. You call me a brute because you couldnt buy a claim on me by fetching my slippers and finding my spectacles. You were a fool: I think a woman fetching a man's slippers is a disgusting sight: did I ever fetch your slippers? I think a good deal more of you for throwing them in my face. No use slaving for me and then saying you want to be cared for: who cares for a slave? If you come back, come back for the sake of good fellowship; for youll get nothing else. Youve had a thousand times as much out of me as I have out of you; and if you dare to set up your little dog's tricks of fetching and carrying slippers against my creation of a Duchess Eliza, I'll slam the door in your silly face.

LIZA

What did you do it for if you didnt care for me?

HIGGINS

[*heartily*] Why, because it was my job.

LIZA

You never thought of the trouble it would make for me.

HIGGINS

Would the world ever have been made if its maker had been afraid of making trouble? Making life means making trouble. Theres only one way of escaping trouble; and thats killing things. Cowards, you notice, are always shrieking to have troublesome people killed.

LIZA

I'm no preacher: I dont notice things like that. I notice that you dont notice me.

HIGGINS

[*jumping up and walking about intolerantly*] Eliza: youre an idiot. I waste the treasures of my Miltonic mind by spreading them before you. Once for all, understand that I go my way and do my work without caring towpence what happens to either of us. I am not intimidated, like your father and your stepmother. So you can come back or go to the devil: which you please.

LIZA

What am I to come back for?

HIGGINS

[*bouncing up on his knees on the ottoman and leaning over it to her*] For the fun of it. Thats why I took you on.

LIZA

[*with averted face*] And you may throw me out tomorrow if I dont do everything you want me to?

HIGGINS

Yes; and you may walk out tomorrow if I dont do everything you want me to.

LIZA

And live with my stepmother?

HIGGINS

Yes, or sell flowers.

LIZA

Oh! if I only could go back to my flower basket! I should be independent of both you and father and all the world! Why did you take my independence from me? Why did I give it up? I'm a slave now, for all my fine clothes.

HIGGINS

Not a bit. I'll adopt you as my daughter and settle money on you if you like. Or would you rather marry Pickering?

LIZA

[*looking fiercely round at him*] I wouldnt marry you if you asked me; and youre nearer my age than what he is.

HIGGINS

[*gently*] Than he is: not "than what he is."

LIZA

[*losing her temper and rising*] I'll talk as I like. Youre not my teacher now.

HIGGINS

[*reflectively*] I dont suppose Pickering would, though. He's as confirmed an old bachelor as I am.

LIZA

Thats not what I want; and dont you think it. I've always had chaps enough wanting me that way. Freddy Hill writes to me twice and three times a day, sheets and sheets.

HIGGINS

[*disagreeably surprised*] Damn his impudence! [*He recoils and finds himself sitting on his heels*].

LIZA

He has a right to if he likes, poor lad. And he does love me.

HIGGINS

[*getting off the ottoman*] You have no right to encourage him.

LIZA

Every girl has a right to be loved.

HIGGINS

What! By fools like that?

LIZA

Freddy's not a fool. And if he's weak and poor and wants me, may be he'd make me happier than my betters that bully me and dont want me.

HIGGINS

Can he make anything of you? Thats the point.

LIZA

Perhaps I could make something of him. But I never thought of us making anything of one another; and you never think of anything else. I only want to be natural.

HIGGINS

In short, you want me to be as infatuated about you as Freddy? Is that it?

LIZA

No I dont. Thats not the sort of feeling I want from you. And dont you be too sure of yourself or of me. I could have been a bad girl if I'd liked. Ive seen more of some things than you, for all your learning. Girls like me can drag gentlemen down to make love to them easy enough. And they wish each other dead the next minute.

HIGGINS

Of course they do. Then what in thunder are we quarelling about?

LIZA

[*much troubled*] I want a little kindness. I know I'm a common ignorant girl, and you a book-learned gentleman; but I'm not dirt under your feet. What I done [*correcting herself*] what I did was not for the dresses and the taxis: I did it because we were pleasant together and I come—came—to care for you; not to want you to make love to me, and not forgetting the difference between us, but more friendly like.

HIGGINS

Well, of course. Thats just how I feel. And how Pickering feels. Eliza: youre a fool.

LIZA

Thats not a proper answer to give me [*she sinks on the chair at the writing-table in tears*].

HIGGINS

It's all youll get until you stop being a common idiot. If youre going to be a lady, youll have to give up feeling neglected if the men you know dont spend half their time snivelling over you and the other half giving you black eyes. If you cant stand the coldness of my sort of life, and the strain of it, go back to the gutter. Work til youre more a brute than a human being; and then cuddle and squabble and drink til you fall asleep. Oh, it's a fine life, the life of the gutter. It's real: it's warm: it's violent: you can feel it through the thickest skin: you can taste it and smell it without any training or any work. Not like Science and Literature and Classical Music and Philosophy and Art. You find me cold, unfeeling, selfish, dont you? Very well: be off with you to the sort of people you like. Marry some sentimental hog or other with lots of money, and a thick pair of lips to kiss you with and a thick pair of boots to kick you with. If you cant appreciate what youve got, youd better get what you can appreciate.

LIZA

[*desperate*] Oh, you are a cruel tyrant. I cant talk to you: you turn everything against me: I'm always in the wrong. But you know very well all the time that youre nothing but a bully. You know I cant go back to the gutter, as you call it, and that I have no real friends in the world but you and the Colonel. You know well I couldnt bear to live with a low common man after you two; and it's wicked and cruel of you to insult me by pretending I could. You think I must go back to Wimpole Street because I have nowhere else to go but father's. But dont you be too sure that you have me under your feet to be trampled on and talked down. I'll marry Freddy, I will, as soon as I'm able to support him.

HIGGINS

[*thunderstruck*] Freddy!!! that young fool! That poor devil who couldnt get a job as an errand boy even if he had the guts to try for it! Woman: do you not understand that I have made you a consort for a king?

LIZA

Freddy loves me: that makes him king enough for me. I dont want him to work: he wasnt brought up to it as I was. I'll go and be a teacher.

HIGGINS

Whatll you teach, in heaven's name?

LIZA

What you taught me. I'll teach phonetics.

HIGGINS

Ha! ha! ha!

LIZA

I'll offer myself as an assistant to that hairyfaced Hungarian.

HIGGINS

[*rising in a fury*] What! That imposter! that humbug! that toadying ignoramus! Teach him my methods! my discoveries! You take one step in his direction and I'll wring your neck. [*He lays hands on her*]. Do you hear?

LIZA

[*defiantly non-resistant*] Wring away. What do I care? I knew youd strike me some day. [*He lets her go, stamping with rage at having forgotten himself, and recoils so hastily that he stumbles back into his seat on the ottoman*]. Aha! Now I know how to deal with you. What a fool I was not to think of it before! You cant take away the knowledge you gave me. You said I had a finer ear than you. And I can be civil and kind to people, which is more than you can. Aha! [*Purposely dropping her aitches to annoy him*] Thats done you, Enry Iggins, it az. Now I dont care that [*snapping her fingers*] for your bullying and your big talk. I'll advertize it in the papers that your duchess is only a flower girl that you taught, and that she'll teach anybody to be a duchess just the same in six months for a thousand guineas. Oh, when I think of myself crawling under your feet and being trampled on and called names, when all the time I had only to lift up my finger to be as good as you, I could just kick myself.

HIGGINS

[*wondering at her*] You damned impudent slut, you! But its better than snivelling; better than fetching slippers and finding spectacles, isnt it? [*Rising*] By George, Eliza, I said I'd make a woman of you; and I have. I like you like this.

LIZA

Yes: you turn round and make up to me now that I'm not afraid of you, and can do without you.

HIGGINS

Of course I do, you little fool. Five minutes ago you were like a millstone round my neck. Now youre a tower of strength: a consort battleship. You and I and Pickering will be three old bachelors instead of only two men and a silly girl.

MRS HIGGINS *returns, dressed for the wedding. Eliza instantly becomes cool and elegant.*

MRS HIGGINS

The carriage is waiting, Eliza. Are you ready?

LIZA

Quite. Is the Professor coming?

MRS HIGGINS

Certainly not. He cant behave himself in church. He makes remarks out loud all the time on the clergyman's pronunciation.

LIZA

Then I shall not see you again, Professor. Goodbye.[*She goes to the door*].

MRS HIGGINS

[*coming to* HIGGINS] Goodbye, dear.

HIGGINS

Goodbye, mother. [*He is about to kiss her, when he recollects something*]. Oh, by the way, Eliza, order a ham and a Stilton cheese, will you? And buy me a pair of reindeer gloves, number eights, and a tie to match that new suit of mine. You can choose the color. [*His cheerful, careless, vigorous voice shews that he is incorrigible*].

LIZA

[*disdainfully*] Number eights are too small for you if you want them lined with lamb's wool. You have three new ties that you have forgotten in the drawer of your washstand. Colonel Pickering prefers double Gloucester to Stilton; and you dont notice the difference. I telephoned Mrs Pearce this morning not to forget the ham. What you are to do without me I cannot imagine. [*She sweeps out*]..

MRS HIGGINS

I'm afraid youve spoilt that girl, Henry. I should be uneasy about you and her if she were less fond of Colonel Pickering.

HIGGINS

Pickering! Nonsense: she's going to marry Freddy. Ha ha! Freddy! Freddy!! Ha ha ha ha ha!!!!! [*He roars with laughter as the play ends*].

From THE SEA GULL
ANTON CHEKHOV

This scene takes place very close to the end of the play. Nina, once a young idealistic neighbor of Trepleff's, has run off to become an actress. Things have not gone well for her. During the course of her struggles, she has an affair with Trigorin, an author and the lover of Trepleff's mother, Irina Nikolayevna. She has returned home briefly and wants some contact with Trepleff, who loves her. The memories are too painful for both of them. Nina departs, seemingly into oblivion, and Trepleff, in the next scene, commits suicide.

Take your time with this scene. Much is said between the lines. Nina remembers in bursts. She is tired and unwell. Fight the tendency to overdramatize.

(All but TREPLEFF *go out. He gets ready to write. Runs his eye over what's already written.)*

TREPLEFF

I've talked so much about new forms, but now I feel that little by little I am slipping into mere routine myself. *(Reads)* "The placards on the wall proclaimed"—"pale face in a frame of dark hair"—frame—that's flat. *(Scratches out what he's written)* I'll begin again where the hero is awakened by the rain, and throw out all the rest. This description of a moonlight night is too long and too precious. Trigorin has worked out his own method, it's easy for him. With him a broken bottleneck lying on the dam glitters in the moonlight and the mill wheel casts a black shadow—and there before you is the moonlit night; but with me it's the beginning light, and the silent twinkling of the stars, and the faroff sound of a piano dying away in the still, sweet-scented air. It's painful. *(A pause)* Yes, I'm coming more and more to the conclusion that it's a matter not of old forms and not of new forms, but that a man writes, not thinking at all of what form to choose, writes because it comes pouring out from his soul. *(A tap at the window nearest the desk.)* What's that? *(Looks out)* I don't see anything. *(Opens the door and peers into the garden)* Someone ran down the steps. *(Calls)* Who's there? *(Goes out. The sound of his steps along the veranda. A moment later returns with* NINA*)* Nina! Nina! *(She lays her head on his breast, with restrained sobbing.)*

TREPLEFF

(Moved) Nina! Nina! It's you—you. I had a presentiment, all day my soul

was tormented. *(Takes off her hat and cape)* Oh, my sweet, my darling, she has come! Let's not cry, let's not.

NINA

There's someone here.

TREPLEFF

No one.

NINA

Lock the doors. Someone might come in.

TREPLEFF

Nobody's coming in.

NINA

I know Irina Nikolayevna is here. Lock the doors.

TREPLEFF

(Locks door on Right. Goes to door on Left) This one doesn't lock. I'll put a chair against it. *(Puts chair against door)* Don't be afraid, nobody's coming in.

NINA

(As if studying his face) Let me look at you. *(Glancing around her)* It's warm, cozy—This used to be the drawing-room. Am I very much changed?

TREPLEFF

Yes—you are thinner and your eyes are bigger. Nina, how strange it is I'm seeing you. Why wouldn't you let me come to see you? Why didn't you come sooner? I know you've been here now for nearly a week. I have been every day there where you were, I stood under your window like a beggar.

NINA

I was afraid you might hate me. I dream every night that you look at me and don't recognize me. If you only knew! Ever since I came I've been here walking about—by the lake. I've been near your house often, and couldn't make up my mind to come in. Let's sit down. *(They sit.)* Let's sit down and let's talk, talk. It's pleasant here, warm, cozy—You hear—the wind? There's a place in Turgenev: "Happy is he who on such a night is under his own roof, who has a warm corner." I—a sea gull—no, that's not it. *(Rubs her forehead)* What was I saying? Yes—Turgenev. "And may the Lord help all homeless wanderers." It's nothing. *(Sobs.)*

TREPLEFF

Nina, again—Nina!

NINA

It's nothing. It will make me feel better. I've not cried for two years. Last night I came to the garden to see whether our theatre was still there, and it's there still. I cried for the first time in two years, and my heart grew lighter and my soul was clearer. Look, I'm not crying now. *(Takes his hand)* You are an author, I—an actress. We have both been drawn into the whirlpool. I used to be as happy as a child. I used to wake up in the morning singing. I loved you and dreamed of being famous, and now? Tomorrow early I must go to Yelets in the third class—with peasants, and at Yelets the cultured merchants will plague me with attentions. Life's brutal!

TREPLEFF

Why Yelets?

NINA

I've taken an engagement there for the winter. It's time I was going.

TREPLEFF

Nina, I cursed you and hated you. I tore up all your letters, tore up your photograph, and yet I knew every minute that my heart was bound to yours forever. It's not in my power to stop loving you, Nina. Ever since I lost you and began to get my work published, my life has been unbearable—I am miserable—All of a sudden my youth was snatched from me, and now I feel as if I'd been living in the world for ninety years. I call out to you, I kiss the ground you walk on, I see your face wherever I look, the tender smile that shone on me those best years of my life.

NINA

(In despair) Why does he talk like that? Why does he talk like that?

TREPLEFF

I'm alone, not warmed by anybody's affection. I'm all chilled—it's cold like living in a cave. And no matter what I write it's dry, gloomy and harsh. Stay here, Nina, if you only would! and if you won't, then take me with you.

(NINA quickly puts on her hat and cape.)

TREPLEFF

Nina, why? For God's sake, Nina. *(He is looking at her as she puts her things on. A pause.)*

NINA

My horses are just out there. Don't see me off. I'll manage by myself. *(Sobbing)* Give me some water.

(He gives her a glass of water.)

TREPLEFF

Where are you going now?

NINA

To town. *(A pause.)* Is Irina Nikolayevna here?

TREPLEFF

Yes, Thursday my uncle was not well, we telegraphed her to come.

NINA

Why do you say you kiss the ground I walk on? I ought to be killed. *(Bends over desk)* I'm so tired. If I could rest—rest. I'm a sea gull. No, that's not it. I'm an actress. Well, no matter— *(Hears* ARCADINA *and* TRIGORIN *laughing in the dining-room. She listens, runs to door on the Left and peeps through the keyhole)* And he's here too. *(Goes to* TREPLEFF*)* Well, no matter. He didn't believe in the theatre, all my dreams he'd laugh at, and little by little I quit believing in it myself, and lost heart. And there was the strain of love, jealousy, constant anxiety about my little baby. I got to be small and trashy, and played without thinking. I didn't know what to do with my hands, couldn't stand properly on the stage, couldn't control my voice. You can't imagine the feeling when you are acting and know it's dull. I'm a sea gull. No, that's not it. Do you remember, you shot a sea gull? A man comes by chance, sees it, and out of nothing else to do, destroys it. That's not it— *(Puts her hand to her forehead)* What was I—? I was talking about the stage. Now I'm not like that. I'm a real actress, I act with delight, with rapture, I'm drunk when I'm on the stage, and feel that I am beautiful. And now, ever since I've been here, I've kept walking about, kept walking and thinking, thinking and believing my soul grows stronger every day. Now I know, I understand, Kostya, that in our work—acting or writing—what matters is not fame, not glory, not what I used to dream about, it's how to endure, to bear my cross, and have faith. I have faith and it all doesn't hurt me so much, and when I think of my calling I'm not afraid of life.

TREPLEFF

(Sadly) You've found your way, you know where you are going, but I still move in a chaos of images and dreams, not knowing why or who it's for. I have no faith, and I don't know where my calling lies.

NINA

(Listening) Ssh—I'm going. Goodbye. When I'm a great actress, come and look at me. You promise? But now— *(Takes his hand)* It's late. I can hardly stand on my feet, I feel faint. I'd like something to eat.

TREPLEFF

Stay, I'll bring you some supper here.

NINA

No, no—I can manage by myself. The horses are just out there. So, she brought him along with her? But that's all one. When you see Trigorin— don't ever tell him anything. I love him. I love him even more than before. "An idea for a short story" I love, I love passionately, I love to desperation. How nice it used to be, Kostya! You remember? How gay and warm and pure our life was; what things we felt, tender, delicate like flowers. Do you remember? "Men and beasts, lions, eagles and partridges, antlered deer, mute fishes dwelling in the water, star-fish and small creatures invisible to the eye—these and all life have run their sad course and are no more. Thousands of creatures have come and gone since there was life on the earth. Vainly now the pallid moon doth light her lamp. In the meadows the cranes wake and cry no longer; and the beetles' hum is silent in the linden groves." *(Impulsively embraces* TREPLEFF, *and runs out by the terrace door.)*

From SCENES FROM A MARRIAGE
INGMAR BERGMAN

This is from Scene Four, "The Vale of Tears." Johan has returned to his wife, Marianne, for a visit, after having left her a year before for another woman. Both characters respond to the fact that they are still attracted to each other. They try to act very sophisticated about their situation, but the frustration, anger, and hurt keep breaking through.

Handle the scene delicately. Take time between the lines for each character to respond and calculate the next move. The stage directions are very important; read them with significance as part of the narrative. For this scene to be successful, the audience must feel the underlying tension between these two people.

An evening in September a year later. The doorbell rings. MARIANNE, *who has been busy in the kitchen preparing a dinner for two, goes to open the door after a quick check-up in front of the mirror.*

JOHAN

Hello.

MARIANNE

Hello. Come in!

JOHAN

Sorry if I'm late. I had trouble with the car. It wouldn't start. *(Kisses her on the cheek)* How pretty you are. And what a nice dress.

MARIANNE

I'm glad you like it. I bought it a couple of days ago but regretted it afterwards. I didn't think it suited me. And it suddenly seemed much too red.

JOHAN

It suits you admirably, I must say.

MARIANNE

Do come in, Johan. I feel nervous standing here in the hall, making polite conversation.

JOHAN

I'm nervous too. I haven't been able to settle down to anything all day. It's ridiculous, really. But I haven't seen you for quite a long time. Over six months.

MARIANNE

How was it that you suddenly . . .?

JOHAN

Paula's in London for a week.

MARIANNE

Oh, I see. Would you like a drink?

JOHAN

Yes, please, I'd love a whisky. Straight. It settles the stomach. I mean, it calms you down.

MARIANNE

Have you taken to drinking whisky?

JOHAN

Yes, just imagine.

MARIANNE

I asked Aunt Berit to take charge of the girls for tonight. So they're staying with her until the day after tomorrow. The delight is mutual. They're going to the theater this evening, and tomorrow they have a holiday from school and are going to the country.

JOHAN

How practical. I mean, it would have been pretty rough going to meet the children too. How are they?

MARIANNE

You needn't ask after them out of politeness. But we'll write down their birthdays in your diary, so that you don't forget them again as you did this year. I bought them each a present from you, but they saw through me. And that wasn't very nice. Couldn't you take them out to dinner sometimes? Or to the movies? It's pretty awful the way you never get in touch with them. They hardly ever mention you nowadays.

JOHAN

That's understandable.

MARIANNE

Why can't Paula let you see us without raising Cain for days on end . . .

JOHAN

If we're meeting just to give you the chance of moralizing, I'd better go at once.

MARIANNE

You've said yourself that Paula is so jealous that you can't see either me or the children without there being a godawful fight.

JOHAN

What do you expect me to do about it?

MARIANNE

Are you so darn yellow that you can't tell her what *you* want to do? Are you so afraid of her making a scene that you let her boss you around?

JOHAN

(Wearily) Yes.

MARIANNE

I'm sorry.

JOHAN

It doesn't matter. I realize you think the situation is absurd. But don't scold me. It's no use.

MARIANNE

Would you like some more whisky?

JOHAN

Yes, please.

MARIANNE

How are things otherwise?

JOHAN

Oh, much the same. What about you?

MARIANNE

I can't complain. It might be worse.

JOHAN

I suppose it was silly of me to call up and suggest we meet. There's nothing we can talk about without hurting each other.

MARIANNE

Then I have an excellent suggestion. Let's have dinner. Undoubtedly we're both ravenous and that's why we're so touchy. Don't you think so?

JOHAN

A good idea.

(As they stand up he puts his arms around her and kisses her on the lips. She submits with a slight protest. Then they look at each other and smile suddenly)

MARIANNE

You look a fright with that haircut. And you've put on weight, I think.

JOHAN

I must admit you really turn me on when we're close together like this. What are we going to do about it?

MARIANNE

Let's have dinner first. Then we'll see.

JOHAN

Have you bought a new dinner service?

MARIANNE

It's family stuff. Dear old Aunt Elsa died six months ago and left me a lot of household things for some obscure reason. She was always under the impression that I was so domestic. Most of it is unusable, but the china is nice. You're only getting a casserole, and wine and cheese. I haven't had time to produce anything fancier. But you usually like my cooking.

JOHAN

It smells wonderful. *(Helping himself)* Have you heard that Martin is going to marry again?

MARIANNE

My dear, I ran into them in town. They were terribly embrarrassed and began to stammer and make excuses for not having called me up or anything the whole year. I felt quite sorry for them.

JOHAN

Anyway, this new one he's got hold of is a flighty little piece. Though she's said to have money.

MARIANNE

As a matter of fact I've heard just the opposite. Her father's firm went bankrupt not long ago.

JOHAN

Then poor old Martin has slipped up again.

MARIANNE

Isn't he one of your closest friends?

JOHAN

Not exactly. Why?

MARIANNE

You sound so smug.

JOHAN

A wise man has said that in our friends' misfortunes there is always something that doesn't entirely displease us. Skoal, Marianne. This is a very good wine.

MARIANNE

My dear, it's nothing very special. Just a rather cheap claret. But it *is* good.

JOHAN

I don't mind telling you that things are going pretty well for me just now. I've been offered a chair at a university in Cleveland for three years. It's a splendid chance, both career-wise and financially. After all, it's over there that things happen in our field. And I'd be more than glad to emigrate, either temporarily or for good. There's nothing to keep me here. I'm fed up with the academic duck-pond. Besides, I have no desire to let myself be fleeced to the bone. So I leave in the spring, if all goes well.

MARIANNE

Congratulations.

JOHAN

And now the unspoken question: Are you taking Paula with you to America? And the answer is no. Call it running away, if you like. Okay, I'm decamping. I've had just about enough. Paula has been good for me. She has taught me a few things about myself which I'm glad to know. But there's a limit. To be quite frank, I'm pretty tired of her. I suppose you think it's disloyal of me to sit here running Paula down. But she forfeited my loyalty long ago. I'm fed up with her. With her emotional storms and scenes and tears and hysterics, then making it all up and saying how much she loves me. (*Checking himself*) I'll tell you this, Marianne. The best thing about Paula was that she taught me to shout and brawl. It was even permissible to strike her. I wasn't aware that I had any feelings at all. If I were to tell you . . . you'd think I was lying. Sometimes I thought I was mixed up in a grotesque play, in which I was both actor and audience. Our fights used to go on for days and nights on end, until we collapsed from sheer exhaustion.

MARIANNE

Would you like another helping?

JOHAN

Thanks, I haven't quite finished this. It's simply delicious. And I'm talking your ear off. But it puts you in such a terribly good mood. I've felt on top of the world ever since I was offered that professorship.

MARIANNE

(Quietly) In that case perhaps we could discuss the divorce. I mean, if you're going to be away for several years it would be better to clinch the matter before you go. Don't you think?

JOHAN

You should do as you see fit.

MARIANNE

Then I suggest that we do get a divorce. One never knows what may happen. I might want to remarry. And it would be awfully complicated if you're in America.

JOHAN

Is something up?

MARIANNE

That made you curious, didn't it?

JOHAN

Look here, Marianne! Suppose you tell me something about yourself. And not just let me rattle on.

MARIANNE

Would you like some more wine?

JOHAN

No thanks. It has already gone to my head. No more of anything. Well, perhaps a little cheese. No, no, we don't need fresh plates. What sort of cheese it this? It looks tasty.

MARIANNE

It's a Bel Paesè. Try it.

JOHAN

Delicious. But don't think you're wriggling out of it. How are things, Marianne? Judging by your appearance, your hairdo, your dress, your figure, and your general amiability, they must be pretty good. What I'm most anxious to know, of course, is whether you have a lover.

MARIANNE

I'll make the coffee. You'd like some, wouldn't you?

(She goes around the table and, taking his head in both hands, bends down and kisses him on the lips. He lends a hand clearing the table. While MARIANNE is making the coffee JOHAN wanders about rather restlessly. He stops in a doorway and looks in)

JOHAN

You've changed things around, I see.

MARIANNE

Any objections?

JOHAN

Oh, none at all.

Chapter 10
Reading Together: Ensemble Techniques

KEY CONCEPTS

Choral speaking

Readers Theatre

Chamber Theatre

One of the most gratifying aspects of the current rising interest in the art of oral interpretation is the concurrent rise of experimentation with ensemble techniques. In this chapter we will examine the three basic techniques— choral speaking, Readers Theatre, and Chamber Theatre—for the purpose of providing an introduction to their methods.

CHORAL SPEAKING

There has always been something thrilling about voices speaking or singing in concert. Certainly the history of choral speaking goes back as far as the art of interpretation itself. Chanting in unison has always been an important part of religious ritual in both Hebrew and Christian services.

In addition to serving a ritualistic purpose, choral speaking was and continues to be recreational and educational. It is a widely used method of teaching language arts in the elementary schools.

Choral speaking is the reading of literature (primarily poetry) either by several persons in unison, responsively, or by large groups of persons, sometimes interspersed with solo voices. The interpreter who engages in choral speaking will derive some important benefits, and some verse choir work should be a basic part of the interpreter's training.

One benefit is speech improvement. In order for large groups speaking together to be understood, they must concentrate on correct articulation, pronunciation, and projection. A great deal can be accomplished along these lines in a short period of time because of the efficiency of choral activity: everybody speaks all the time.

Another benefit is the development of literary appreciation. Some interpreters have their first meaningful experience with poetry while working in a group. The sound and rhythm generated by a group reading of a poem can penetrate the thickest skin. In addition, because the group affords a degree of anonymity, fears, complexes, and anxieties which may occur in an individual performance diminish.

SELECTING MATERIALS

Materials for choral speaking should, of course, be suited to the group. Factors such as size, background, and purpose should be considered. Also, since almost all choral-speaking materials will be poetry, attention should be paid to the variety and flexibility of tone and emotion. As the group becomes more experienced, difficult arrangements of long duration will provide a delightful challenge.

Selections can be made from the Bible, ancient Greek plays, modern poetry, Old English and American ballads, American Indian rituals, Black spiritual poetry, and song lyrics. The selections which seem to work best for choral arrangements are those with strong rhythmical qualities.

TYPES OF CHORAL SPEECH

Choral speaking lends itself to various structures. The four most common are *refrain, antiphonal, group*, and *unison*.

THE REFRAIN

This type of choral speech is most appropriate for young children and other beginners. Selections which work with this treatment have lines, either exactly alike or similar, which are repeated throughout the poem. These lines are spoken by the whole chorus, in the same way as for some songs. A soloist delivers the remaining lines of the selection.

Old ballads are particularly good for refrain work. An example is the following poem, which is an excerpt from an Old English ballad entitled ''Robin-A-Thrush.''

Solo:	Old Robin-a-thrush he married a wife.
Chorus:	With a hoppitty, moppitty mow now.
Solo:	She proved to be the plague of his life.
Chorus:	With a hig jig jiggitty, ruffetty petticoat
Chorus:	Robin-a-thrush cries mow now.
Solo:	She never got up till twelve o'clock.
Chorus:	With a hoppitty, moppitty mow now.
Solo:	Put on her gown above her smock.
Chorus:	With a jig jiggitty, ruffetty petticoat.
Chorus:	Robin-a-thrush cries mow now.

The solo lines can be delivered either by the same soloist or by a different soloist for each line.

ANTIPHONAL

The antiphonal approach divides the choral group in half, and the selection is read responsively. The main element in this approach is contrast. That is, the two halves of the group must consist of voices with distinct differences. A simple arrangement would be to separate the light from the heavy voices. Where a selection contains questions and answers, the light voices usually ask the questions and the heavy voices respond with the replies.

This type of choral speech is more advanced than the refrain, because it requires more complete participation. The following short poem illustrates one type of antiphonal arrangement.

FAREWELL TO THE FARM
ROBERT LOUIS STEVENSON

Light: The coach is at the door at last;
The eager children, mounting fast
And kissing hands in chorus sing;
"Good-bye, good-bye, to everything."

Heavy: "To house and garden, field and lawn,
The meadow gates we swung upon,
To pump and stable, tree and swing,
Good-bye, good-bye, to everything."

Light: "And fare you well for evermore,
O ladder at the hayloft door,
O hayloft where the cobwebs cling,
Good-bye, good-bye, to everything."

Heavy: Crack goes the whip, and on we go;
The trees and houses smaller grow,
Last, round the woody turn we swing;
"Good-bye, good-bye, to everything."

There are several ways that choral groups can be divided. The selection might lend itself to a division of women and men, or high voices and low voices.

GROUP SPEAKING

Sometimes called *part speaking*, this type of choral speech divides the group into more than two parts. Soloists, duets, trios, and quartets of voices are used in combination with the whole chorus.

The best poems for group arrangements are those which contain a series of images, ideas, or episodes, since they provide for the widest variety of potential arrangements. Some selections which lend themselves to group speaking, such as Vachel Lindsay's "Mysterious Cat," are included at the end of the chapter. A good working chorus can find an infinite number of ways to divide up the lines, producing very interesting and exciting results.

UNISON

It is a mistake to consider unison arrangements easy. In fact, unison is the most difficult form of choral speaking to carry off well. It can become sing-song and ragged because of all the voices attempting to perform at the same time. Also, shadings and mood changes can be difficult to produce from large groups speaking in unison.

On the other hand, a large group speaking effectively in unison can provide some thrilling effects. The sheer weight and volume of twenty or thirty voices can add a dimension to a poem which could never be achieved by a single reader.

In sum, a knowledge of the techniques of choral speaking is invaluable to the interpreter, particularly when a group of interpreters consider the possibility of developing a program. Rather than presenting only a series of individual readings, they can add something special to the performance. Functioning as a chorus can give a group of interpreters a real sense of rapport, make them feel like an ensemble or a company, and, at the same time, provide some excellent voice training and discipline.

READERS THEATRE

Although the distinction is becoming somewhat blurred, Readers Theatre generally refers to the group reading of drama, while Chamber Theatre designates the group reading of narrative prose. A third category, which I call the Interpreter's Ensemble, is the group presentation of several different pieces of literature in the same program. This last form has grown in popularity primarily because programs can be developed around a theme.

Some writers, like Joanna Hawkins Maclay, tend to group all the forms under the heading of Readers Theatre.

> There is no essential difference between Chamber Theatre and Readers Theatre as we have defined it; Chamber Theatre is Readers Theatre whose literary text is in narrative form.[1]

It is useful to cut down on terminology, and, in time, the term Readers Theatre will apply to all forms. The interpreter must be aware, however, that the differences in material will demand somewhat different approaches.

As with the individual reading of drama, the Readers Theatre approach calls more attention to the text than the usual theatrical production. Although

---

[1] Joanna Hawkins Maclay, *Readers Theatre: Toward a Grammar of Practice,* Random House, New York, 1971, p. 10.

279

the production is a bit more elaborate, the relationship between the performers and the audience remains presentational rather the representational. That is, there is no "fourth wall." The audience does not magically eavesdrop on the characters of the play as they interact, and the performers do not immerse themselves totally in the characters. The material is projected to the audience, and, as in the individual performance, the main depiction of the action takes place in the minds of the audience.

One of the advantages of Readers Theatre as a method of presenting plays is that more characters can be illustrated than in the usual interpretive performance. Three, four, five, and even more characters can be presented within the same scene. Since as interpreters we always remain narrators, it is possible for each interpreter to sketch more than one character. The most prevalent arrangement uses one interpreter for each character, or "one-on-one." The audience quickly comes to associate the particular character with the interpreter who speaks the lines of that character, thus eliminating any confusion which may arise about who is speaking to whom during the performance.

Some interesting experiments have been carried out using more than one interpreter to sketch the same character. At Baylor University in the late 1950s such experiments were conducted by Paul Baker. He cast three performers in the role of Hamlet, each one focusing on a different aspect of Hamlet's character.

PROJECTIVE TECHNIQUE

The projective technique described in Chapter 8 is applicable to Readers Theatre as well. If you are doing a two-character scene with another interpreter reading the second part, you do not look at the other interpreter when you say a line. Two interpreters reading lines to each other in front of an audience with scripts in their hands, devoid of scenery, props, lights, costumes, etc., will always apppear to be two actors rehearsing a scene which isn't quite ready.

Place yourself at some distance from the other interpreter. Experiment with various distances, until both of you are comfortable. Too close together, you will confuse your perspective; too far apart, you will split the focus, and the audience will feel as if they are at a tennis match. Then, "project" the other character to the back wall. Even though you hear the line coming from the other person next to you, respond as if it is coming from out front. The following diagram illustrates the basic reader-audience perspective for Readers Theatre.

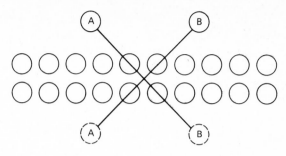

When there are several characters being sketched by several inter-preters, care must be taken not to place two interpreters in close proximity who have a great deal of dialogue to deliver to each other.

STAGING TECHNIQUE

Elaborate staging of a dramatic reading should be avoided. Even though there is much to be gained from staging an interpretive performance of a play, adding too many theatrical elements will diminish the focus on the text. Many effective Readers Theatre presentations take place with the readers lined up in front of the audience, situated on stools or behind reading stands.

Some directors of Readers Threatre prefer to work with areas or levels in the playing area. The readers are arranged according to their relationships in the play. These relationships can be literal (such as husband and wife, friend and foe) or figurative (such as dominant versus submissive).

Most staging factors are determined by some combination of the text, the space, and the conception of the play. In the main, though, movement should be used with the greatest economy. The audience is occupied with the problem of visualizing the scene and a great deal of moving and shifting around can become confusing. Also, since the interpreters have so little help in producing effects, a well-directed move will have extraordinary impact if the audience has not already witnessed a great deal of movement.

There are many variations of the basic staging technique, some of which run counter to what has been said above. But, the interpreter—like all artists—should be firmly grounded in the rules before experimenting with various ways of breaking them.

One staging variation is especially interesting to the beginning student, because it can help the student, whose performance orientation has been acting courses, to grasp the difference in perspective which oral intepretation creates. When space permits, it is conceivable to establish a small playing area, usually down center, where short scenes can be played out in the conventional fourth-wall manner. This variation, however, should be attempted only within the context of a Readers Theatre production, where the intent of the total performance is clearly understood by the audience. That is, the audience must not be confused about what they are seeing. They should recognize such a variation as just that—a variation. Usually, short two-character scenes, which require no essential props or scenery, work best. The area should be set with some furniture to distinguish it from the remaining space—just stools will do.

While one interpreter reads a pertinent stage direction to the audience, which signals the beginning of the scene, two other interpreters move to occupy the playing area. The effect will be enhanced if it is possible to make a lighting change which will place the remaining readers in limbo. The two interpreters then play the scene to each other, as they would in a full production. At the conclusion of the scene, they return to their original positions, and the reading continues as before. This variation is most effective when used only two or three times for the reading of a whole play, and only when such scenes are of extraordinary importance.

In sum, Readers Theatre can provide a very enjoyable and important experience for the interpreter. The practice with ensemble work, with Readers Theatre techniques, and with the dramatic texts will broaden the outlook and increase the skill of the interpreter. Many of the skills learned from Readers Theatre are applicable to careers involving commercials and animated voice-overs for television and film.

CHAMBER THEATRE

The term *Chamber Theatre* is generally attributed to Robert S. Breen of Northwestern University. The technique is similar to that of Readers Theatre, in that several interpreters work together to present a literary work, but the material used in Chamber Theatre is narrative prose rather than drama. In addition, Readers Theatre tends to simplify the presentation of drama, while Chamber Theatre productions can be very elaborate, complete with scenery, lights, costumes, props, furniture, and makeup.

We have all experienced dramatizations of narrative prose in one form or another. One can hardly get through high school without seeing one of the many films based on novels, such as *Great Expectations* or *For Whom the Bell Tolls*. The stage production of *The Diary of Ann Frank*, while adapted to more usual theatrical conventions, was essentially a Chamber Theatre production. Chamber Theatre can be viewed as the dramatization of narrative prose without rewriting.

As in all forms of oral interpretation, the narrator is a central figure in the Chamber Theatre presentation. As the performers who represent the characters in the story act out the passages of dialogue as if they were in a play, the narrator interrupts the flow of events to describe and explain thoughts, feelings, actions, and motives—exactly as the text does.

In addition to the narrator who represents the author's point of view, each character can also assume a narrative function. The following passages from Erskine Caldwell's "Daughter" has been arranged to demonstrate the potential for multiple narrative perspective.

Narrator:	The sheriff got in front of the barred window.
Sheriff:	You ought to go to the bunk now and rest some, Jim boy.
Narrator:	He was elbowed out of the way.
First Man:	You didn't kill the mule, did you Jim?
Jim:	The mule dropped dead in the barn,
Narrator:	Jim said.
Jim:	I wasn't nowhere around it. It just dropped dead.
Narrator:	The crowd was pushing harder. The men in front were jammed against the jail, and the men behind were trying to get within earshot. Those in the middle were squeezed against each other so tightly they could not move in any direction. Everyone was talking louder.
Jim:	(*to the audience*) Jim's face pressed between the bars and his fingers gripped the iron until the knuckles were white.
Narrator:	The milling crowd was moving across the street to the vacant lot. Somebody was shouting. He climbed up on an automobile and began swearing at the top of his lungs.
First Man:	(*to the audience*) A man in the middle of the crowd pushed his way out and went to his automobile. He got in and drove off alone (*leaves stage*).
Jim:	(*to the audience*) Jim stood holding to the bars and looking through the window.
Sheriff:	(*to the audience*) The sheriff had his back to the crowd, and he was saying something to Jim.
Narrator:	Jim did not hear what he said.

In the preceding passage, Jim, the sheriff, and an anonymous man speak both as the character and as the narrator describing the activity of the character. The narrator always maintains contact with the audience and delivers the more general descriptive material.

STAGING TECHNIQUE

Chamber Theatre is most effective when full production resources are available. Along with the scenery, light, etc., Chamber Theatre also borrows much of its staging technique from conventional theater. The material is most easily handled if it is reconstituted in script form. The performers should memorize their parts. It might be desirable for the narrator to carry the script, as this can become a very complicated part to memorize due to the lack of interaction. In addition, the presence of the script in some form helps to emphasize that it's an interpretive performance.

The entire show must be *blocked*. That is, the movements of the performers must be planned and executed in the same way one would direct a play. The biggest problem occurs when the perspective shifts from the action to the narrator. This problem can be handled in several ways. The most obvious is the *freeze technique*. The performers stop action while the narrator speaks to the audience. The freeze technique tends to become tedious and distracting, however, when used throughout an entire presentation.

A second possibility is *subdued action*. While the narrator is speaking, the level of the noise and activity lowers significantly, but continues. When the focus returns to the action, the level is raised.

Lighting changes can also be of great help in making these transitions between action and narrative. Pantomime should also be considered as a possible variation.

It is quite possible during the course of a long Chamber Theatre presentation to use many different staging techniques. In fact, variety in staging technique will add interest and hold attention.

In sum, Chamber Theatre is a very effective and exciting form of oral interpretation. It presents the narrative prose on stage more or less as written, rather than as an adaptation into a play. It does not, however, share the virtue of economy with other forms of oral interpretation. Interest in the form is spreading, and many colleges and universities are including a Chamber Theatre performance in their regular schedule of shows for the academic season. There have been a few professional successes with this form as well. For example, *Story Theatre* enjoyed a long run on Broadway and then was developed into several half-hour segments which played on television for two seasons.

Like other ensemble forms, Chamber Theatre provides the interpreter the opportunity to work in concert with other performers. Its greatest benefit to the individual interpreter is the demand it makes on the performer to explore the problem of double perspective, that is, of coping with character and narrator at the same time.

THE INTERPRETER'S ENSEMBLE

The headings of Readers Theatre and Chamber Theatre do not encompass the many variations in group interpretive performance which exist today. The Interpreter's Ensemble is the group presentation of several different literary selections in the same program. Basic to this form is a thematic rather than a story focus. For example, programs on ecology are very popular now. Such a program could contain selections of prose, poetry, and drama that all relate to the ecology theme.

It is not unusual to find the Interpreter's Ensemble combined with other art forms, such as music, dance, and multimedia.

STAGING TECHNIQUE

Staging for these programs can be either quite simple, or as elaborate as your budget and imagination allow. Since several different types of literature are being brought together into one unified whole, staging techniques must be flexible enough to accommodate the variety.

While there are always exceptions, scenery is usually kept to a minimum. It would be difficult to create either the right scenery or enough scenery to cover all the potential scenic situations represented in the several selections.

The following selections have been included as examples for choral treatment. Selections for the other approaches should be made from the various materials provided throughout this text.

Selections for Analysis and Performance

ELEPHANT SONG
DON BLANDING

Tong!   Tong!
Tong-a . . . tong-a . . . .   tong.
That is the rhythm of the elephant song.
As the big gray elephants shuffle along.
To the sing-song-singing of the old brass bells,
To the shrill harsh stridence of the mahout's yells,
To the shuff-shuff-shuffle of the great round feet.
The elephants are swinging down the village street.
   A priest peers out from his white-washed cell
   When he hears the ringing of the elephant bell.
   A wild-eyed faquir flings a membling curse.
   A baby peers from the arms of its nurse.
   A cobra dances to a charmer's tune.
   The incense wavers in the shrine of the moon.
   The street dogs scamper, the children scurry,
   A woman hum-hums as she fixes curry,
   And the bells keep ringing like a distant gong.
      Tong!   Tong!
      Tong-a . . . tong-a . . . .   tong.
The swing-along rhythm of the elephant song.

JIMMIE'S GOT A GOIL
From IS 5
e. e. cummings

Jimmie's got a goil

goil
goil,
Jimmie

's got a goil and
she coitnly can shimmie

when you see her shake
shake
shake,
when

you see her shake a
shimmie how you wish that you was Jimmie.

Oh for such a gurl
gurl
gurl,
oh

for such a gurl to
be a fellow's twistandstwirl
talk about your Sal-
Sal-
Sal-,
talk

about your Salo
-mes but gimmie Jimmie's gal.

EVER
EVERLAND
e. e. cummings

(of Ever-Ever Land I speak
sweet morons gather roun'
who does not dare to stand or sit
may take it lying down)

Down with the human soul
and anything else uncanned
for everyone carries canopeners
in Ever-Ever Land

(for Ever-Ever Land is a place
that's as simple as simple can be
and was built that way on purpose
by simple people like we)

down with hell and heaven
and all the religious fuss
infinity pleased our parents
one inch looks good to us

(and Ever-Ever Land is a place
that's measured and safe and known
where it's lucky to be unlucky
and the hitler lies down with the cohn)

down above all with love
and everything perverse
or which makes some feel more better
when all ought to feel less worse

(but only sameness is normal
in Ever-Ever Land
for a bad cigar is a woman
but a gland is only a gland)

FOREBODING
From Vagabond's House
DON BLANDING

. . . zoom . . . zoom . . . zoom . . .
that is the sound of the surf . . .
as the great green waves rush up the shore
with a murderous thundering ominous roar
and leave drowned dead things at my door
. . . zoom . . . zoom . . . zoom . . .

. . . suish . . . suish . . . suis-s-h . . .
that is the sound of the tow . . .
as it slips and slithers along the sands
with terrible groping formless hands

that drag at my beach-house where it stands
. . . suish . . . suis-h . . . suis-s-h . . .

   eeeie-u-u . . . eeeie-u-u . . . eeeie-u-u . . .
   that is the wound of the wind
it wails like a banshee adrift in space
and threatens to scatter my driftwood place.
it slashes the sand like spit in my face
   eeeie-u-u-u . . . eeeie-u-u . . . eeeie-u-u . . .

   Surf . . . tow . . . or the wind . . .
   which of the three will it be . . .
the surf . . . will it bludgeon and beat me dead . . .
or the tow drag me down to its ocean bed . . .
or the wind wail a dirge above my head . . .
   zoom . . . suis-h . . . eeeie-u-u . . .

THE MYSTERIOUS CAT
VACHEL LINDSEY

I saw a proud, mysterious cat,
I saw a proud, mysterious cat,
Too proud to catch a mouse or rat—
Mew, mew, mew.

But catnip she would eat, and purr,
But catnip, she would eat, and purr,
And goldfish she did much prefer—
Mew, mew, mew.

I saw a cat—'twas but a dream,
I saw a cat—'twas but a dream,
Who scorned the slave that brought her cream—
Mew, mew, mew.

Unless the slave were dressed in style,
Unless the slave were dressed in style,
And knelt before her all the while—
Mew, mew, mew.

Did you ever hear of a thing like that?
Did you ever hear of a thing like that?
Did you ever hear of a thing like that?
Oh, what a proud mysterious cat.
Oh, what a proud mysterious cat.
Oh, what a proud mysterious cat.
Mew . . . mew . . . mew.

Sources and Credits

Sources and Credits

W. H. Auden, "The Unknown Citizen," from *Collected Poems*, edited by Edward Mendelson (New York: Random House, Inc., 1940). Copyright © 1940 by W. H. Auden. Reprinted by permission of Random House, Inc.

William E. Barrett, "Señor Payroll." Copyright © 1943 by *Southwest Review*. Reprinted by permission of Harold Ober Associates Incorporated. First published in *Southwest Review*, Autumn 1943.

Ingmar Bergman, from *Scenes from a Marriage*, translated by Alan Blair (New York: Random House, Inc., 1974). Copyright © 1973 by Ingmar Bergman. Reprinted by permission of Random House, Inc.

William Blake, "London" and "The Tiger," from *Poems*, 3d ed., edited by C. F. Main and Peter G. Seng (Belmont, Calif.: Wadsworth Publishing Co., Inc., 1973).

Don Blanding, "Elephant Song," from *Memory Room* (New York: Dodd, Mead & Co., Inc., 1935). Copyright © 1935 by Don Blanding. Copyright renewed. Reprinted by permission of Dodd, Mead & Co., Inc.

Don Blanding, "Foreboding," from Vagabond's House (New York: Dodd, Mead & Co., Inc., 1928). Copyright © 1928 by Don Blanding. Copyright renewed. Reprinted by permission of Dodd, Mead & Co., Inc.

Julian Bond, "Rotation," from *Poems*, 3d ed., edited by C. F. Main and Peter J. Seng (Belmont, Calif.: Wadsworth Publishing Co., Inc., 1973). Reprinted by permission of the author.

Richard Brautigan, "The Chinese Checker Players," from *The Pill Versus the Springhill Mine Disaster* (New York: Delacorte Press, 1968). Copyright © 1968 by Richard Brautigan. Reprinted by permission of Delacorte Press/ Seymour Lawrence.

Gwendolyn Brooks, "The Ballad of Rudolph Reed," from *The World of Gwendolyn Brooks* (New York: Harper & Row, Publishers, Inc., 1960). Copyright © by Gwendolyn Brooks. Reprinted by permission of Harper & Row, Publishers, Inc.

Robert Browning, "Meeting at Night" and "My Last Duchess," from *A Journey of Poems,* edited by Richard Niebling (New York: Dell Publishing Co., 1964).

Robert Browning, "Prospice," from *Poems,* 3d ed., edited by C. F. Main and Peter J. Seng (Belmont, Calif.: Wadsworth Publishing Co., Inc., 1973).

Ventura Garcia Calderón, "The Lottery Ticket," translated by Richard Phibbs, from *Seventy-Five Short Masterpieces,* edited by Roger Goodman (New York: Bantam Books, 1961). Reprinted by permission of the Golden Cockerel Press.

Erskine Caldwell, "Daughter," from *The Complete Stories of Erskine Caldwell* (Boston: Little, Brown and Company, 1935). Copyright © 1935, 1963 by Erskine Caldwell. Reprinted by permission of McIntosh and Otis, Inc.

Anton Chekhov, "A Wicked Boy," translated by Helen Reeve, from *Seventy-Five Short Masterpieces,* edited by Roger Goodman (New York: Bantam Books, Inc., 1961). Copyright © 1961 by Bantam Books, Inc. All rights reserved. Reprinted by permission of Bantam Books, Inc.

Anton Chekhov, from *The Sea Gull,* translated by Stark Young (New York: Samuel French, Inc., 1950). Copyright © 1950 by Stark Young. Reprinted by permission of Samuel French, Inc.

John Collier, "The Chaser." Copyright © 1941, 1968 by John Collier. Reprinted by permission of the Harold Matson Co., Inc. First appeared in *The New Yorker.*

Hilary Corke, "The Choice," from *The Early Drowned* (London: Martin Secker & Warburg Ltd., 1961). Reprinted by permission of Martin Secker & Warburg Ltd.

Malcolm Cowley, "The Long Vogage," from *Blue Juniata: Collected Poems* (New York: Viking Penguin, Inc., 1968). Copyright © 1968 by Malcolm Cowley. Reprinted by permission of Viking Penguin, Inc.

Hart Crane, "The Air Plant," from *The Complete Poems and Selected Letters*

Harper and Bros., Publishers, Inc., 1954). Reprinted by permission of Yvette S. Eastman.

James T. Farrell, "The Scoop," from *The Short Stories of James T. Farrell* (New York: Vanguard Press, Inc., 1937). Copyright © 1937, 1964, by James T. Farrell. Reprinted by permission of Vanguard Press.

Kenneth Fearing, "Requiem," from *New and Selected Poems* (Bloomington, Ind.: Indiana University Press, 1956). Copyright © 1956 by Kenneth Fearing. Reprinted by permission of Indiana University Press.

Kenneth Fearing, "King Juke" and "Travelogue in a Shooting Gallery," from *Afternoon of a Pawnbroker* (New York: Harcourt Brace Jovanovich, Inc., 1943). Copyright © 1943 by Kenneth Fearing, renewed 1971 by Bruce Fearing. Reprinted by permission of Harcourt Brace Jovanovich, Inc. "Travelogue in a Shooting Gallery" was first published in *The New Yorker*.

Robert Frost, "An Old Man's Winter Night," "The Road Not Taken," "The Wood-Pile," and selection from "Provide, Provide," from *The Poetry of Robert Frost,* edited by Edward Connery Lathem (New York: Holt, Rinehart and Winston, Publishers, 1916). Copyright © 1916, 1930, 1939, 1969 by Holt, Rinehart and Winston. Copyright © 1936, 1944, 1958 by Robert Frost. Copyright © 1964, 1967 by Lesley Frost Ballantine. Reprinted by permission of Holt, Rinehart and Winston, Publishers.

Herbert Goldstone, "Virtuoso." Copyright © 1953 by Mercury Press, Inc. Reprinted from *The Magazine of Fantasy and Science Fiction* and by permission of Herbert Goldstone.

Donald Hall, "The Sleeping Giant." Copyright © 1955 by Donald Hall. Reprinted by permission of Curtis Brown, Ltd. First published in *The New Yorker* (1955).

Ben Hecht, "The Lost Soul," from *A Book of Miracles* (New York: Viking Penguin Inc., 1939). Copyright © 1939 by Ben Hecht, renewed 1967 by Rose Hecht. Reprinted by permission of Viking Penguin Inc.

Gerard Manley Hopkins, "Spring and Fall: To a Young Child," from *Poems,* 3d ed., edited by C. F. Main and Peter J. Seng (Belmont, Calif.: Wadsworth Publishing Co., Inc., 1973).

Rolfe Humphries, "Night Game," from *Collected Poems of Rolfe Humphries* (Bloomington, Ind.: Indiana University Press, 1968). Copyright © 1968 by Indiana University Press. Reprinted by permission of Indiana University Press.

Rolfe Humphries, "Polo Grounds," from *Collected Poems of Rolfe Hum-*

Robert H. Woodward, *The Craft of Prose,* 2d ed. (Belmont, Calif.: Wadsworth Publishing Company, Inc., 1968).

Edna St. Vincent Millay, "Exiled," from *Collected Poems* (New York: Harper & Row, Publishers, Inc., 1921). Copyright © 1921, 1948, by Edna St. Vincent Millay. Reprinted by permission of Harper and Row, Publishers, Inc.

Arthur Miller, from *A View from the Bridge* (New York: Viking Penguin, Inc., 1955). Copyright © 1955 by Arthur Miller. All rights reserved. Reprinted by permission of Viking Penguin, Inc.

John Milton, "How Soon Hath Time," from *Twelve Poets: Alternate Edition,* edited by Glenn Leggett and Henry-York Steiner (New York: Holt, Rinehart and Winston, Publishers, 1967).

Liam O'Flaherty, "The Sniper," from *Spring Sowing* (New York: Harcourt Brace Jovanovich, Inc.). Reprinted by permission of Harcourt Brace Jovanovich, Inc.

Kenneth Patchen, "An Easy Decision," from *Collected Poems* (New York: New Directions Publishing Corp., 1952). Copyright © 1952 by Kenneth Patchen. Reprinted by permission of New Directions.

Sylvia Plath, "Edge," from *Ariel* (New York: Harper & Row, Publishers, Inc., 1963). Copyright © 1963 by Ted Hughes. Reprinted by permission of Harper & Row, Publishers, Inc.

Sylvia Plath, "Frog Autumn," from *The Colossus and Other Poems* (New York: Random House, Inc., 1959). Copyright © 1959 by Sylvia Plath. Reprinted by permission of Alfred A. Knopf, Inc.

Alexander Pope, from "Ode on Solitude," from *A Journey of Poems,* edited by Richard Niebling (New York: Dell Publishing Co., 1964).

Ezra Pound, "The Bath Tub," from *Personae* (New York: New Directions Publishing Corp., 1926). Copyright © 1926 by Ezra Pound. Reprinted by permission of New Directions.

Edward Arlington Robinson, "Mr. Flood's Party," from *Collected Poems* (New York: Macmillan Publishing Co., Inc., 1921). Copyright © 1921 by Edward Arlington Robinson, renewed 1949. Reprinted by permission of Macmillan Publishing Co., Inc.

Edward Arlington Robinson, "Richard Cory," from *Poems,* 3d ed., edited by C. F. Main and Peter J. Seng (Belmont, Calif.: Wadsworth Publishing Co., Inc., 1973).

Edmond Rostand, from *Cyrano de Bergerac,* translated by Brian Hooker

(New York: Holt, Rinehart and Winston, Publishers, 1923). Copyright © 1923 by Henry Holt and Co.; renewed 1951 by Doris C. Hooker. Reprinted by permission of Holt, Rinehart and Winston, Publishers.

Muriel Rukeyser, "Effort at Speech Between Two People," from *Theory of Flight* (New Haven, Conn.: Yale University Press, 1935). Copyright © 1935 by Yale University, 1960, 1979 by Muriel Rukeyser. Reprinted by permission of Monica McCall, International Creative Management.

Siegfried Sassoon, "Everyone Sang," from *Collected Poems* (New York: E. P. Dutton Co., 1948). Copyright © 1948 by Seigfried Sassoon. Reprinted by permission of The Viking Press.

George Bernard Shaw, from *Pygmalion,* from *Bernard Shaw: Collected Plays with Prefaces,* Vol. 4 (New York: Dodd Mead & Co., 1975). Copyright © 1913, 1914, 1916, 1930, 1941, 1944 by George Bernard Shaw; 1957 by The Public Trustee as Executor of the Estate of George Bernard Shaw; 1972 by The Trustees of the British Museum, The Governors and Guardians of the National Gallery of Ireland and Royal Academy of Dramatic Art. Reprinted by permission of The Society of Authors on behalf of the Bernard Shaw Estate.

Paul Simon, "Richard Cory." Copyright © 1966 by Paul Simon. Used by permission.

Sophocles, from *Electra,* translated by Francis Fergusson, from *Greek Plays in Modern Translation,* edited by Dudley Fitts (New York: Dial Press, 1947). Copyright © 1938 by Francis Fergusson. All rights renewed. Reprinted with permission of Theatre Arts Books, New York.

Theodore Spencer, "The Day," from *Poems 1940–1947* (Cambridge, Mass.: Harvard University Press, 1948). Copyright © 1944, 1948 by the President and Fellows of Harvard College, renewed 1972 by Eloise Spencer Bender. Reprinted by permission of Harvard University Press.

James Stephens, "In Waste Places," from *Collected Poems* (New York: Macmillan Publishing Co., Inc., 1916). Copyright © 1916 by Macmillan Publishing Co., Inc., renewed 1944 by James Stephens. Reprinted by permission of Macmillan Publishing Co., Inc.

James Stephens, "The Shell," from *Collected Poems* (New York: Macmillan Publishing Co., Inc., 1915). Copyright © 1915 by Macmillan Publishing Co., Inc., renewed 1943 by James Stephens. Reprinted by permission of Macmillan Publishing Co., Inc.

Cj Stevens, "Secrets" and "The Firebird." Printed by permission of the author.

August Strindberg, "An Attempt at Reform," from *Seventy-Five Short Masterpieces,* edited by Roger Goodman (New York: Bantam Books, 1961).

John Updike, "Ex-Basketball Player," from *The Carpentered Hen and Other Stories* (New York: Harper & Row, Publishers, Inc., 1954). Copyright © 1954 by John Updike. Reprinted by permission of Harper & Row, Publishers, Inc. Originally published in *The New Yorker.*

Robert Vas Dias, "Saturday Poem," from *Speech Acts and Happenings: Poetry by Robert Vas Dias* (Indianapolis and New York: Bobbs-Merrill, 1967). Copyright © 1967, 1972 by Robert Vas Dias. Reprinted by permission of Bobbs-Merrill.

Robert Penn Warren, "Original Sin: A Short Story," from Norman Friedman and Charles A. McLaughlin, *Poetry: An Introduction to its Form and Art* (New York: Harper & Row, Publishers, Inc., 1961).

E. B. White, "The Hour of Letdown," from *The Second Tree from the Corner* (New York: Harper & Row, Publishers, Inc., 1951). Copyright © 1951 by E. B. White. Reprinted by permission of Harper & Row, Publishers, Inc. Originally published in *The New Yorker.*

Walt Whitman, "Animals" from "Song of Myself," from *A Journey of Poems,* edited by Richard Niebling (New York: Dell Publishing Co., 1964).

William Carlos Williams, "The Drunkard," from *Collected Earlier Poems* (New York: New Directions Publishing Corp., 1938). Copyright © 1938 by New Directions Publishing Corp. Reprinted by permission of New Directions.

William Wordsworth, "Composed Upon Westminister Bridge" and "Strange Fits of Passion Have I Known," from *Poems,* 3d ed., edited by C. F. Main and Peter J. Seng (Belmont, Calif.: Wadsworth Publishing Co., Inc., 1973).

William Butler Yeats, "Leda and the Swan," from *Collected Poems* (New York: Macmillan Publishing Co., Inc., 1928). Copyright © 1928 by Macmillan Publishing Co., Inc., renewed 1956 by Bertha Georgie Yeats. Reprinted by permission of Macmillan Publishing Co., Inc.

William Butler Yeats, "Father and Child," from *Collected Poems* (New York: Macmillan Publishing Co., Inc., 1928). Copyright © 1933 by Macmillan Publishing Co., Inc., renewed 1961 by Bertha Georgie Yeats. Reprinted by permission of Macmillan Publishing Co., Inc.

William Butler Yeats, "The Second Coming," from *Collected Poems* (New York: Macmillan Publishing Co., Inc., 1928). Copyright © 1924 by Macmillan Publishing Co., Inc., renewed 1952 by Bertha Georgie Yeats. Reprinted by permission of Macmillan Publishing Co., Inc.

Elsa Zantner, "How Grandpa Came into the Money," from *Seventy-Five Short Masterpieces,* edited by Roger Goodman (New York: Bantam Books, Inc., 1961).

Index

Index